MOMENTS OF BEING

BOOKS BY VIRGINIA WOOLF

VIRGINIA WOOLF
Moments of Being

UNPUBLISHED AUTOBIOGRAPHICAL
WRITINGS

*Edited and
with an Introduction and Notes
by*
JEANNE SCHULKIND

HARCOURT BRACE JOVANOVICH
NEW YORK AND LONDON

Printed in the United States of America

Library of Congress Catalog Card Number 76-27410
ISBN 0-15-162034-2

First American edition

B C D E

Contents

Acknowledgements

This edition of Virginia Woolf's autobiographical writings has been made possible by the consent and cooperation of Peter Lewis, Librarian of the University of Sussex Library, and the owners of the copyright, Quentin Bell and Angelica Garnett. Professor Bell and his wife, Olivier, have been characteristically kind and obliging in giving aid at whatever inopportune moments they have been called upon. They have provided me with much indispensable information and have often saved me from error for which I am most grateful. The courtesy of the staff of the University of Sussex Library, and in particular Adrian Peasgood who has been unflagging in providing invaluable assistance at every stage of the preparation, has been greatly appreciated. I am especially indebted to Professor David Daiches for his encouragement, sound advice and unfailing generosity.

I wish also to thank the publishers of Virginia Woolf's writings for permission to quote from them in my Introduction and Mrs Lola Szladits for making possible the presentation of a complete text of "Old Bloomsbury" by giving permission to use material from the Berg Collection. It is a pleasant task to recall my obligation to many people, too numerous to mention, who have assisted me in resolving minor problems.

Finally, thanks must go to my husband and to my daughter for their patience and good humour.

Editor's Note

This collection of autobiographical writings by Virginia Woolf brings together unpublished material selected from the Woolf archive at the University of Sussex Library. The 'Monks House Papers', as they are called, belonged to Leonard Woolf. When he persuaded Quentin Bell to write the authorized biography of Virginia Woolf he placed the papers at the disposal of Professor Bell who quoted brief passages from them in the biography. After the death of Leonard Woolf the papers passed, through the generosity of the executrix of the estate, Mrs Trekkie Parsons, to The University of Sussex.

The decision to publish material which would have been extensively revised by Virginia Woolf and most of which—unlike the essays published posthumously by Leonard Woolf—was never intended for publication, was not taken without the most careful consideration. The undeniable interest and value of these memoirs, however, left those involved in the decision to publish with no doubts. Publication which would make readily available to a wide audience material that so richly illuminates the vision and sensibility of a writer whose contribution to the history of English literature was so profoundly individual could not but be a tribute honouring her memory. Knowledge of Virginia Woolf will be invaluably and copiously supplemented by the eventual publication of the complete Diary and the Letters,* but these memoirs have their unique contribution to make to the documentation of her life and art.

It was Virginia Woolf's practice to write out one or more rough drafts of a work and then to type out complete revisions, sometimes as many as eight or nine. The material in this collection is in various stages of revision—most of it exists in typescript, a part of one section is in manuscript only—but with the exception of the first memoir the scripts bear signs of 'work in progress', notwithstanding that the last three selections were in fact read by Virginia Woolf to the audiences for whom they were intended. Corrections, additions, deletions, sometimes hastily made and incomplete, are scattered throughout the work and in the case where only the manuscript

---

* Edited by Nigel Nicolson assisted by Joanne Trautmann (*The Letters of Virginia Woolf, Vol. I: 1888–1912*; The Hogarth Press; London, 1975).

exists whole passages are revised within the text. No attempt has been made in this edition to present a record of these textual revisions and variations. To have done so would have greatly impaired the enjoyment of most readers. For anyone seriously interested in studying this aspect of Virginia Woolf's memoirs, the material is available at the University of Sussex Library. However, the desire to present a readable text has at no point been allowed to take precedence over what must be the commitment of primary importance, that of following faithfully Virginia Woolf's last intentions regarding the material as far as they are known or can be reasonably surmised, or to state the reason for not doing so and to indicate doubt where it exists. It is hoped that the 'editorial machinery' will not be unpleasantly obtrusive to the general reader — and Editor's Notes to the individual texts have been provided to minimize this danger — but that it is in evidence has at least the advantage of keeping before the reader the fact that these texts were not prepared for publication by Virginia Woolf, and hence they should not be judged by the same criteria as would be applied to texts published during her lifetime.

Because the selections that follow are in different stages of revision it has occasionally been necessary to adapt editorial practice to deal with specific problems. When this has been done, mention has been made in the appropriate preface. With that exception, the following editorial principles have been applied to the texts uniformly.

Deletions made by Virginia Woolf have not been included unless they are necessary for the sense of the passage and no substitute has been provided. In such cases the deleted words have been enclosed in square brackets. Partial deletions, which are not uncommon, have been silently completed. In those few cases where Virginia Woolf added a word or a phrase but failed to make the deletion necessary to accommodate the addition, the oversight has been silently corrected. For example, in "Old Bloomsbury", the first version of one passage reads: "True, we still had Thursday evenings as before. But they were always strained and ended generally in dismal failure." Virginia Woolf then added 'often' before 'ended' but failed to delete 'generally'. Where an addition has made it necessary to alter the grammatical form of a word, the change has been listed in the Appendix. Deletions which are of interest have been noted.

Just as some of Virginia Woolf's deletions were incomplete, so were some of her additions and corrections. When it was impossible to incorporate them into the text without serious disruption to the thought they have been omitted and noted. In those instances where a word or phrase was added by Virginia Woolf in such a way as to make it clear that it was merely being considered as an alternative, the later version has been used except where the first is clearly preferable. In very few instances indeed is any point of significance involved; however, alternative readings have been noted if they are of interest or if there is doubt as to the choice Virginia Woolf would have made.

In early drafts, Virginia Woolf's practice regarding punctuation, spelling and capitalization was highly erratic and she often used abbreviations which never appeared in her published work. On occasion, obvious oversights coupled with typing mistakes and incomplete or hastily made corrections have resulted in a profusion of errors; at others, the careful attention to these matters which characterizes her published works is evident. It was Virginia Woolf's practice to submit her work to her husband, Leonard, for revision of these details and he, in publishing her posthumous works, did not hesitate, as he writes in the editorial preface to *The Death of the Moth,** 'to punctuate' the essays and correct 'obvious verbal mistakes'. Although the liberties that Leonard Woolf would have been justified in taking could not be similarly justified by anyone else, his practice has at least served as a general guideline for the kinds of corrections which have been made in the present text; for it is equally clear that in the case of these memoirs—unlike that of the Diary or the Letters —Virginia Woolf would most certainly have made the spelling, punctuation and capitalization conform to standard usage, except where a nuance was involved, had she decided to publish them.

Hence punctuation has been altered to conform to Virginia Woolf's own practice in her published works. Hyphens, italics, question marks, full stops, double quotes for dialogue, apostrophes for possessives and contractions have been added where appropriate; 'and' has been substituted for the ampersand; abbreviations and numbers have been written out where it was her practice to do so. Apart from these uncontroversial examples, punctuation has been altered only to avoid ambiguity, to correct obvious oversights, or to conform to a pattern established in a sentence or passage which was momentarily overlooked. No attempt has been made to make Virginia Woolf's idiosyncratic and highly expressive punctuation conform in other respects to conventional usage. When, for example,

* The Hogarth Press; London, 1942.

an exclamation point occurs in the middle of a sentence, it is retained
if it is appropriate to the sense of the passage. All typing errors have
been corrected. Spelling and capitalization have been regularized
to conform to common usage unless a nuance is involved.

The sense or the grammar of a sentence has occasionally necessita-
ted the addition of a word which has been enclosed in brackets.
However, more than one word in brackets without a note indicates
words deleted by Virginia Woolf as explained above. All doubtful
readings and illegible words have been noted except in those few
cases where a legible and acceptable alternative is available.

The individual prefaces contain a brief description of the subject
matter of the memoir in order to avoid cumbersome annotations of
the text; the date and circumstances of writing; and a description of
the typescript or manuscript on which the edited text is based as well
as any unusual problems.

For the sake of brevity, the initials 'VW' and 'LW', for Virginia
and Leonard Woolf respectively, have been used in the footnotes.
The manuscripts and typescripts (ms and ts) are referred to by their
Library reference numbers, for example, 'MH/A.5a', except that
after the initial mention, the 'MH' (Monks House) has been omitted
because all the papers come from that collection. The two-volume
biography by Quentin Bell* is referred to simply as 'QB' followed
by the appropriate volume and page numbers. The Letters, edited
by Nigel Nicolson, are referred to as '*Letters*, I'. No attempt has been
made to be exhaustive in the identification of persons mentioned in
the memoirs. In those cases where the individual was of minor or
passing significance to Virginia Woolf, or significant because of being
representative of a type, as the context makes clear, identification
has not generally been made. Quentin Bell's biography is available
for those interested in such details and it will soon be supplemented
by further volumes of the Letters as mentioned above. The period in
general and 'Bloomsbury' in particular are amply documented.

* The Hogarth Press; London, 1972.

Introduction

This collection of autobiographical writings, although diverse, nevertheless reveals the remarkable unity of Virginia Woolf's art, thought and sensibility. The beliefs and values that underlie her work are shown in these pages to be an outgrowth of the sensibility which marked her responses to the world from the very beginning, with a distinctive quality. The need to express this vision was perhaps the chief impetus behind the experiments with structures, techniques and style which place Virginia Woolf's novels among the most highly innovative and personal contributions in the history of the genre. These memoirs also reveal the unusual degree to which Virginia Woolf wove the facts of her life—the people, the incidents, the emotions—into the fabric of her fiction, thus testifying to the firm artistic control she exercised over that material in creating works having the coherence and inner necessity which distinguish the highest artistic achievement.

The first selection, "Reminiscences", begun in 1907, eight years before the publication of Virginia Woolf's first novel, *The Voyage Out*, belongs to the period of her apprenticeship. At that time, she regularly assigned herself literary exercises which often took the form of short descriptive essays to be shown only to a few intimates and as much, one suspects, for their reactions and judgements as for their amusement. "Reminiscences" was intended as a 'life' of her sister Vanessa, but it is in fact a memoir of the childhood and adolescence they shared. The second item of the collection, "A Sketch of the Past", was written at the end of her career and was clearly intended to provide relief from particularly taxing literary commitments and from the deepening gloom of the second world war. The two selections are juxtaposed here because they concern the same period of Virginia Woolf's life, that is, the early years before the move to Bloomsbury.

The three pieces that follow were papers delivered between 1920 and 1936 to the Memoir Club, a group of close friends of long standing who gathered at intervals to read memoirs in which they were committed to complete candour. The intimate character of the Memoir Club is evident in the tone that pervades the three papers and contrasts sharply with that of the other selections, different as they are from one another. The order in which the papers were written coincides with the chronological order of the events described; the first paper takes up where the preceding selection, "A Sketch of the Past", ends. The first two papers, "22 Hyde Park Gate" and "Old Bloomsbury", were written in the early 1920s when Virginia Woolf was on the threshold of artistic maturity and about to create for the novel new forms and techniques so admirably adapted to the expression of her highly personal vision. The last selection of the present volume, "Am I a Snob?", was written in the late 1930s and is, if a state of mind can be pinned down to a period, concerned chiefly with events of that decade.

The diversity of purpose which characterizes these memoirs—written for different audiences and occasions and spanning a career that lasted almost four decades—might well have resulted in an absence of coherence, a random heaping together of fragments of a life. Yet the fragments do arrange themselves into a meaningful order; a pattern emerges which expresses Virginia Woolf's view of the self generally, and herself in particular, in ways that a conventional autobiography could not have done.

That self was an elusive will o' the wisp, always just ahead on the horizon, flickering and insubstantial, yet enduring. She believed the individual identity to be always in flux, every moment changing its shape in response to the forces surrounding it: forces which were invisible emerge, others sink silently below the surface, and the past, on which the identity of the present moment rests, is never static, never fixed like a fly in amber, but as subject to alteration as the consciousness that recalls it. As she writes in "A Sketch of the Past", when she thinks she may have discovered a possible form for the memoirs: "That is, to make them include the present—at least enough of the present to serve as platform to stand upon. It would be interesting to make the two people, I now, I then, come out in contrast. And further, this past is much affected by the present moment. What I write today I should not write in a year's time."*

Thus, in "A Sketch of the Past", this belief in the ceaseless transformation of personality is formally expressed in the juxtaposition of the present self and the past self. Virginia Woolf's present self is conveyed in the fragments of her daily life that preface each entry and in the reflective, mature consciousness which is continually

* p. 75.

searching and probing the past for meanings that could not have been evident to the self who had the experience. The collection taken as a whole, composed as it is of material written at such widely different stages in her life and in her development as a writer, also dramatizes this point of view by filtering the past through a succession of present selves. Even the last selection, "Am I a Snob?", which deals more with contemporary events than any of the other selections, leads back to Hyde Park Gate, albeit through a side entrance. In short, the collection emphasizes the active interpenetration of past and present that continually results in fresh arrangements of that elusive identity which is 'the subject of these memoirs'.

In the first selection, for example, Julia Stephen, Virginia's mother, is an enigmatic, revered, perhaps slightly resented, certainly distant figure who, though dead some dozen years, remains for the daughter a powerful, almost obsessive presence, but is not after all very credible. When Virginia Woolf writes again of Julia in "A Sketch of the Past", long after the cathartic experience of writing *To the Lighthouse*, she does so with perception and understanding gained partly, no doubt, through abandoning the unwitting subterfuge of reverence and honestly confronting her feelings towards her mother in all their ambivalence and complexity. As a result, both Julia Stephen and Virginia Woolf are much more fully realized; the slightly implausible, superficial identities created in the first memoir now reveal nuances and depths of meaning which were barely suggested in the earlier sketch. A similar increase in honesty and perception can be seen in the two portraits of Leslie Stephen. In the first sketch, Virginia Woolf's harsh but muted resentment of her father after Stella's death is at least partly responsible for the distorted and incomplete view of him and of their relationship. One would not easily sense the intensity of her feeling for him, so skilfully is it concealed. This emerges only in the later memoir where shading is added to the spare lines of the sketch, creating around Leslie Stephen a complex psychological space in which he achieves a convincing existence. In frankly acknowledging the vehemence of her anger against him she is free to acknowledge the depth of her love and affection for him.

If life then is 'a bowl which one fills and fills and fills', each new experience added to the existing ones displaces them ever so slightly and alters their previous meaning by forcing them into new combinations. The present moment is enriched by the past but the past

is also enriched by the present. This view of the self which emphasizes simultaneously the change and continuity of the individual
identity is of central importance in Virginia Woolf's fiction; it lies
behind her attitudes to the characters she creates—Mrs Dalloway,
for example, Mr and Mrs Ramsay, the six characters of *The Waves*,
Mrs Swithin—endowing them with the elusiveness and complexity
of figures in the real world. Her characters are marked by the infinite
variability which she admired in Mme. de Sévigné: "And then
something she says rouses us. We add it to her character, so that the
character grows and changes, and she seems like a living person,
inexhaustible."* There is a roominess about so many of Virginia
Woolf's characters, a sense of mystery and of the inexplicable; they
are rarely enclosed in precise outlines.

This conviction that the outer crust of the self, one's personality, is
a finely tuned mechanism, sensitive as a seismograph to the slightest
vibration in the social environment, and hence volatile like the flux
and multiplicity of experience to which it is exposed, inspired a
particular concern in her novels with just those moments when
identities are created out of situations and relationships through the
chameleon transformations of the responsive personality. Bernard,
in *The Waves*, aware of his doffing and donning of carapaces, reflects
how: "The tree alone resisted our eternal flux. For I changed and
changed; was Hamlet, was Shelley, was the hero, whose name I now
forget, of a novel by Dostoevsky; was for a whole term, incredibly,
Napoleon; but was Byron chiefly. For many weeks at a time it
was my part to stride into rooms and fling gloves and coat on the
back of chairs, scowling slightly."† He seeks to crystallize his
identity, to put his finger on it and halt the flux: "But now let me
ask myself the final question, as I sit over this grey fire, with its
naked promontories of black coal, which of these people am I? It
depends so much upon the room. When I say to myself, 'Bernard,'
who comes?"‡ Susan echoes his thought as she muses: "For there is
nothing to lay hold of. I am made and remade continually. Different
people draw different words from me."§

* *Collected Essays*, Vol. III, ed. Leonard Woolf (The Hogarth Press;
London, 1967), p. 66.
† (The Hogarth Press; London, 1943, new edition), p. 177. *The Waves*
was first published in 1931.
‡ *op. cit.*, p. 58.
§ *op. cit.*, p. 96.

And so the audiences for which these memoirs were written draw out different sides of Virginia Woolf's personality, and so demonstrate just this facet of her belief in the continuously changing identity in the context of her own life and personality. In "A Sketch of the Past" she puts it this way: "This influence, by which I mean the consciousness of other groups impinging upon ourselves; public opinion; what other people say and think; all those magnets which attract us this way to be like that, or repel us the other and make us different from that; has never been analysed in any of those Lives which I so much enjoy reading, or very superficially. Yet it is by such invisible presences that the 'subject of this memoir' is tugged this way and that every day of his life; it is they that keep him in position . . . if we cannot analyse these invisible presences, we know very little of the subject of the memoir; and again how futile life-writing becomes. I see myself as a fish in a stream; deflected; held in place; but cannot describe the stream."*

These memoirs reveal, by their variously shaded tones, 'other groups impinging' on Virginia Woolf's consciousness, how 'what other people say and think' subtly alters the shape of the self that is presented to the world. In the first memoir, "Reminiscences", there is a self-conscious adoption of a literary 'manner', not unexpected in a writer just learning to gauge the spread of her wings but nonetheless distracting, particularly at those moments when the forced flights of the poetic imagination leave feeling far behind on the ground or the tentative starts into areas of originality are cut short by hasty retreats into the safety of conventional formulas. The self-consciousness, with its hint of vulnerability, no doubt reflects a slight unease regarding her audience. Virginia Woolf had intended the 'life' of Vanessa to be read by her new brother-in-law with whom she was not yet on a completely free and easy footing and by her sister with whom she was conscious of reestablishing relations on a new basis. Indeed, so omnipresent was Clive Bell at this period that she felt she might never see Vanessa alone again.† This situation may partially account for the occasional disconcerting shifts of tone, from an affectionate intimacy to a stilted, formal manner like that

* p. 80.
† In a letter to Violet Dickinson (3 January 1907) she writes: "I did not see Nessa alone, but I realise that that is all over, and I shall never see her alone any more; and Clive is a new part of her, which I must learn to accept." (*Letters*, I, No. 336.)

which Virginia Woolf later associated with the 'Victorian tea table manner'.

"A Sketch of the Past" provides a sharp contrast with its easy, unaffected manner revealing an ego so unaware of itself that it appears almost impersonal. So confident is she now, so much a master of her material, that she need not even be bothered to decide on a form before beginning: "So without stopping to choose my way, in the sure and certain knowledge that it will find itself—or if not it will not matter—I begin: the first memory."* The memoir is characterized by a flowing, ruminative expansiveness; it presents a consciousness which follows its own peculiar byways rather than a pre-ordained route as it ponders the meaning of reality and the mystery of identity.

The Memoir Club contributions expose yet another side of Virginia Woolf. The expanding, reflective self of "A Sketch of the Past" is contracted into a sharper, more definite shape, a well-known and predictable personality confronting a group of old friends who, though intimate, are nonetheless demanding. They expect total frankness, some originality, and certainly they expect to be amused. These requirements are met in full and Virginia Woolf's enjoyment of the informality of the occasion is obvious. Her wit sparkles and not infrequently she adds a playful malice to her flights of candour, as she peers into dark cupboards and under beds, stripping bare the heavy padding of suppression and evasion which characterized Victorian attitudes to sexuality.

The memoirs bring to the surface other invisible forces mentioned in "A Sketch of the Past" which deflect the fish in the stream 'this way and that'—namely 'society [that] changes from decade to decade, and also from class to class.' The worlds described in the memoirs are remarkably varied. With great economy, Virginia Woolf describes the pressures exerted by the conventions and beliefs dominant in the late Victorian, upper middle class family life of the Stephens and Duckworths at Hyde Park Gate. The family is set in a broad historical perspective as the disparate forces which contributed to its making are analysed: the literary, free-thinking world of Leslie Stephen and his friends; the puritanical, socially conscious attitudes of the Clapham Sect; the painters and poets at Little Holland House; the 'Society' of the well-connected Duckworths. As the Victorian age passes imperceptibly into the Edwardian the young

* p. 64.

Stephens develop interests which lead them in different directions: Thoby goes to Cambridge, Vanessa has her painting, and Virginia her writing. Then Hyde Park Gate is left behind and 'Bloomsbury' gradually takes shape. Virginia Woolf charts the development of 'Bloomsbury' from its serious, truth-seeking, Cambridge-oriented origins, through its period of notoriety, to what, in some respects at least, was its antithesis, the society of London hostesses such as Margot Asquith and Sibyl Colefax.

The greatest insights afforded by these memoirs into Virginia Woolf's life, her thought and sensibility and the development of her art, are not, however, those brought about thus fortuitously but those which emerge when she consciously sets out to explore the origins of the beliefs and intuitions which shaped and ordered her vision of life and which, as she began to write fiction, gradually came to shape and order that as well.

One such belief is that the individual in his daily life is cut off from 'reality' but at rare moments receives a shock. These shocks or 'moments of being' are not, as she had imagined as a child, simply random manifestations of some malevolent force but 'a token of some real thing behind appearances'. The idea of a privileged moment when a spiritually transcendent truth of either personal or cosmic dimensions is perceived in a flash of intuition is, of course, a commonplace of religious experience and in particular of mystical traditions of thought, as well as a recurrent feature of idealist philosophies from Plato onwards. But in these memoirs Virginia Woolf sets this belief in a uniquely personal context and shows it emerging, almost inevitably, from her own intense and highly individual susceptibility.

In a few words she sets forth that fundamental conviction which underlies the meaning she finds in her own life and that which she creates in her fiction: "From this I reach what I might call a philosophy; at any rate it is a constant idea of mine; that behind the cotton wool is hidden a pattern; that we—I mean all human beings—are connected with this; that the whole world is a work of art; that we are parts of the work of art. *Hamlet* or a Beethoven quartet is the truth about this vast mass that we call the world. But there is no Shakespeare, there is no Beethoven; certainly and emphatically there is no God; we are the words; we are the music; we are the thing itself."*

* p. 72.

Here, so succinctly stated, is the explanation why the search for 'Mrs Brown' — Virginia Woolf's shorthand for the idea of character in the novel — cannot be purposefully separated from the search for reality, why the subject of the memoir cannot be separated from "the stream". The questions repeatedly posed by the characters of her novels — What is life? What is love? What is reality? Who are you? Who am I? — lead to this one end, the spiritual continuum which embraces all of life, the vision of reality as a timeless unity which lies beneath the appearance of change, separation and disorder that marks daily life. As one of the characters in *The Waves* remarks: "It is Percival . . . who makes us aware that these attempts to say, 'I am this, I am that,' which we make, coming together, like separated parts of one body and soul, are false. Something has been left out from fear. Something has been altered, from vanity. We have tried to accentuate differences. From the desire to be separate we have laid stress upon our faults, and what is particular to us. But there is a chain whirling round, round, in a steel-blue circle beneath."*

The emphasis on the change and continuity of personal identity discussed above applies only to the self that inhabits the finite world of physical and social existence. During moments of being, this self is transcended and the individual consciousness becomes an undifferentiated part of a greater whole. Thus, just as the outer limits of personality are blurred and unstable because of the responsiveness of the self to the forces of the present moment, so the boundaries of the inner self are vague and, at moments, non-existent. For Virginia Woolf, when the self merges with reality, all limits associated with the physical world cease to exist. Mrs Dalloway, so definite and dartlike on the surface, becomes a consciousness transcending all temporal and physical boundaries, merging, through her imaginative, intuitive identification with Septimus Warren Smith, with the impersonal, universal consciousness that lies behind all of those characters in the novel not irrevocably sealed off from reality. In *To the Lighthouse*, there is a picture of Mrs Ramsay, after the children have gone to bed and quiet has descended on the house, sinking slowly but deeply into one of those moments of being characterized by intimations of profound understanding and communion against which a sense of what one is to others seems trivial, transitory and illusory. "All the being and the doing, expansive, glittering, vocal,

* p. 98.

evaporated; and one shrunk, with a sense of solemnity, to being oneself, a wedge-shaped core of darkness, something invisible to others ... and this self having shed its attachments was free for the strangest adventures. When life sank down for a moment, the range of experience seemed limitless."*

To convey these two levels of being—the surface and the spreading depths—was the challenge taken up by Virginia Woolf the memoir writer as well as by Virginia Woolf the novelist. As she once wrote of De Quincey: "To tell the whole story of a life the autobiographer must devise some means by which the two levels of existence can be recorded—the rapid passage of events and actions; the slow opening up of single and solemn moments of concentrated emotion."† In "A Sketch of the Past" the two levels are interwoven. The moments of being, sometimes charged with revelations of astonishing intensity, are threaded in among scenes, of typical days and occasions, describing the physical environment, the social forces, the family and personal attachments and passions, which shape the outer self.

The moment of intensity may come, as it once did in Virginia Woolf's own experience, from something as apparently trivial as seeing a flower and understanding it as part of a greater whole; such an experience was, for her, one of those moments which she described in the essay on De Quincey that 'transcend in value fifty years'. Such a moment for Virginia Woolf is one of recognition and then revelation—the value of which is independent of the object that is catalyst—and, as such, is very close to Joyce's notion of epiphany. One is reminded of the young Stephen Daedalus solemnly telling his friend Cranly 'that the clock of the Ballast office was capable of epiphany.'‡ The difficulties facing the writer who seeks to convey a value of this order are daunting in a special way; for such a moment has few consequences which can be objectively demonstrated. Furthermore, the experience of the moment of being is so personal, the belief in a transcending order so intuitive, that, as Virginia Woolf herself wrote in describing her 'philosophy': 'it will not bear arguing about; it is irrational'.

* The Hogarth Press; London, 1943. Uniform Edition, p. 99. *To the Lighthouse* was first published in 1927.

† *Collected Essays*, Vol. IV, p. 6.

‡ *Stephen Hero*, ed. T. Spencer, rev. ed. (New English Library; London, 1966), p. 216.

Although Virginia Woolf never believed that these moments of being were reserved for an élite she did believe that they were withheld from some. In both the memoirs and in the novels there are figures around whom precise outlines are drawn, in contrast to the supple, fluid lines which she commonly used to portray character. Such figures are so encrusted with the trivia of daily life, so attached to objects and values which are in the last analysis irrelevant, or so imprisoned by their egocentricity, that they are incapable of cutting themselves free from the material world: George Duckworth, Sibyl Colefax, Margot Asquith, in the memoirs; Hugh Whitbread, Miss Kilman and Charles Tansley in the novels. Reality never penetrates the cotton wool of their daily lives.

Belief in these moments of being both motivated and determined the direction of Virginia Woolf's experiments with the forms of fiction which eventually resulted in her discovery of a method — indeed a variety of methods — for recording the two worlds of being and non-being. Success, however, was only achieved through continuous and exacting experimentation. A comparison of her first two novels, *The Voyage Out* and *Night and Day*, with *To the Lighthouse* and *The Waves*, or of the early "Reminiscences" with the later memoir, "A Sketch of the Past", shows vividly the difficulties Virginia Woolf had to overcome before she successfully fused form, method and idea.

In "A Sketch of the Past" she considers, almost parenthetically, how her instinctive way of responding to experience cannot be separated from her literary methods nor from her belief in the pattern of significance behind the apparent contingency of the present moment. "Whatever the reason may be, I find that scene making is my natural way of marking the past. Always a scene has arranged itself: representative; enduring. This confirms me in my instinctive notion . . . the sensation that we are sealed vessels afloat on what it is convenient to call reality; and at some moments, the sealing matter cracks; in floods reality; that is, these scenes. . . ."*
In "A Sketch of the Past", as in most of her fiction, she imposed an order based on these moments of being and conveyed by means of these scenes.

Many of her novels are similarly organized; that is, scenes, characters, images and so on, that might initially appear to have been selected arbitrarily are subsequently revealed to be pieces of the hidden pattern. During the day of Mrs Dalloway's party not only

* p. 122.

do the scenes in the minds of the major characters suggest patterns of significance built up over a lifetime, of which only fragments are brought to the surface, but the sharp differences between Clarissa Dalloway and Septimus Warren Smith, reinforced by the implausible juxtapositions of scenes from their respective lives, are shown, by the revelation of this other reality—to be merely superficial. Similarly, in *To the Lighthouse* two passages of time separated by an interval of ten years and seemingly selected at random are ultimately locked in a pattern of significant moments in the minds of several of the characters.

Implicit in this approach to the past is the role of memory: for the moment of being is most often a 'sledge-hammer blow', a shock; the meaning unfolds after the experience. The decisive role which memory plays in Virginia Woolf's moments of being brings out her affinity with Wordsworth, specifically with his emphasis on 'emotion recollected in tranquillity'. Often, for Virginia Woolf, an experience would only begin to seem real once she had written about it; only then was its import recognized. Apparently she attached importance to the element of reflection involved from an early age: " 'That is the whole', I said. I was looking at a plant with a spread of leaves; and it seemed suddenly plain that the flower itself was a part of the earth; that a ring enclosed what was the flower; and that was the real flower; part earth; part flower. It was a thought I put away as being likely to be very useful to me later."* Thus memory, itself the test of the enduring quality of the moment of being, is invaluable in extending the dimensions of the moment; memory is the means by which the individual builds up patterns of personal significance to which to anchor his or her life and secure it against the 'lash of the random unheeding flail'. Witness the case of Septimus Warren Smith: when he lost his power to recall the past, he lost his will to survive the present.

Inseparable from this 'scene making' which is characteristic of both the memoirs and the fiction of Virginia Woolf is the 'symbol making' quality of her vision. In *To the Lighthouse*, 'a symbolical outline' transcends the 'real figures of Mr and Mrs Ramsay' as Lily and Mr Bankes approach them: "And suddenly the meaning which, for no reason at all, as perhaps they are stepping out of the Tube or ringing a doorbell, descends on people, making them symbolical, making them representative, came upon them, and made them in

* p. 71.

the dusk standing, looking, the symbols of marriage, husband and wife."* In "A Sketch of the Past", Virginia Woolf describes a similar personal experience of an ordinary object gradually being invested with just such a symbolic meaning. "And the tree, outside in the dark garden, was to me the emblem, the symbol, of the skeleton agony to which her (Stella's) death had reduced him (Jack); and us; everything."†

Certain images—involving sights, sounds, odours—also appear to have permeated the innermost fibres of her being, so that they too assume a symbolic significance: the waves breaking; the acorn of the blind being drawn across the floor; the nutty smelling gorse; the rooks cawing; the colour of the flowers on her mother's dress. Though these experiences occur on a purely sensual level they have that enduring force for Virginia Woolf which makes them no less moments of being than those flashes of recognition involving understanding.

In the mature fiction, the moments of being are threaded on a 'steel ring'—to borrow a phrase from *The Waves*. The ring exists beyond space and time, beyond the individual. When Mrs Dalloway experiences that reality most intensely, in the moment of identification with Septimus, she adds her moment to the 'steel ring'. She becomes—for that moment—part of the impersonal consciousness which is expressed through intricately woven patterns constructed out of recurring rhythms, symbols, images and phrases, patterns which deliberately violate the laws of probability governing the finite, material world. The ring is the pattern, the hidden order: "a steel ring of clear poetry", which Louis in *The Waves* searches for, "that shall connect the gulls and the women with bad teeth, the church spire and the bobbing billycock hats. . . ."‡

It is not however only the genesis of Virginia Woolf's vision and art which is shown with such clarity in these memoirs but also much of the raw material of her fiction. An appreciation of the fiction by no means requires a knowledge of its autobiographical roots but such knowledge cannot but enrich one's reading of the fiction, giving it a density of association like that which memory gives to the present moment. That Virginia Woolf's personal relationships have generated whole novels has been widely known since the publication

* pp. 114–15.
† p. 121.
‡ p. 92.

of *A Writer's Diary* and Quentin Bell's biography. There is her relationship with her father and mother which lies behind *To the
Lighthouse*; her brother Thoby whose memory is honoured in *Jacob's
Room* and in the character of Percival in *The Waves*; Kitty Maxse
who contributed to the portrait of Mrs Dalloway. The present collection brings to light many sources for minor characters. George
Duckworth pondering the question of whether the crest on the post
office notepaper would look well picked out in red bears a striking
resemblance to Hugh Whitbread in *Mrs Dalloway*, 'carrying a
despatch box stamped with the Royal Arms', or 'drafting sentiments
in alphabetical order of the highest nobility'. George's 'saintliness',
the eagerness with which he always did 'the tactful thing', is woven
into Hugh's reputation for being 'indispensable to hostesses'.
Virginia Woolf's ruthless attentiveness to George's greed helps to
explain the note of vindictiveness in the attack on Hugh's greediness.
Lady Bruton's supreme nonchalance as well as her difficulties with
the English language recall the portrait of the Marchioness of Bath
lounging on her sofa and appealing to her butler: "what's marl,
Middleton?"

The extent to which the most minor details in Virginia Woolf's
fiction were drawn from specific experiences is perhaps less well
known. The story of her father throwing the flower pot at his mother,
whether apocryphal or not, is clearly the prototype for the incident
in which Mr Ramsay "finding an earwig in his milk at breakfast had
sent the whole thing flying through the air on to the terrace outside."
The brooch which Minta lost in *To the Lighthouse* was most probably
inspired by the one lost by a visitor to Talland House and 'cried' by
Charlie Pearce, the town crier. Cam, at loggerheads with James
because she insists that a shawl be thrown over the boar's skull,
recreates the situation in the Stephen nursery when Virginia and
Adrian argued about the fire which Adrian liked but which
frightened Virginia if it burned after she had gone to bed. "As a
compromise Nurse folded a towel over the fender . . . ." Innumerable
incidents in the memoirs reappear in the novels, although almost
always in slightly altered forms or new arrangements. But not only
incidents, the images too which recur in novel after novel are so
often those which seem to have been fixed immutably in Virginia
Woolf's early consciousness. Certain sounds form the basis of
rhythmic patterns which appear in the novels—for example, the
waves breaking on the shore which reverberate throughout the

novel named after them. Other sounds play a less dramatic role, but are not less memorable, such as the sound of the latch on the gate at Talland House which can be heard again as Mrs Dalloway remembers: "For so it had always seemed to her when, with a little squeak of the hinges, which she could hear now. . . ."

But the material of the fiction, however directly it appears to have been taken from her life, was nevertheless subtly transmuted in the creative process. Bits of one individual or incident are not infrequently found mixed with bits of another, but more significantly, the meaning of the thing created, whether character or incident, is rigorously subordinated to the design of the novel which, once established, generated its own principles of harmony and coherence. Apart from this caution against expecting the autobiographical material to 'explain' the fiction, the memoirs, whose undeniable intrinsic merit enables them to stand richly on their own, cannot but deepen the experience of reading the fiction by rooting it more firmly in the context of Virginia Woolf's life.

REMINISCENCES

(*Editor's Note*)

These reminiscences of Julia Stephen, Stella Duckworth and Vanessa Bell, the three figures who stood successively at the heart of the Stephen/Duckworth ménage at 22 Hyde Park Gate, were addressed to the first child of Vanessa and Clive Bell. Julian, however, can only be held responsible in a very remote sense for inspiring this memoir; for, according to Quentin Bell, it was begun before Julian's birth (February 1908) when Virginia was spending the summer holidays of 1907 in Playden, just north of Rye, where the Bells were staying.* The memoir is mentioned in two letters after Julian's birth: one, from Virginia to Clive, written on 15 April 1908, and another from Vanessa to Virginia from Cleeve House, of 20 April 1908.† In the letter to Clive it is clear that Virginia's feeling for Vanessa was a major source of inspiration: "I have been writing Nessa's life; and I am going to send you 2 chapters in a day or two. It might have been so good! As it is, I am too near, and too far; and it seems to be blurred, and I ask myself why write it at all? seeing I never shall recapture what you have, by your side this minute."‡

At the age of twenty-five, Virginia Woolf was very conscious of being an apprentice at her chosen craft. She had been reviewing since the end of 1904 but her own first 'work of imagination' as she called 'Melymbrosia' (published in 1915 as *The Voyage Out*) was only just begun. Of the exercises which she conscientiously assigned herself, descriptions of places visited and the lives of close friends or relations formed an important part.§ She showed these experiments only to a few intimates and on various occasions she declared her intention of rewriting them at set intervals. It is in such a provisional light that the "Reminiscences" should be read.

* QB, I, p. 122.
† In The Berg Collection, the New York Public Library.
‡ *Letters*, I, No. 406.
§ At this period of her life she wrote, for example, "lives" of her intimate friend Violet Dickinson, her Quaker Aunt Caroline Emelia Stephen and her Aunt Mary Fisher. The 'Life' of Violet is in the Berg Collection ("Friendship's Gallery") but the comic lives of the two aunts have not come to light. See *Letters*, I, No. 199.

Yet, in addressing the memoir to the next generation and in broadening her subject to include the Stephen family so that no meaningful distinction can be made here between biography (of Vanessa) and autobiography, Virginia Woolf continued a practice which might almost be said to have attained the status of a family tradition. For her great grandfather, James Stephen, had written his memoirs for the use of his children* and her father, Leslie, had followed suit in writing the 'Mausoleum Book', addressed to his children and step-children.†

Virginia Woolf begins the memoir with her childish impressions of Vanessa, who was three years her senior, recreating as she goes a vivid impression of the vitality, affection and security which distinguished life in the Stephen family. This family life was brutally transformed by the deaths of Julia, her mother, and then Stella, those traumatic events which seemed to bear the message that life had begun in earnest for the Stephen children.

Julia Jackson, daughter of Maria, one of the beautiful Pattle sisters, and Dr Jackson, was born in 1846. In 1867, when she was twenty-one, she married Herbert Duckworth, a barrister, who died three years later on 19 September 1870. The three children of the marriage were George (b. 1868); Stella (b. 1869); and Gerald, born after the death of his father in 1870. Eight years of widowhood ended in 1878 when Julia married Leslie Stephen whose first wife Minny, daughter of Thackeray, had died in 1875 leaving one child, Laura, whose mental deficiency was becoming increasingly apparent. There were four children born to Julia and Leslie Stephen: Vanessa (b. 1879); Thoby (b. 1880); Virginia (b. 1882) and Adrian (b. 1883). When Julia died in 1895 Stella assumed her responsibilities in the house at Hyde Park Gate. She married John Waller (Jack) Hills in 1897; she died three months later. It was now Vanessa's turn to be her father's 'angel in the house', a role which ill suited her. Jack is just emerging from the black grief into which Stella's death had plunged him when the memoir ends somewhat abruptly—perhaps because of the difficulty, as Quentin Bell has suggested, of describing Vanessa's affair with Jack.

The text that follows (Library reference number MH/A. 6) is based on fifty-six pages typed by Virginia Woolf, with corrections

* *The Memoirs of James Stephen. Written by Himself for the Use of His Children*, ed. M. M. Bevington (The Hogarth Press; London, 1954).
† This manuscript is now in the British Museum.

by her in soft black and blue lead pencil and black ink.* The corrections are minor, confined for the most part to single words or phrases which involve matters of style rather than changes of thought. The typing, for Virginia Woolf, is unusually careful. There are a number of infelicitous phrases, inelegant repetitions, grammatical confusions and obscurities of thought such as are rarely found in her later work and which she would surely have resolved had she prepared the text for publication.

* The finer, hard lead pencil marks date from after VW's death and were made by Clive Bell.

Reminiscences
CHAPTER ONE

Your mother was born in 1879, and as some six years at least must have passed before I knew that she was my sister, I can say nothing of that time.* A photograph is the best token there is of her appearance, and the face in this instance shows also much of the character. You see the soft, dreamy and almost melancholy expression of the eyes; and it may not be fanciful to discover some kind of test and rejection in them as though, even then, she considered the thing she saw, and did not always find what she needed in it. But certainly it would be mere fancy to conceive that this was other than unconscious at that age. For the rest, a mother who gazed in her face might feel her heart leap at the endowment already promised her daughter, for she was to have great beauty. And in this case the mother would also feel tender joy within her, and some bright amusement too, for already her daughter promised to be honest and loving; already, as I have heard, she was able to care for the three little creatures who were younger than she was, teaching Thoby his letters, and giving up to him her bottle. I can imagine that she attached great importance to the way in which Thoby sat in his highchair, and appealed to Nurse to have him properly fastened there before he was allowed to eat his porridge. Her mother would smile silently at this.

Our life was ordered with great simplicity and regularity. It seems to divide itself into two large spaces, not crowded with events, but in some way more exquisitely natural than any that follow; for our duties were very plain and our pleasures absolutely appropriate. Earth gave all the satisfaction we asked. One space was spent indoors, in the drawing room and nursery, and the other in Kensington Gardens. There were a number of little warfares, and sometimes Nessa and Thoby fought with us and sometimes they were our friends. I remember too the great extent and mystery of the dark land under the nursery table, where a continuous romance seemed to go forward, though the time spent there was really so short. Here

* 'Your mother' is of course Julian Bell's mother, Vanessa. 'The three little creatures' whom she cares for are her younger brothers and sister — Thoby, Virginia and Adrian Stephen.

I met your mother, in a gloom happily encircled by the firelight, and peopled with legs and skirts. We drifted together like ships in an immense ocean and she asked me whether black cats had tails. And I answered that they had not, after a pause in which her question seemed to drop echoing down vast abysses, hitherto silent. In future I suppose there was some consciousness between us that the other held possibilities. But though shot occasionally by stormy passions, when sympathies seemed to waken beyond the reach of circumstances, the great satisfaction was to be had from impersonal things. There were smells and flowers and dead leaves and chestnuts, by which you distinguished the seasons, and each had innumerable associations, and power to flood the brain in a second. There were long summer evenings, with white moths abroad; and bright winter evenings when the fire-wood could be cut into shape. "The others" were not brothers and sister,* but beings possessed of knives, or enviable gifts for running or carving; and your mother, partly because she did not seem to hold these views as completely as we did, was the first to disturb me from my contentment. Another influence was even then astir in her, the influence of an affection only to be gratified by people. No hole dug in the gardens however deep, so that it was possible to extract clay of a malleable quality from it, gave her all that she needed. Dolls did not satisfy her. At present, until she was fifteen indeed, she was outwardly sober and austere, the most trustworthy, and always the eldest; sometimes she would lament her "responsibilities". Other children had their stages, and sudden gifts and failings; she seemed to draw on steadily, as though with her eye on some far object, which attained, she might reveal herself. She was very silent, and the only peculiar tastes which she seemed encouraged to show were those that people called out; she cried when Thoby went to school, and she minded more than the rest when your grandmother declared with some passion and humour, as I think, that she could never trust a single one of us again; had we not gone hunting for a dead cat against her commands? But beneath the serious surface only legitimately broken by such affections, there burnt also the other passion, the passion for art. She drew indeed under the care of a Mr Cook, but talk of art, talk of her own gifts and loves, was unknown to her. What did she think then? For with her long fingers grouping, and her eye considering, she surely painted many pictures without a canvas. Once I saw her scrawl on a black

* 'The others' are George, Stella and Gerald Duckworth.

door a great maze of lines, with white chalk. "When I am a famous painter—" she began, and then turned shy and rubbed it out in her capable way. And when she won the prize at her drawing school, she hardly knew, so shy was she, at the recognition of a secret, how to tell me, in order that I might repeat the news at home. "They've given me the thing—I don't know why." "What thing?" "O they say I've won it—the book—the prize you know." She was awkward as a long-legged colt.

When I try to see her I see more distinctly how our lives are pieces in a pattern and to judge one truly you must consider how this side is squeezed and that indented and a third expanded and none are really isolated, and so I conceive that there were many reasons then to make your mother show herself a little other than she was. We lived in a state of anxious growth; school, reports, professions to be chosen, marriage for the elders, books coming out, bills, health—the future was always too near and too much of a question for any sedate self expression. All these activities, too, charged the air with personal emotions and urged even children, and certainly "the eldest", to develop one side prematurely. To help, to do something was desirable, not to obtrude diffident wishes, irrelevant and possibly expensive.

So your mother, whose sight seemed in some ways so clear, took it upon her to be what people call 'practical' though a generous talent for losing umbrellas and forgetting messages showed that nature sometimes delighted to laugh at the pretence. But the power which was not feigned and was probably recognized by those who trusted her, was what I call variously sagacity, and common sense, and more rightly perhaps, honesty of mind. She might not see all, but she would not see what was not there. Stories, shallow though they seem, and I cannot be sure that to other eyes they will show what they show to mine, float upon the surface and must be made to illustrate this flying narrative. One August night, very much later in date, when your grandmother was dead we walked in the garden at Ringwood.* Your grandfather sat indoors alone, and might at any moment call us in to play whist with him as usual; and the light and the cards and the shouting seemed to us that night too crude and close to be tolerable. So we walked in the shade, and when we heard him come to the window and call we stood silent. Then he came out onto the lawn, and peered round him and called us each by name.

* Julian's grandparents were, of course, Julia and Leslie Stephen.

But still we persisted, and at length he went in and left us to walk alone. But as we knew from the first perhaps, such joy is not for mortals; we wandered without delight, and at last went in and found him impressive, consciously but truly impressive, old, solitary and deserted. "Did you hear me call?" he said, and I was silent, and so was Adrian; your mother hesitated, and then said "Yes".

But this shows her quality in a tragic light; exposed to the fiercest strain. In earlier years it was most often the characteristic laughable token by which we knew her; "Old Nessa's honesty" or "The Old Creature is so matter-of-fact" or "She means well". For sometimes she clung to truth too tenaciously, too simply; and we, flippant or sometimes insolent, persecuted her with horrid titles, 'Saint', and so on; for children so soon as they have any wit to direct are apt to use it cruelly. But there were then days of pure enjoyment — I conceive them at St Ives most readily,* when your mother trotted about on various businesses, considering the characters and desires of dogs very gravely, skilfully contriving butterfly nets, under your Uncle Waller's tuition,† accepting his law as the divine law, painting in water-colours, and scratching a number of black little squares, after Ruskin's prescription.‡ She played cricket better for the same reasons, with her straight forward stroke, calculated to meet all emergencies; and began by means of such fidelity and outward simplicity to win respect for herself from those tyrants and demigods who ruled our world; George, Waller, and Madge Symonds.§ She was a happy creature! beginning to feel within her the spring of unsuspected gifts, that the sea was beautiful and might be painted some day, and perhaps once or twice she looked steadily in the glass when no one was by and saw a face that excited her strangely; her being began to have a definite shape, a place in the world — what was it like? But her natural development, in which the artistic gift, so sensitive and yet so vigorous, would have asserted itself, was checked;

* St Ives, Cornwall, where the Stephen family spent summer holidays from 1882 to 1894.

† John (Jack) Walter Hills. See p. 47. "It was natural to be indebted to him . . . and to requite him by . . . the title of uncle to some one else's children."

‡ John Ruskin, *The Elements of Drawing* (London, 1857).

§ Madge Symonds, a daughter of J. A. Symonds, married Virginia's cousin, William Wyamar Vaughan. Madge was the object of Virginia's first passion, the intensity of which is echoed in Mrs Dalloway's memories of Sally Seton. (See QB, I, pp. 60–61.)

the effect of death upon those that live is always strange, and often terrible in the havoc it makes with innocent desires.

In this sense your grandmother's death was disastrous; for you must conceive that she was not only the most beautiful of women as her portraits will tell you, but also one of the most distinct. Her life had been so swift, it was to be so short, that experiences which in most have space to expand themselves and bear leisurely fruit, were all compressed in her; she had married, borne children, and mourned her husband by the time she was twenty-four. For eight years she pondered that active season, and as I guess, formulated then in great part the judgement of life which underlay her future. She had been happy as few people are happy, for she had passed like a princess in a pageant from her supremely beautiful youth to marriage and motherhood, without awakenment. If I read truly, indeed the atmosphere of her home flattered such dreams and cast over the figure of her bridegroom all the golden enchantments of Tennysonian sentiment. But it would need a clearer vision than mine to decide how far her husband, though now so obviously her inferior in all ways, was able then to satisfy noble and genuine passions in his wife. Perhaps she made satisfaction for herself, cloaking his deficiencies in her own superabundance. At any rate when he was dead she determined to consecrate those years as the golden ones; when as she phrased it perhaps, she had not known the sorrow and the crime of the world because she had lived with a man, stainless of his kind, exalted in a world of pure love and beauty. The effect of his death then was doubly tremendous, because it was a disillusionment as well as a tragic human loss. She had by nature a keen brain, remorseless of all insincerity and even too much inclined to insist that all feeling has an equivalent in action or is worthless. And now that she had none to worship she worshipped the memory, and looking on the world with clear eyes, was more scornful than was just of its tragedy and stupidity because she had lived in a dream and still cherished a dream. She flung aside her religion, and became, as I have heard, the most positive of disbelievers. She reversed those natural instincts which were so strong in her of happiness and joy in a generous and abundant life, and pressed the bitterest fruit only to her lips. She visited the poor, nursed the dying, and felt herself possessed of the true secret of life at last, which is still obscured from a few, though they too must come to know it, that sorrow is our lot, and at best we can but face it bravely. All these things certainly she would have learnt had her husband lived, but learnt them with wisdom and temperance, delighting, rejoicing in the exercise of her own gifts and in the enjoyment of blessings which, surely, were not singular. But it would be easy to exaggerate the significance of this attitude, for much of its crudeness came, not from native harshness, but from the mutilation which her natural growth had undergone. Slowly, as I believe, she came to exercise her mind, and sadly enough to determine that much of the interest of the world must come in future from the satisfaction of her intellect. She saw many clever people, and read with a desire to establish her own sad faith, the works of disbelievers who spelt God without a capital G. In particular she read some early articles by your grandfather and liked them better than she liked him.

Fate, who is thought by some to arrange human lives to her liking, chose that your grandfather, with his first wife, should live in the same street with your grandmother and further decreed that Minny was to die there, and that your grandmother thus should be thrown into contact with her learned and formidable friend under the conditions which she of all people felt most poignantly. Would any other arrangement of circumstances have so brought about the miracle? For she found one who had equal reasons with herself to believe in the sorrow of life and every incentive to adopt her own stoic philosophy; he also was of the giant breed, no light lover, no superficial optimist. She might go hand in hand with him through the shadows of the Valley—but, of a sudden, her companion became her guide, pointed on, urged her to follow, to hope, to strive once more. She could not so soon throw off what had come to be a habit of suffering almost, and yet his reason was the stronger, his need was the greater. At length with pain and remorse she, courageous as she was, more truly courageous perhaps than her husband, bade herself face the truth and realize in all its aspects the fact that joy was to be endured as well as sorrow. She rose to the heights, wide-eyed and nobly free from all illusion or sentiment, her second love shining pure as starlight; the rosy mists of the first rapture dispelled for ever. Indeed it is notable that she never spoke of her first love; and in treasuring it changed it perhaps to something far fairer than it could have been, had life allowed it to endure. The second marriage was the true though late fulfilment of all that she could be; and, but that it was rather late, rather crowded, and rather anxious, no match was more truly equal, or more ceaselessly valiant. Large words, perhaps, to use of fifteen years! with all their opportunity for smallness, failure, tolerance of mediocrity. But, although there were certain matters which seem to us now decided by her too much in a spirit of compromise, and exacted by him without strict regard for justice or magnanimity, still it is true whether you judge by their work or by themselves that it was a triumphant life, consistently aiming at high things.

These circumstances had taken their part in forming your grand-mother's character; and by the time we, her children, knew her, she was the most prompt, practical and vivid of human beings. It was as though she had made up her mind definitely upon certain great matters and was never after troubled to consider herself at all; but every deed and word had the bright, inexorable, swift stamp of something struck clearly by a mass of hoarded experience. Four children were born to her; there were four others already, older, demanding other care;* she taught us, was their companion, and soothed, cheered, inspired, nursed, deceived your grandfather; and any one coming for help found her invincibly upright in her place, with time to give, earnest consideration, and the most practical sympathy. Her relations with people indeed were all through her life remarkable; and after her second marriage this decision, of which I speak, seemed to make her spend herself more freely than ever in the service of others. And as that phrase has a doubtful reputation, and might well lead you to imagine a different woman from the real one, I must explain that her conduct in this matter was singular, and by no means of a piece with the mischievous philanthropy which other women practise so complacently and often with such disastrous results.

Her view of the world had come to be very comprehensive; she seemed to watch, like some wise Fate, the birth, growth, flower and death of innumerable lives all round her, with a constant sense of the mystery that encircled them, not now so sceptical as of old, and [with] a perfectly definite idea of the help that was possible and of use. Her intellectual gifts had always been those that find their closest expression in action; she had great clearness of insight, sound judgement, humour, and a power of grasping very quickly the real nature of someone's circumstances, and so arranging that the

* The 'four others' were Julia's three children by her first husband, Herbert Duckworth, and Laura, the daughter of Leslie Stephen and his first wife, Minny.

matter, whatever it was, fell into its true proportions at once. Sometimes with her natural impetuosity, she took it on herself to despatch
difficulties with a high hand, like some commanding Empress. But
most often I think her service, when it was not purely practical, lay
in simply helping people by the light of her judgement and experience, to see what they really meant or felt. But any sensible woman
may have these qualities, and yet be none of the things that your
grandmother was. All her gifts had something swift, decisive, witty
even, in their nature; so that there could be no question of dulness
or drudgery in her daily work, however lugubrious it seemed of
itself. She was sensitive by temperament and impatient of stupidity;
and while she was there the whole of that interminable and incongruous procession which is the life of a large family, went
merrily; with exquisite humour in its incidents very often, or something grotesque or impressive in its arrangement, perpetually lit up
by her keen attention, her amazing sense of the life that is in the
weakest or most threadbare situations. She stamped people with
characters at once; and at St Ives, or on Sunday afternoons at Hyde
Park Gate, the scene was often fit for the stage; boldly acting on her
conception she drew out from old General Beadle, or C. B. Clarke, or
Jack Hills, or Sidney Lee, such sparks of character as they have never
shown to anyone since. All lives directly she crossed them seemed to
form themselves into a pattern and while she stayed each move was
of the utmost importance. But she was no aesthetic spectator, collecting impressions for her own amusement.*

Life rather had taught her that facts, as she interpreted them,
were by themselves of supreme importance; it was a matter of
anxious moment to her that Lisa Stillman should like her brother-
in-law, or that a workman wounded in an accident should find
healthy employment. She kept herself marvellously alive to all the
changes that went on round her, as though she heard perpetually the
ticking of a vast clock and could never forget that some day it would
cease for all of us. People of the most diverse kinds came to her when
they had reason to rejoice or to weep; she seemed, if anything, a little
indiscriminate in her choice of friends; but bores and fools have their
moments. And it must be owned that living thus at high pressure she
contrived to invest the whole scene with an inimitable bravery as

* The ts (p. 14) is torn at mid-page. After 'amusement', instead of a full
stop, there is a semi-colon and four deleted words. There is no doubt that the
next page is meant to follow directly.

though she saw it properly composed, of fools, clowns and splendid
Queens, a vast procession on the march towards death. This intense
preoccupation with the event of the moment arose partly no doubt
because nature had fitted her to deal victoriously with such matters ;
but also because she had inborn in her and [had] acquired a deep
sense of the futility of all effort, the mystery of life. You may see the
two things in her face. 'Let us make the most of what we have, since
we know nothing of the future' was the motive that urged her to toil
so incessantly on behalf of happiness, right doing, love; and the
melancholy echoes answered 'What does it matter? Perhaps there is
no future.' Encompassed as she was by this solemn doubt her most
trivial activities had something of grandeur about them; and her
presence was large and austere, bringing with it not only joy and life,
exquisite fleeting femininities, but the majesty of a nobly composed
human being.

Written words of a person who is dead or still alive tend most unfortunately to drape themselves in smooth folds annulling all evidence of life. You will not find in what I say, or again in those sincere
but conventional phrases in the life of your grandfather, or in the
noble lamentations with which he fills the pages of his autobiography,* any semblance of a woman whom you can love. It has
often occurred to me to regret that no one ever wrote down her
sayings and vivid ways of speech since she had the gift of turning
words in a manner peculiar to her, rubbing her hands swiftly, or
raising them in gesticulation as she spoke.† I can see her, standing by
the open door of a railway carriage which was taking Stella and some
others to Cambridge, and striking out in a phrase or two pictures of
all the people who came past her along the platform, and so she kept
them laughing till the train went.

What would one not give to recapture a single phrase even! or the
tone of the clear round voice, or the sight of the beautiful figure, so
upright and so distinct, in its long shabby cloak, with the head held
at a certain angle, a little upwards, so that the eye looked straight
out at you. "Come children," she would say directly she had waved
her last fantastic farewell, and one would grasp her umbrella, and

---

* The 'Mausoleum Book', begun by Leslie Stephen in 1895 after the
death of Julia. The last entry, dictated to Virginia, was made in 1903. See
QB, "The Mausoleum Book", *A Review of English Literature*, VI, No. 1 (Jan.
1965), 9–19.
    † Mrs Carlyle reminds me oddly of her, with her 'coterie' speech. (VW).

another her arm, and one no doubt would stand gaping, and she would call sharply, "Quick, quick". And so she would pass with her swift step, through the crowds, and into some dingy train or omnibus, where perhaps she would ask the conductor why the company did not give him straw to stand on—"Your feet must be cold"—and hear his story and make her comment, until we were home just in time for lunch. "Don't keep father waiting." And at lunch in answer to some languid question, "So those young people are gone? We...ll, I don't envy 'em", she would have her little story to tell, or perhaps her cryptic phrase which we could not interpret, but knew from the shrugs and "Perhaps" that it bore on one of those romances which they both loved to discuss. The relationship between your grandfather and mother was, as the saying is, perfect, nor would I for a moment dispute that, believing as I do that each of these much tried and by no means easy-going people found in the other the highest and most perfect harmony which their natures could respond to. Beautiful often, even to our eyes, were their gestures, their glances of pure and unutterable delight in each other. But, if I can convey my meaning by the metaphor, the high consonance, the flute voices of two birds in tune, was only reached by rich, rapid scales of discord, and incongruity. After all she was fifteen years the younger, and his age was made emphatic by the keen intellect, always voyaging, as she must have thought, alone in ice-bound seas. Her pride in it was like the pride of one in some lofty mountain peak, visited only by the light of the stars, and the rain of snow; it was enthusiastic, but very humble.

She delighted to transact all those trifling businesses which, as women feel instinctively, are somehow derogatory to the dignity which they like to discover in clever men; and she took it as proud testimony that he came to her ignorant of all depressions and elations but those that high philosophy bred in him. But she never belittled her own works, thinking them, if properly discharged, of equal, though other, importance with her husband's. Thus in those moments, breathing spaces in the incessant conflict, when each rested secure for a second in the other's embrace, she knew with just but always delighted pride, that he worshipped in her something as unchallengeably high as the lofty remote peak which she honoured in him. And each sprang rejoicing to do homage to qualities unlike their own—how sweet, released from the agony and loneliness of thought to recognize instantly the real presence of unquestionable human loveliness! as a seafarer wrapt for many days in mist on the fruitless waters lands at dawn upon a sunlit shore, where all nature enfolds him and breathes in his ear rest and assurance. She too whose days were spent in labours often trifling, and often vain, exulted as one clasped suddenly in strong arms and set above it all, silent, still and immortal. She was always the first to reinforce his own impulse towards the most remote and unprofitable tasks; it was on her assurance I think that he began his last long book, *The Utilitarians*,* which would yield no wealth and very little fame, for she undertook that all other matters would prosper meanwhile.

But these are the pinnacles of life, and as time drew on, the struggle grew sharper, and the buoyancy of youth diminished. His health was worn, and the kind of praise which would have encouraged him, delayed unduly, as he complained. And by this time she had expanded so far, into such remote recesses, alleys in St Ives, London slums, and many other more prosperous but no less exacting quarters, that retrenchment was beyond her power. Every day brought her, it seemed, a fresh sprung harvest that must be despatched and would flourish infallibly tomorrow. Each evening she sat at her table, after some laborious afternoon, her hand moving ceaselessly, at the last a little erratically, as she wrote answers, advice, jests, warning, sympathy, her wise brow and deep eyes presiding, so beautiful still, but now so worn, so profoundly experienced that you could hardly call them sad. When she was dead I found a desk shut when we left St Ives with all the letters received that morning freshly laid in it, to be answered perhaps when she got to London. There was a letter from a woman whose daughter had been betrayed and asked for help; a letter from George, from Aunt Mary,† from a nurse who was out of work, some bills, some begging letters, and many sheets from a girl who had quarrelled with her parents and must reveal her soul, earnestly, diffusely. "Ah, thank Heaven, there is no post tonight!" she would exclaim, half smiling and half sighing, on Saturday; and even your grandfather would look up from his book, press her hand, and vainly protest, "there must be an end of this, Julia!"

In addition to all her other labours she took it on herself to teach us our lessons, and thus established a very close and rather trying

* *The English Utilitarians*, published in 1900; shorter works were to follow.
† Aunt Mary Fisher. See p. 100n.

relationship, for she was of a quick temper, and least of all inclined to spare her children. "Your father is a great man." But in no other way could we have learnt, in the short time we had, so much of her true nature, obscured by none of those graceful figments which interpose themselves generally in the gulf which lies between a middle-aged woman and her children. It might have been better, as it certainly would have tired her less, had she allowed that some of those duties could be discharged for her. But she was impetuous, and also a little imperious; so conscious of her own burning will that she could scarcely believe that there was not something quicker and more effective in her action than in another's. Thus when your grandfather was ill she would never suffer a nurse to be with him, nor could she believe that a governess would teach us as well as she did. And apart from economy, which always weighed with her, she had come to attach a desperate importance to the saving of time, as though she saw heap themselves all round her, duties and desires, and time to embrace them slipped from her and left her with grasping fingers. She had constantly in mind that comprehensive view of the final proportions of things which I have noticed; for her words were never trivial; but as her strength lessened her respites were fewer; she sank, like an exhausted swimmer, deeper and deeper in the water, and could only at moments descry some restful shore on the horizon to be gained in old age when all this toil was over. But when we exclaim at the extravagant waste of such a life we are inclined no doubt to lose that view of the surrounding parts, the husband and child and home which if you see them as a whole surrounding her, completing her, robs the single life of its arrow-like speed, and its tragic departure. What is noticeable about her, as I am come to think, is not the waste and the futile gallantry, but the niceness, born of sure judgement, with which her effort matched her aim. There was scarcely any superfluity; and it is for this reason that, past as those years are, her mark on them is ineffaceable, as though branded by the naked steel, the sharp, the pure. Living voices in many parts of the world still speak of her as of someone who is actually a fact in life. Whether she came merry, wrathful or in impulsive sympathy, it does not matter; they speak of her as of a thing that happened, recalling, as though all round her grew significant, how she stood and turned and how the bird sang loudly, or a great cloud passed across the sky. Where has she gone? What she said has never ceased. She died when she was forty-eight, and your

mother was a child of fifteen.* If what I have said of her has any
meaning you will believe that her death was the greatest disaster that
could happen; it was as though on some brilliant day of spring the
racing clouds of a sudden stood still, grew dark, and massed themselves; the wind flagged, and all creatures on the earth moaned or
wandered seeking aimlessly. But what figure or variety of figures will
do justice to the shapes which since then she has taken in countless
lives? The dead, so people say, are forgotten, or they should rather
say, that life has for the most part little significance to any of us. But
now and again on more occasions than I can number, in bed at
night, or in the street, or as I come into the room, there she is;
beautiful, emphatic, with her familiar phrase and her laugh; closer
than any of the living are, lighting our random lives as with a
burning torch, infinitely noble and delightful to her children.

CHAPTER TWO

Her death, on the 5th of May, 1895, began a period of Oriental
gloom, for surely there was something in the darkened rooms, the
groans, the passionate lamentations that passed the normal limits of
sorrow, and hung about the genuine tragedy with folds of Eastern
drapery. Your grandfather had in him much of the stuff of a Hebrew
prophet; something of the amazing vigour of his youth remained to
him, but he no longer spent his strength in climbing mountains or
coaching crews; all his devotion for many years had concentrated
itself upon his home. And now that against all his expectations, his
wife had died before him, he was like one who, by the failure of some
stay, reels staggering blindly about the world, and fills it with his
woe. But no words of mine can convey what he felt, or even the
energy of the visible expression of it, which took place in one scene
after another all through that dreadful summer. One room it
seemed was always shut, was always disturbed now and then, by
some groan or outburst. He had constant interviews with sympathetic women, who went in to see him nervously enough, and
came out flushed and tear-stained, confused as people are who have
been swept away on the tide of someone else's emotion, to give their
report to Stella. Indeed all her diplomacy was needed to keep him

* Julia died at the age of forty-nine on 5 May 1895. Vanessa became
sixteen on 30 May.

occupied in some way, when his morning's work was over; and there were dreadful meal-times when, unable to hear what we said, or disdaining its comfort, he gave himself up to the passion which seemed to burn within him, and groaned aloud or protested again and again his wish to die. I do not think that Stella lost consciousness for a single moment during all those months of his immediate need. She would always have some little device to offer him, observing him so closely that she would suddenly beg one of us to speak to him directly, or ask him to walk with us. Sometimes at night she spent a long time alone in his study with him, hearing again and again the bitter story of his loneliness, his love and his remorse. For exhausted and unstrung as he was he came to torment himself piteously with the idea that he had never told his wife how much he had loved her, that she had endured anxiety and suffering by his side in silence.

"I was not as bad as Carlyle, was I?" I have heard him ask. Stella perhaps knew little of Carlyle, but her assurance came over and over again, tired but persistent. There is, no doubt, a strange comfort in making the living hear your confession of wrong done to the dead; not only can they reassure you from their own observation, but they also represent, mysteriously, a power which can be appeased by your confession, and can grant you something approaching a final absolution. For these reasons, then, and also because it was his nature and habit to find ease in the expression of his feelings, he did not scruple to lay before her his sufferings and to demand perpetual attention, and whatever comfort she had to give. But what comfort could she give? From the nature of the case there was little to be done; all depended therefore upon what she was, for suddenly she was placed in the utmost intimacy with a man who as her stepfather and an elderly man of letters she had hitherto regarded only with respect and a formal affection. Stella's position, until this crisis, had been in some ways peculiar; indeed her character altogether, as one sees it now illuminated afresh by one's own equality of age, was remarkable; remarkable for what it was, and for its destiny; great issues hung upon her life; but the shortness and almost tremulous quality of the early years make it hard to tell the story with any decision.

She was not clever, she seldom read a book; and this fact had I think an immense influence upon her life, a disproportionate influence, indeed. She exaggerated her own deficiency, and, living in close companionship with her mother, was always contrasting their differences, and imputing to herself an inferiority which led her from the first to live in her mother's shade. Your grandmother too was, I have said, ruthless in her ways, and quite indifferent, if she saw good, to any amount of personal suffering. It was characteristic of her to feel that her daughter was, as she expressed it, part of herself, and as a slower and less efficient part she did not scruple to treat her with the severity with which she would have treated her own failings, or to offer her up as freely as she would have offered herself. Once before your grandparents' marriage, when your grandfather remarked to her upon the harshness with which she treated Stella in comparison with the other children who were both boys, she gave the answer I have written.*

As a child then, Stella was suppressed, and learned early to look upon her mother as a person of divine power and divine intelligence. But later as Stella grew older and developed her own beauty, her own singular charm and temperament, her mother ceased her harshness, if it were ever rightly called so, and showed only the true cause of it, a peculiar depth and intimacy of feeling. They always kept in the main the relationship which nature perhaps had ordained. Stella was always the beautiful attendant handmaid, feeding her mother's vivid flame, rejoicing in the service, and making it the central duty of her life. But besides this she began very soon to enjoy the influence of her gifts on others; she was beautiful, more beautiful than her pictures show, for much of her phantom loveliness came from accidents of the moment—the pale luminous complexion, the changing light in the eyes, the movement and ripple of the whole. If your grandmother's was a head of the finest period of Greek art, Stella's was Greek too, but it was Greek of a later and more decadent age, making with its softer lines and more languid shape, a closer appeal. But in each case, their beauty was the expression of them. Stella was mutable, modest, but somehow with what is called charm or magic possessed of wonderful distinction, and the power of penetrating deeply into people's minds. It was not I suppose for what she said, for that was simple enough; but for her ripple of sweetness and laughter over a shape, dimly discerned, as of statuesque marble. She was so gay, so feminine, and at the same time had about her something of the large repose which in her mother, under stress of circumstance, had resolved itself into an enduring melancholy. Stella and her coming out, and her success and her lovers, excited many

* See p. 96.

instincts long dormant in her mother; she liked young men, she enjoyed their confidences, she was intensely amused by the play and intrigue of the thing; only, as she complained, Stella would insist upon going home, long before the night was over, for fear lest she should be tired. That indeed was what, with desperate use of imagery, I have called her marble shape; for all her triumphs were mere frippery on the surface of this constant preoccupation with her mother. It was beautiful, it was almost excessive; for it had something of the morbid nature of an affection between two people too closely allied for the proper amount of reflection to take place between them; what her mother felt passed almost instantly through Stella's mind; there was no need for the brain to ponder and criticize what the soul knew. Your grandmother would no doubt have liked some brisker resistance, some intellectual opposition, calling out a different sort of care; she may well have felt that the tie was too close to be wholesome, and might hinder Stella from entertaining those natural feelings upon which she set so high a value. Even a short parting was unduly painful; Stella was white as a ghost for days before she went abroad, and broke once into a passion of tears. "What can it matter where we are", she said, "so long as we are all together?"

Her feeling during the last years became ever more anxious, as she detected signs of failing health in her mother, and could not contrive in any way to give her the rest which of all things she needed. Her silence with her stepfather almost gave way now and then to sharp and open remonstrance; for he never seemed to see, what was so plain to her eye, the innumerable things that his wife did, or how terribly she was worn. Then, in the spring of 1895 Stella was driven abroad, and half-way through the journey she became convinced by sign of handwriting or phrase, that her mother lay ill at home. She appealed to Vanessa, who could only send an answer dictated by her mother. Slight illness had indeed attacked her, but with the strange and ghastly fantasy of one who plays a part to the end, she would insist that the truth should not yet be told. Stella came home with a consciousness like that of some tormented dumb animal, that she had been deceived; and found her mother in bed, with the chill which was to end ten days later, in her death.

The shock to Stella was complete; she began, by sheer pure beauty of character, to do all that she could for everyone; but almost automatically. The future held nothing for her; the present was, I suppose, with a stepfather whom she barely knew, and four children who needed care and could as yet help her little, constantly painful. She was only just twenty-six, and in a moment she had to relinquish not only the chief source of all her life, but also the peculiar ways in which she best enjoyed her gifts. Indeed whoever she had been the position must have been painfully hard, but with her great distrust of her own powers, and her dread of books in particular, her task was terribly painful and almost bewildering. But still, had it not been for this desolation, laying her whole nature bare, and bidding it put forth its powers in entire loneliness, could she ever have shown herself as noble and as true as she was? All that she became in the future was firmly grounded, her own achievement; no one ever again was to serve her for prop; never again, perhaps, did she care for anyone as she had cared for her mother. That, whatever gain is to be set beside it, was the permanent loss.

Directly your grandmother was dead, Stella inherited all the duties that she had discharged; and like some creaking old waggon, pitifully rusted, and yet filled with stirring young creatures, our family once more toiled painfully along the way.

CHAPTER THREE

Your grandmother's position in the family was such that her death not only removed the central figure from our eyes, but brought about such a shifting of relationships that life for a long time seemed incredibly strange. Your grandfather in his natural but surely unwise desire to do for us all that your grandmother had done, began to teach us our lessons; and gave up half his morning to us; a sacrifice indeed but that did not make his mood the easier. Then George, on the full tide of emotion, insisted upon a closer and more mature friendship with us; Gerald even became for the time serious and sentimental; and round this centre of profound emotion circled a number of friends, suddenly become conscious of a desire to take part in our lives, and of their right to have the depth of their own feelings recognized. Stella herself, almost stunned though she was at the moment, was never driven from her calm attitude of infinite consideration for others, of silence with respect to her own feelings; but this very calmness seemed to suffer, indifferently, a number of trials, and in particular to admit of quite unqualified self-surrender to

your grandfather's needs. Any comfort, whatever its nature, that
came to hand, she offered him to stay his anguish; all her day was at
his service, she exerted herself as I have said, to find people to visit
him, to help her in some of her innumerable minute plans for his
welfare. It is easy to see now that where she failed for the time was in
proper discrimination. Her own disbelief in herself, and her long
season of dependence made her incapable of trusting her own clear
instincts in the matter. Her stepfather was the charge bequeathed
her by her mother. She gave indiscriminately, conscious that she had
not the best of all to give; and your grandfather who would doubtless have understood a clear statement of the position, took all that
she offered him failing this as his right. But one of the consequences
was that for some time life seemed to us in a chronic state of confusion. We were quite naturally unhappy; feeling a definite need,
unbearably keen at moments, which was never to be satisfied. But
that was recognizable pain, and the sharp pang grew to be almost
welcome in the midst of the sultry and opaque life which was not
felt, had nothing real in it, and yet swam about us, and choked us
and blinded us. All these tears and groans, reproaches and protesta-
tions of affection, high talk of duty and work and living for others,
were doubtless what we should feel if we felt properly, and yet we
had but a dull sense of gloom which could not honestly be referred to
the dead; unfortunately it did not quicken our feeling for the
living; but hideous as it was, obscured both living and dead; and for
long did unpardonable mischief by substituting for the shape of a true
and most vivid mother, nothing better than an unlovable phantom.

That summer, after some hot months in London, we spent in
Freshwater; and the heat there in the low bay, brimming as it
seemed with soft vapours, and luxuriant with lush plants, mixes,
like smoke, with other memories of hot rooms and silence, and an
atmosphere all choked with too luxuriant feelings, so that one had at
times a physical need of ruthless barbarism and fresh air. Stella
herself looked like the white flower of some teeming hot-house, for a
change had come over her that seemed terribly symbolical. Never
did anyone look so pale. And yet unexpected as it might seem, but
still was most natural, the first impulse to set us free came from
your grandfather; it came and went again. On a walk perhaps he
would suddenly brush aside all our curiously conventional relationships, and show us for a minute an inspiriting vision of free life,
bathed in an impersonal light. There were numbers of things to be

learnt, books to be read, and success and happiness were to be attained there without disloyalty. Indeed it seemed possible at these moments, to continue the old life but in a more significant way, using as he told us, our sorrow to quicken the feeling that remained. But such exaltations doubtless depended for their endurance upon a closer relationship than age made possible. We were too young, and for sympathy that required less effort, he had to turn to others, whose difference of blood and temperament, made it harder for them to recognize as we did — by glimpses — his most urgent need. Beautiful was he at such moments; simple and eager as a child; and exquisitely alive to all affection; exquisitely tender. We would have helped him then if we could, given him all we had, and felt it little beside his need — but the moment passed.

It was exhilarating at times to peer above our immature world, and fancy that the actual conflict of recognized human beings had already begun for us. In truth the change which declared itself when we were once more settled in London and gone about our tasks, was partly invigorating; for we tried to prove ourselves equal companions for Stella and our lives were much quickened by the chivalrous devotion she roused in us. It was chivalrous because she was too remote for real companionship, so that there was always a kind of chance in one's offering; perhaps she would not perceive it; perhaps she would kindle rapture by a sudden recognition; her distance made such close moments exquisitely sweet. But alas, no such humble friendship however romantic, could give her the sense that we completely shared her thoughts; the nature of them made it hard for anyone to understand; and her sorrow was very lonely. Perhaps one would come into a room unexpectedly, and surprise her in tears, and, to one's miserable confusion, she would hide them instantly, and speak ordinary words, as though she did not imagine that one could understand her suffering.

And this, as I think, was the time when your mother first came somewhat tentatively upon the scene, her age being then almost seventeen. Her qualities of honesty and wisdom were precisely those that Stella was then most inclined to appreciate, both because she was often bewildered by the eccentric storms in which your grandfather indulged, ascribed by her too simply to the greatness of his intellect, and also because she found in Vanessa both in nature and in person something like a reflection of her mother. Vanessa too might be treated almost as a confidante, the single person who did not need any kind of sacrifice to be made for her. And Stella felt also, no doubt, that curiously intimate pride which a woman feels when she sees womanly virtues beautifully expressed by another, the torch still worthily carried; and the pride was very tender in this case and mixed with much of a maternal joy. I do not know how far I shall be guilty of over-ingenuity if I discover another, though an unspoken, cause for the growth of natural sympathy with Vanessa. For two or three years now the one suitor who stood out above other suitors and was greatly liked by your grandmother and tolerated by Stella herself was John Waller Hills. He was then a lean, rather threadbare young man, who seemed to force his way by sheer determination and solid integrity; suggesting the figure of some tenacious wire-haired terrier, in whose obstinacy and strength of jaw there seemed, at a time when all the fates were against him, something honourable, which appealed to one's half humorous sense of sport as even pathetic. He would come, Sunday after Sunday, and sit his hour out, worrying his speech as a terrier a bone; but sticking doggedly to the word, until at last he got it pronounced. His method was the same always. He knew what he wanted, and unless there occurred a sudden bursting of his stout skull and soft illimitable prospects opened on each side, which was incredible, there was little doubt that he would come by it—except indeed in this very instance. For, with so much that everyone could respect, and find admirable in his relations with others, there was yet very little that anyone seemed called on to love at first hand. It was natural to be indebted to him, for faithful services rendered over a score of years, and to requite him by a perpetual seat at the fireside, or a cover laid for him on Sundays, or the title of uncle to some one else's children. But to disregard all these oblique services, and meet him face to face, as one capable of the supreme gift of all, needed as Stella found, prolonged consideration and repeated rejection. He satisfied so many requirements, but the sum of all he gave did not need love to reward it. After her mother's death however, Stella became far less exacting, as indeed she lost interest in her fate, and had no contrast to oppose to it; Jack was persistent as ever, almost a natural if secondary part of oneself. No doubt he had a system plainly marked in front of him, arranged on paper in his little room in Ebury Street, and was simply following it out in detail. But that even had a kind of fascination for one so prone now to consider herself merely as the atmosphere that enclosed solid bodies. The long visits, when there were such long pauses, or spasmodic talk of indifferent matters, salmon fishing or Stevenson's novels, had yet an undeniable glow, a conviction of meaning lying at the base of them, which made them remarkable, and wore, like some dull heat, into her mind. It made her realize herself, turning solid much that floated vague as mist around her as she went about her daily life. But it threatened to be destructive of the compact which she had made with her stepfather, upon which by this time he had come to depend. It was natural then that she should turn instinctively to Vanessa, for many unformulated reasons, and for this obvious one, that Vanessa alone could justify her action if, as it sometimes seemed possible, she consented to marry Jack in the end. And also your mother was sympathetic without words; she had a great respect for Mr Hills, and her respect was warmed and at the same time sanctioned by the knowledge which was common to us all of his devotion. Insensibly, Stella grew to depend upon Jack's visits, for though she was sad to the point of despair, and physically tired, there was a pale flame in her which leapt at the prospect of an independent life, a life at least which depended upon one person only. For when some months had passed, and the first storm of distress was over, she found that she had completely pledged herself to her stepfather; he expected entire self-surrender on her part, and had decided apparently, and with sufficient reason, that she possessed one of those beautiful feminine natures which are quite without wishes of their own. She had to acquiesce, partly because it was easier to go on as she had begun, and partly because as she could not give him intellectual companionship she must give him the only thing she had. But Jack, with the shrewdness of a businessman who is in love, quickly saw how matters stood, and offered a very refreshing revolt. He considered Stella's wishes and Stella's health far more important than those of one whom he treated as an encyclopaedia who should be kept on the shelf, and must be humoured and tolerated in all his irrational desires if he chose to come downstairs. Stella would not have been human if she had not found this change of view a relief to her. Slowly then she admitted the thought of new life, and recognized that it was Jack and Jack only who inspired [it.]

But she had lapsed very far, into a kind of snowy numbness, nor could she waken at the first touch. He proposed to her in March (I think), almost a year after her mother's death, and she refused him. The thought of the break, the havoc played with delicate webs just

beginning to spin themselves across the abyss, may well have deterred
her; and, when she came face to face with her love, and tried to
yield herself to his passion, his honesty, all his canine qualities glowing with their utmost expressiveness, did she still find something in
her left cold and meditative, reflecting, when all should have been
consenting? She remembered what she had felt before. But the
summer wore on, and she looked with comfort at Vanessa, and there
were not wanting authoritative voices who declared that such a
sacrifice, for they gave it the definite name, was cowardly and short-
sighted too. For in years to come, they argued, her stepfather would
draw his best comfort from her home. Jack meanwhile, was persistent, and patient; and she had to confess that she had accumulated
a reckoning with him that was serious however she looked at it; he
meant a great deal in her life. The summer wore on, nor did anyone,
unless it were your mother, suspect the change in Stella's mind; we
depended on her as thoughtless men on some natural power; for it
seemed to our judgement obvious enough that there must be someone always discharging the duties that Stella discharged. We had
been lent a house at Hindhead, and one afternoon at the end of
August, Jack came there, bicycling to some place in the neighbour-
hood. His visits were so often forced in this way that we suspected
nothing more than the usual amount of restraint from his explosive
ways, and much information about dogs and bicycles. His opinion
on these matters stood very high with us. He stayed to dinner, and
that also was characteristic of his method; but after dinner a strange
lapse occurred in the usual etiquette. Stella left the room with him, to
show him the garden or the moon, and decisively shut the door
behind her. We had our business to attend to also, and followed
them soon with a lantern, for we were then in the habit of catching
moths after dinner. Once or twice we saw them, always hasting
round a corner; once or twice we heard her skirts brushing, and
once a sound of whispering. But the moon was very bright, and there
were no moths; Stella and Jack had gone in, it seemed, and we
returned to the drawing room. But father was alone, and he was
unusually restless, turning his pages, crossing his legs, and looking
again and again at the clock. Then he sent Adrian to bed; then me;
then Nessa and Thoby; and still it was only ten, and still Stella and
Jack stayed out! There was then a pause, and we sat together in
Adrian's room, cold, melancholy and strangely uncomfortable.
Your Uncle Thoby discovered a tramp in the garden, who begged

for food and Thoby sent him away with great eloquence, and we felt a little frightened, for it was no ordinary night, and ominous things were happening. Your grandfather was tramping the terrace, up and down, up and down; we were all awake, all expectant; and still nothing happened. At length, someone looking from the window, exclaimed, "Stella and Mr Hills are coming up the path together!" Were their arms locked? Did we know immediately all that we had not dared to guess? At any rate we ran to our rooms, and in a few minutes Stella came up herself, blushing the loveliest rose colour, and told us — how she was very happy.

The news was met, of course, by the usual outburst of clamorous voices which always threatens on such occasions to drown the single true utterance. Families at these moments touch their high, and perhaps also their low, watermarks. Your grandfather, I remember, spoke sharply to one whom he found in tears, for it should make us only happy, he said, that Stella should be happy; true words! But the moment after he was groaning to her that the blow was irreparable. Then George and Gerald, who lavished kisses and did their best to arrange that she and Jack should be left alone together, soon let her see that there would be difficulties if Jack came too much to the house. "It won't do; men are like that", she said once, without complaint; and Kitty Maxse,* who had the reputation with us of profound knowledge and exquisite sympathy, an irresistible combination, confirmed her no doubt in her sad estimate of mankind. "It won't do."

Their engagement then was at the mercy of many forces from the outset; still there were some walks at Hindhead, a week spent together at Corby,† and Jack found excuses for dining with us every night in London, and stayed on very late, till George came down and invoked the proprieties, or with some reason, insisted that Stella must rest. One thing seemed to survive all these vexations, and was miraculous to see; the exquisite tremor of life was once more alight in Stella; her eye shone, her pale cheeks glowed constantly with a faint rose. She laughed and had her tender jokes. Sometimes a fear came over her, possessed her; she had had her life; but then there was Jack to reason her out of her alarms, to kiss her, and show her a sane future, with many interests and much substance. She had come

* Kitty Maxse (née Lushington) was a frequent visitor to Hyde Park Gate. She became a close friend of Vanessa's after Stella's death.

† Corby Castle, just east of Carlisle, was the home of the Hills.

to stand by herself, with a painful footing upon real life, and her love now had as little of dependence in it as may be. He, it is true, had more wish to live than she had, but she took and gave with open eyes. It was beautiful; it was, once more, a flight of unfurled wings into the upper air.

But all these difficulties and jealousies resolved themselves shortly into one formidable question; where were they to live after their marriage? Your grandfather had taken it for granted that Stella would not leave him, since she had become indispensable; and in the first flush of their joy both Stella and Jack had agreed that it would be possible to live on at Hyde Park Gate. Then they began to consider rooms, and habits, conveniences and rights, and it soon became obvious that the plan was impossible. And if they started wrong disasters would accumulate. Stella was convinced, for she began to entertain a just idea of her independence as a wife; and George and Gerald agreed also. It is significant however of your grandfather's temper at the time that he continued to count upon their rash promise as though it were the natural and just arrangement, which did not need further consideration. His awakenment was bound to be painful, and there were many painful words to be said on his side; they had promised and they had deserted him. One night however Stella went up into his study alone, and explained what they felt. What she said, what he answered, I cannot tell; but for some time afterwards he could never hear the marriage spoken of without a profound groan, and the least encouragement would lead him to explain precisely how much he suffered, and how little cause there was for him to rejoice. But Stella was very patient, and just capable now under Jack's influence of seeing another side to her stepfather's remarks. There were signs that in years to come she would enjoy a lively and delightful companionship with him. They took a house at the end of the street, for that was the compromise, and in the beginning of April, 1897, they were married.

There had been so much talk of loss, loneliness and change that it was surprising to find that the house went on next day very much as usual. We went to Brighton, and letters began to come from Stella in Florence and from Jack giving promise, stirring as Spring, of happy new intimacies in the future. Indeed it was already a relief that there should be a separate house with a different basis from ours, untinged presumably with our gloom; under these influences that gloom itself seemed to lighten. For your grandfather, left alone

with us, found doubtless much to try him in our crudeness and lack
of sympathy but there was also great interest in our development,
and we began to surprise him with voluntary remarks, bearing on
matters of art and literature. Thoby was becoming, he said, 'a fine
fellow'; he discovered that suddenly your mother was grown 'very
handsome'; friendship with us, in short, was the great desire of his
life, and Stella's marriage seemed to clear the way for it. We had our
theory too, of the way to manage him, and it was not Stella's way,
but promised well. Thus, when it was time to come back to London
we were eager to see Stella again, and had many things to tell her,
and much curiosity to see how she would live. But on the very
morning of our return a letter came from George saying that Stella
was in bed with a chill. When we got back home she was a little
worse; almost immediately it seemed we were in the midst of serious
illness, nurses, consultations, interviews and whispers. Like a nightmare it came upon us, waking terrible memories, confronting us
with a possibility which we could not even believe, and then, like a
nightmare, it was gone; Stella was said to be recovered. Indeed she
went about a little, came in to tea and lunch with us, and walked out
in Kensington Gardens. But she had a relapse, and then another;
and the doctors ordered that for a certain time she should stay in her
room. But she could see us; and it seemed that although the time was
interrupted by terrible fears, to which we got accustomed however,
and was never quite secure, our hopes were realized. She was certainly happy; she was less despondent, less modest than ever before,
as though Jack had finally convinced her of her worth. That indeed
was a service for which one might forgive much, and under the
influence of her large presence and repose he lost many of his difficult ways, his emphatic insistence upon the commonplaces of life,
and showed himself loyal and kind as he had always been, but more
gentle, and far more sensitive of perception than he was of old. He
only needed perhaps some such happiness to discard all his angulari-
ties, which were partly produced, no doubt, by the need he had been
in for so many years of forcing his way through obstacles. All her
arrangements prospered; she had her stepfather to tea with her
regularly, and marvelled at his good spirits and health, and he was
very tender to her when he heard that she was to be a mother.
George and Gerald had their interviews alone. And your mother
'came out' that summer, and Stella had one of the purest pleasures of
her life in gazing on her beauty and speculating on her success. She

felt what a mother would have felt, and this was the sort of triumph that she could herself understand to the uttermost; she had attempted it. But once more she fell ill; again, almost in a moment, there was danger, and this time it did not pass away, but pressed on and on, till suddenly we knew that the worst had actually come to pass. Even now it seems incredible.

CHAPTER FOUR

It generally happens in seasons of such bewilderment as that in which we now found ourselves, that one person becomes immediately the central figure, as it were the solid figure, and on this occasion it was your mother. Many reasons combined to give her this prominence. She fulfilled the duties which Stella had but lately fulfilled; she had much of the beauty and something of the character which with but little stretch of the imagination we could accept as worthy to carry on the tradition; for in our morbid state, haunted by great ghosts, we insisted that to be like mother, or like Stella, was to achieve the height of human perfection. Vanessa then at the age of eighteen was exalted, in the most tragic way, to a strange position, full of power and responsibility. Everyone turned to her, and she moved, like some young Queen, all weighed down with the pomp of her ceremonial robes, perplexed and mournful and uncertain of her way. The instant need was to comfort, say rather, to be with, Jack. He had lost infinitely more than anyone could calculate; his sorrow seemed to stretch over years to come, withering them, and to cast a bitter light on his past. Never was there so cruel a loss, for it was cruel in the harshest way, in that it somehow seemed to damage him. Like some animal stunned by a blow on the head he went methodically about his work, worn and grim enough to behold, taking an abrupt mechanical interest in substantial facts, the make of a bicycle, or the number of men killed at the battle of Waterloo. But in the evenings he would come and sit with your mother, and loosen this tight tension and burst out what he could speak of his sorrow. Poor inarticulate man! In his dumb way he had worshipped beauty; it had been a long discipline; and he may well have doubted half consciously, whether he could ever achieve such heights again. Stella had been his pinnacle, all through his tenacious youth; he had loved her and her mother with all that he had of love; they had been to him poetry and youth. A very high nature perhaps might have preserved the echo; but Jack was more inclined to set his eye upon the hardship of his loss, unflinchingly, as he would have considered the harm done him by some unscrupulous human enemy. His attitude was courageous indeed, in a dogged way; but there was little of hope in it, and it threatened to cramp his future.

Your mother, as I have said, coming into this inheritance, with all its complications, was bewildered; so many demands were made on her; it was, in a sense, so easy to be what was expected, with such models before her, but also it was so hard to be herself. She was but just eighteen, and when she should have been free and tentative, she was required to be definite and exact. It came to pass then that she acted at first as though she had her lesson by heart but did not attach much meaning to it; to George she would be devoted and submissive; to Gerald affectionate; to her father helpful; to us protective. She was more than anyone, I suppose, left desolate by Stella's death, bereft of happy intercourse, which had grown daily more intimate, and also she had much responsibility and there was no woman older than herself to share it with her. Strange was her position then; and an affectionate onlooker might well have asked himself anxiously what kind of nature she was able to oppose to it. One glance at her might have reassured him and yet served but to shift his anxiety. She looked so self-contained, and so mature that clearly she would never act foolishly; but also there was so much promise of thought and development in eye and brow, and passionate mouth, that it was certain she would not long stay quiescent. The calm of the moment was as an instinctive shield to cover her wounded senses; but soon they would collect themselves and fall to work upon all these difficult matters so lavishly heaped upon them — and with what result?

She was beautiful, but she had not lived for eighteen years without revealing that she was also strong of brain, agile and determined; she had revealed so much in the nursery, where she would meet Thoby in argument, and press on to the very centre of the matter, whether it were question of art or morality. She was also, on her secret side, sensitive to all beauty of colour and form; but she hid this, because her views did not agree with those current around her, and she feared to give pain. Again, she was as quick to detect insincerity of nature as fallacy of argument, and the one fared as ill with her as the other; for her standard was rigid. But then she was bound to certain people by a kind of instinctive fidelity, which admitted of no question; it was, if anything, too instinctive. Such was the feeling she had for Jack before his marriage, and it was the first thread in her devotion to her mother or to Thoby. If her mother had lived it is easy to imagine how Vanessa, questing about her, like some active dog, would have tried one experiment after another, arguing, painting, making friends, disproving fallacies, much to her mother's amusement; she would have delighted in her daughter's spirit and adventures, mourned her lack of practical wisdom, and laughed at her failures, and rejoiced in her sense. But that is one of the things, which though they must have happened, yet, incredible though it seems, never did happen, death making an end of all these exquisite preparations. Instead Vanessa was first baffled by her mother's death, and the unnatural life which for a time was entailed upon us, and now again, Stella's death set her among entirely new surroundings.

People who must follow obvious tokens, such as the colour of the eye, the shape of the nose, and love to invent a melodramatic fitness in life, as though it were a sensational novel, acclaimed her now the divinely appointed inheritor of all womanly virtues, and with a certain haziness forgot your grandmother's sharp features and Stella's vague ones, and created a model of them for Vanessa to follow, beautiful on the surface, but fatally insipid within. Once again we went through the same expressions of sympathy; we heard again and again that so great a tragedy had never happened; sometimes it appeared almost in the light of a work of art; more often it revealed a shapeless catastrophe, from which there could be no recovery. But happily it was time for us to leave London; we had taken a house at Painswick; and the ghastly mourners, the relations and friends, went back to their own homes.

But for us the tragedy was but just beginning; as in the case of other wounds the pain was drugged at the moment, and made itself felt afterwards when we began to move. There was pain in all our circumstances, or a dull discomfort, a kind of restlessness and aimlessness which was even worse. Misery of this kind tends to concentrate itself upon an object, if it can find one, and there was a figure, unfortunately, who would serve our purpose very well. Your grandfather showed himself strangely brisk, and so soon as we came to think, we fastened our eyes upon him, and found just cause for anger. We remembered how he had tasked Stella's strength, embittered her few months of joy, and now when he should be penitent, he showed less grief than anyone. On the contrary none was more vigorous, and there were signs at once which woke us to a sort of frenzy, that he was quite prepared to take Vanessa for his next victim. When he was sad, he explained, she should be sad; when he was angry, as he was periodically when she asked him for a cheque, she should weep; instead she stood before him like a stone. A girl who had character would not tolerate such speeches, and when she connected them with other words of the same kind, addressed to the sister lately dead, to her mother even, it was not strange that an uncompromising anger took possession of her. We made him the type of all that we hated in our lives; he was the tyrant of inconceivable selfishness, who had replaced the beauty and merriment of the dead with ugliness and gloom. We were bitter, harsh, and to a great extent, unjust; but even now it seems to me that there was some truth in our complaint; and sufficient reason why both parties should be unable at the time and without fault, to come to a good understanding. If he had been ten years younger, or we older, or had there been a mother or sister to intervene, much pain and anger and loneliness might have been spared. But again, death spoilt what should have been so fair.

There was also another cause to fret us and forbid us from judging clearly. Jack who was spending a terrible summer in London came to us regularly on Sunday. He was tired and morose, and it seemed that his only relief was to spend long hours with your mother or with me in a little summer house in the garden; he talked, when he talked, of Stella and the past; there were silences when no words seemed to have meaning; I remember the shape of a small tree which stood in a little hollow in front of us, and how, as I sat holding Jack's hand, I came to conceive this tree as the symbol of sorrow, for it was silent, enduring and without fruit. But now and then Jack would say something bitter though restrained, about your grandfather and his behaviour to Stella, and how her death had not saddened him. That was enough to sharpen all our feelings against him; for we had an enthusiastic wish to help Jack, and in truth he seemed the person who best understood our misery. But although I shared these vigils equally at first with Vanessa she, by degrees, began to have more of Jack's favour and confidence than I did; and directly any such favour is shown it becomes more marked and endures. She was the natural person to be with him, and also, as I have said, she had of old an affection for him, which although immature, was easily the starting point of much quicker and more fervent feelings, and the incentive now was urgent.

Profoundly gloomy as this all was, the intolerable part of it was the feeling of difference of temper and aim revealed day by day, among people who must live together. For Stella had united many things otherwise incompatible. We, (in future this 'we' must stand for your mother and me) walked alone when we could, and discussed the state of the different parties, and how they threatened to meet in conflict over her body. So far they did not more than threaten; but a man, or woman, of the world, George, for example or Kitty Maxse, might already foretell the supreme struggle of the future. Decency at present forbade open speech, but no doubt the suspicion was alive, and made itself felt in an unrest and intensity of feeling on George's part which we saw, but failed as yet to interpret. George indeed had become and was to remain, a very important figure. He had advanced so suddenly into the closest intimacy with us, that it was not strange if in our blindfold state we made rash and credulous judgements about him. He had been once, when we were children, a hero to us; strong and handsome and just; he taught us to hold our bats straight and to tell the truth, and we blushed with delight if he praised. All the world so far as we could tell, applauded him too. Your grandmother showed keen delight in his presence, and, sentimental as children are, we believed that he was like her dead husband, and perhaps we were not wrong. His triumphs over Italian Countesses and watchmakers in the slums, who all revealed to him at once their inmost hearts, were part of our daily legend; and then he would play with us in the back garden, and pretend, for we guessed that it was pretence, that he read our school stories. His affections, his character, his soul, as we understood, were immaculate; and daily achieved that uncomfortable and mysterious victory which virtue, in books, achieves over intellect. Gerald, strange though it may seem, represented intellect in the contest. George was in truth, a stupid, good natured young man, of profuse, voluble affections, which during his mother's lifetime were kept in check. When she died however, some restraint seemed to burst; he showed himself so sad, so affectionate, so boundlessly unselfish in his plans, that the voices of all women cried aloud in his praise, and men were touched by his modest virtues, at the same time that they were puzzled. What was it that made him so different from other men?

Stupid he was, and good natured; but such qualities were not simple; they were modified, confused, distorted, exalted, set swimming in a sea of racing emotions until you were completely at a loss to know where you stood. Nature, we may suppose, had supplied him with abundant animal vigour, but she had neglected to set an efficient brain in control of it. The result was that all the impressions which the good priggish boy took in at school and college remained with him when he was a man; they were not extended, but were liable to be expanded into enormous proportions by violent gusts of passion; and [he] proved more and more incapable of containing them. Thus, under the name of unselfishness he allowed himself to commit acts which a cleverer man would have called tyrannical; and, profoundly believing in the purity of his love, he behaved little better than a brute. How far he wilfully deceived himself, how far he was capable of understanding, what juggleries went on in that obscure mind, is a problem which we at any rate could never solve. But the combination of something like reason and much unlike anything but irrational instinct was for ever confusing us, deceiving us and leading us alternately to trust and suspect him, until his marriage happily made such speculations but an occasional diversion for the intellect.* But at the moment his position seemed perfectly accountable; he was the simple domestic creature, of deep feeling, who, from native goodness now that his chief joy was gone, was setting himself to do all he could to be mother and sister and brother to us in one. He spent his holiday with us and was always ready to take your grandfather for a walk, to discuss her difficulties with Vanessa, to arrange little plans for our amusement. Who shall say that there was not some real affection in this? some effort to do what he thought right against his will? But who again can distinguish the good from the bad, the feeling from the sentiment, the truth from the pose? We however were simply credulous, and ready to impose our conventional heroic shape upon the tumult of his character. Virtue it seemed was always victorious. Such were the figures that seemed unnaturally brought together in the great whirlpool; and it did not need the eye of a seer to foretell collision, fracture, and at length a sundering of the parts. Where are we today, indeed, who used to stand so close?

At the end of the summer Jack pressed us very hard to spend a week at Corby; we were to soothe the first shock of his home-coming,

* George was married to Lady Margaret Herbert on 10 September 1904.

or to know something which we could not know else; for when you examine feelings with the intense microscope that sorrow lends, it is amazing how they stretch, like the finest goldbeater's skin, over immense tracts of substance. And we, poor children that we were, conceived it to be our duty evermore to go searching for these atoms, wherever they might lie sprinkled about the surface, the great mountains and oceans, of the world. It is pitiable to remember the hours we spent in such minute speculations. Either Jack expressed some wish, or we thought we guessed it, and then we must devise the appropriate solace, the tiny, but to us gigantic, inflection this way or that, of the course of events. And so some grain would be saved, or some pin-point closed, and our immense task of piecing together all the torn fragments of his life would progress by the breadth of an atom. Jack himself could not recognize what we were doing for him in its detail; but he certainly had come to realize the mass of our, say rather of Vanessa's, endeavour. He began to take a regular and unthinking satisfaction in being with her, without I suppose, for I was sometimes jealous, perceiving a single one of the multitude of fine adjustments that composed her presence. But that was proof, like a healthy sleep, that the healing process was well begun. We went to Corby and spent there one of the most acutely miserable weeks of our lives; and perhaps something of our misery came from the suspicion that Jack did not see all our efforts, and the outer world was grossly ignorant of them. Now and again I rebelled in the old way against him, but with an instant sense of treason, when I realized with what silence, as of one possessed of incommunicable knowledge, Vanessa met my plaints.*

* Jack Hills was elected to Parliament in 1906. In 1931 he married Mary Grace Ashton.

A SKETCH OF THE PAST

(*Editor's Note*)

"A Sketch of the Past" covers some of the same ground as the preceding memoir but from such a different angle of vision that there is not, in a significant sense, any repetition. Virginia Woolf is near sixty when she begins this memoir. The present moment— 1939–1940—is the platform on which she stands to explore the meaning behind certain indelibly printed experiences of her childhood and the figures who dominated that world. The first memories lead her, through the central figure of her mother, to St Ives, Cornwall, and Talland House where the Stephens spent their summer holidays from 1882 to 1894. This idyllic 'country' world is countered by descriptions of life in London, of the young Stephens growing up at 22 Hyde Park Gate enmeshed in a large network of relations and friends at the very nub of which is always Julia Stephen. Once again the shattering effect of her death is described and the reordering of family life around the eldest daughter, Stella, begins. Virginia's first mental illness occurs at this time but it is mentioned only in an earlier, rejected version, MH/A.5c. The new arrangement of family life is first disturbed by Stella's marriage to Jack Hills and then destroyed by her death a bare three months later. The tensions within the household which hardly seemed to exist in Julia's lifetime and which were glossed over during Stella's reign become more pronounced: the serious, open-minded Stephen girls are forced to submit to George Duckworth's plans for their advancement, to enter 'Society' with its glitter, emptiness and rigid conventions; the young Stephens are silently antagonistic to the ageing Leslie Stephen who is increasingly deaf, increasingly isolated from reality and, at times, rudely tyrannical to his daughters. The outside world begins to exert a greater influence on the lives of the Stephens and the memoir closes on a typical day, around 1900, in this Victorian upper middle class family.

"A Sketch of the Past" was begun by Virginia Woolf on 18 April 1939, as relief from the exacting labours imposed by the writing of the biography of Roger Fry. The last date entered in the manuscript is 17 November 1940, some four months before her death. The text that follows is based on two separate items in the Monks House

Papers, in different stages of revision, which were nonetheless clearly intended to run consecutively: the typescript, MH/A.5a and the manuscript, MH/A.5d. Had this memoir been completed, it would undoubtedly have been considerably revised and extended.

A.5a consists of seventy pages typed by Virginia Woolf with corrections by her in black ink and soft lead pencil and by Leonard Woolf in blue ink. Leonard Woolf's corrections involve punctuation, spelling, clarification of Virginia's manuscript additions and the sorting out of the more obscure typing errors. These corrections have been retained when they conform to the principles set forth in the introductory 'Editor's Note'.

A.5d is in the form of a makeshift notebook held together by metal rings and containing sixty-four pages of manuscript and eleven blank pages. The manuscript begins with an entry dated '8 June 1940', that is, the date of the last entry in the 'a' typescript. The first nine pages of this entry are clearly an earlier version of the last entry in the 'a' typescript. The latter incorporates all the marginal corrections of the 'd' manuscript; its style is far more polished and the sentence construction is often more complex than the earlier 'd' version. Comparison of these two versions gives some insight into the extent and nature of the revisions which Virginia Woolf would probably have made on the 'd' manuscript had she reworked it. As it stands, A.5d, unlike the 'a' manuscript, contains some rewriting. In most cases, Virginia Woolf did not trouble to delete material which she proceeded directly to rework. Such passages have been omitted in the present edition and the relevant manuscript page numbers given in the footnotes. A number of sections are marked by false starts, partial or ambiguous deletions, coupled with obvious oversights and words on the verge of legibility. Such instances, while presenting difficulties, have been noted only when there are reasonable grounds to consider the reading doubtful, or when the difficulties are themselves of interest.

Other items in the Monks House Papers are connected with the two used for the present text: A.5b; A.5c; A.5e; and A.13a. Their value lies chiefly in the insight they afford into Virginia Woolf's working methods. The most interesting of them is A.5c, a twenty-one page manuscript, a part of which is an earlier version of a section of A.5a. On occasion it has proved useful in resolving obscurities in the latter. The remainder of the material of A.5c consists of lists of names, events and ideas to be developed later or brief sketches of other figures related to the Stephens which were not included in the 'a' revision. An eight page autobiographical manuscript fragment in the Berg Collection ("The tea table was the centre of Victorian family life . . . ") contained in a notebook dated 28 January 1940 is closely related to "A Sketch of the Past" but the date and the paper used suggest that it does not belong to the 'd' manuscript. It is perhaps an early version. However, the description there of Virginia's room at Hyde Park Gate no doubt accounts for the reference to 'that room' which occurs at the point where the present text takes up the 'd' manuscript. These items taken together with the more carefully revised 'a' typescript and the less revised 'd' manuscript, represent a cross-section of various stages through which a work of Virginia Woolf's might characteristically pass — from the rough notes and first tentative sketches to a draft approaching the final stage of preparation — with, of course, the important exception of the complete typed revisions of which there might be many.

A Sketch of the Past

Two days ago—Sunday 16th April 1939 to be precise—Nessa said that if I did not start writing my memoirs I should soon be too old. I should be eighty-five, and should have forgotten—witness the unhappy case of Lady Strachey.* As it happens that I am sick of writing Roger's life, perhaps I will spend two or three mornings making a sketch.† There are several difficulties. In the first place, the enormous number of things I can remember; in the second, the number of different ways in which memoirs can be written. As a great memoir reader, I know many different ways. But if I begin to go through them and to analyse them and their merits and faults, the mornings—I cannot take more than two or three at most—will be gone. So without stopping to choose my way, in the sure and certain knowledge that it will find itself—or if not it will not matter —I begin: the first memory.

This was of red and purple flowers on a black ground—my mother's dress; and she was sitting either in a train or in an omnibus, and I was on her lap. I therefore saw the flowers she was wearing very close; and can still see purple and red and blue, I think, against the black; they must have been anemones, I suppose. Perhaps we were going to St Ives; more probably, for from the light it must have been evening, we were coming back to London. But it is more convenient artistically to suppose that we were going to St Ives, for that will lead to my other memory, which also seems to be my first memory, and in fact it is the most important of all my memories. If life has a base that it stands upon, if it is a bowl that one fills and fills and fills—then my bowl without a doubt stands upon this memory. It is of lying half asleep, half awake, in bed in the nursery at St Ives. It is of hearing the waves breaking, one, two, one, two, and sending a splash of water over the beach; and then breaking, one, two, one, two, behind a yellow blind. It is of hearing the

* Lady Strachey, mother of Lytton, died at the age of eighty-nine, in 1928. In old age she wrote "Some Recollections of a Long Life" which were very short—less than a dozen pages in *Nation and Athenaeum*. This may indicate, as Michael Holroyd has suggested, that by the early 1920s she had forgotten more than she remembered.

† VW was at work on *Roger Fry: A Biography* (The Hogarth Press; London, 1940).

blind draw its little acorn across the floor as the wind blew the blind
out. It is of lying and hearing this splash and seeing this light, and
feeling, it is almost impossible that I should be here; of feeling the
purest ecstasy I can conceive.

I could spend hours trying to write that as it should be written,
in order to give the feeling which is even at this moment very strong
in me. But I should fail (unless I had some wonderful luck); I dare
say I should only succeed in having the luck if I had begun by
describing Virginia herself.

Here I come to one of the memoir writer's difficulties—one of the
reasons why, though I read so many, so many are failures. They
leave out the person to whom things happened. The reason is that it
is so difficult to describe any human being. So they say: "This is
what happened"; but they do not say what the person was like to
whom it happened. And the events mean very little unless we know
first to whom they happened. Who was I then? Adeline Virginia
Stephen, the second daughter of Leslie and Julia Prinsep Stephen,
born on 25th January 1882, descended from a great many people,
some famous, others obscure; born into a large connection, born not
of rich parents, but of well-to-do parents, born into a very communi-
cative, literate, letter writing, visiting, articulate, late nineteenth
century world; so that I could if I liked to take the trouble, write a
great deal here not only about my mother and father but about
uncles and aunts, cousins and friends. But I do not know how much
of this, or what part of this, made me feel what I felt in the nursery
at St Ives. I do not know how far I differ from other people. That is
another memoir writer's difficulty. Yet to describe oneself truly one
must have some standard of comparison; was I clever, stupid, good
looking, ugly, passionate, cold—? Owing partly to the fact that I was
never at school, never competed in any way with children of my own
age, I have never been able to compare my gifts and defects with
other people's. But of course there was one external reason for the
intensity of this first impression: the impression of the waves and the
acorn on the blind; the feeling, as I describe it sometimes to myself,
of lying in a grape and seeing through a film of semi-transparent
yellow—it was due partly to the many months we spent in London.
The change of nursery was a great change. And there was the long
train journey; and the excitement. I remember the dark; the lights;
the stir of the going up to bed.

But to fix my mind upon the nursery—it had a balcony; there

was a partition, but it joined the balcony of my father's and mother's
bedroom. My mother would come out onto her balcony in a white
dressing gown. There were passion flowers growing on the wall;
they were great starry blossoms, with purple streaks, and large green
buds, part empty, part full.

If I were a painter I should paint these first impressions in pale
yellow, silver, and green. There was the pale yellow blind; the
green sea; and the silver of the passion flowers. I should make a
picture that was globular; semi-transparent. I should make a
picture of curved petals; of shells; of things that were semi-transparent; I should make curved shapes, showing the light through,
but not giving a clear outline. Everything would be large and dim;
and what was seen would at the same time be heard; sounds would
come through this petal or leaf—sounds indistinguishable from
sights. Sound and sight seem to make equal parts of these first
impressions. When I think of the early morning in bed I also hear the
caw of rooks falling from a great height. The sound seems to fall
through an elastic, gummy air; which holds it up; which prevents
it from being sharp and distinct.* The quality of the air above
Talland House seemed to suspend sound, to let it sink down slowly,
as if it were caught in a blue gummy veil. The rooks cawing is part
of the waves breaking—one, two, one, two—and the splash as the
wave drew back and then it gathered again, and I lay there half
awake, half asleep, drawing in such ecstasy as I cannot describe.

The next memory—all these colour-and-sound memories hang
together at St Ives—was much more robust; it was highly sensual.
It was later. It still makes me feel warm; as if everything were ripe;
humming; sunny; smelling so many smells at once; and all making
a whole that even now makes me stop—as I stopped then going
down to the beach; I stopped at the top to look down at the gardens.
They were sunk beneath the road. The apples were on a level with
one's head. The gardens gave off a murmur of bees; the apples were
red and gold; there were also pink flowers; and grey and silver
leaves. The buzz, the croon, the smell, all seemed to press voluptu-
ously against some membrane; not to burst it; but to hum round one
such a complete rapture of pleasure that I stopped, smelt; looked.
But again I cannot describe that rapture. It was rapture rather than
ecstasy.

* VW has written 'made it seem to fall from a great height' above
'prevents . . . distinct.'

The strength of these pictures—but sight was always then so much mixed with sound that picture is not the right word—the strength anyhow of these impressions makes me again digress. Those moments —in the nursery, on the road to the beach—can still be more real than the present moment. This I have just tested. For I got up and crossed the garden. Percy was digging the asparagus bed; Louie was shaking a mat in front of the bedroom door.* But I was seeing them through the sight I saw here—the nursery and the road to the beach. At times I can go back to St Ives more completely than I can this morning. I can reach a state where I seem to be watching things happen as if I were there. That is, I suppose, that my memory supplies what I had forgotten, so that it seems as if it were happening independently, though I am really making it happen. In certain favourable moods, memories—what one has forgotten—come to the top. Now if this is so, is it not possible—I often wonder—that things we have felt with great intensity have an existence independent of our minds; are in fact still in existence? And if so, will it not be possible, in time, that some device will be invented by which we can tap them? I see it—the past—as an avenue lying behind; a long ribbon of scenes, emotions. There at the end of the avenue still, are the garden and the nursery. Instead of remembering here a scene and there a sound, I shall fit a plug into the wall; and listen in to the past. I shall turn up August 1890. I feel that strong emotion must leave its trace; and it is only a question of discovering how we can get ourselves again attached to it, so that we shall be able to live our lives through from the start.

But the peculiarity of these two strong memories is that each was very simple. I am hardly aware of myself, but only of the sensation. I am only the container of the feeling of ecstasy, of the feeling of rapture. Perhaps this is characteristic of all childhood memories; perhaps it accounts for their strength. Later we add to feelings much that makes them more complex; and therefore less strong; or if not less strong, less isolated, less complete. But instead of analysing this, here is an instance of what I mean—my feeling about the looking-glass in the hall.

There was a small looking-glass in the hall at Talland House. It had, I remember, a ledge with a brush on it. By standing on tiptoe I could see my face in the glass. When I was six or seven perhaps, I

* The gardener and daily help, respectively, at Monks House, the country home of the Woolfs in Rodmell, Sussex from 1919.

got into the habit of looking at my face in the glass. But I only did this if I was sure that I was alone. I was ashamed of it. A strong feeling of guilt seemed naturally attached to it. But why was this so? One obvious reason occurs to me—Vanessa and I were both what was called tomboys; that is, we played cricket, scrambled over rocks, climbed trees, were said not to care for clothes and so on. Perhaps therefore to have been found looking in the glass would have been against our tomboy code. But I think that my feeling of shame went a great deal deeper. I am almost inclined to drag in my grand-father—Sir James, who once smoked a cigar, liked it, and so threw away his cigar and never smoked another. I am almost inclined to think that I inherited a streak of the puritan, of the Clapham Sect.* At any rate, the looking-glass shame has lasted all my life, long after the tomboy phase was over. I cannot now powder my nose in public. Everything to do with dress—to be fitted, to come into a room wearing a new dress—still frightens me; at least makes me shy, self-conscious, uncomfortable. "Oh to be able to run, like Julian Morrell, all over the garden in a new dress", I thought not many years ago at Garsington; when Julian undid a parcel and put on a new dress and scampered round and round like a hare.† Yet femininity was very strong in our family. We were famous for our beauty—my mother's beauty, Stella's beauty, gave me as early as I can remember, pride and pleasure. What then gave me this feeling of shame, unless it were that I inherited some opposite instinct? My father was spartan, ascetic, puritanical. He had I think no feeling for pictures; no ear for music; no sense of the sound of words. This leads me to think that my—I would say 'our' if I knew enough about Vanessa, Thoby and Adrian—but how little we know even about brothers and sisters—this leads me to think that my natural love for beauty was checked by some ancestral dread. Yet this did not prevent me from feeling ecstasies and raptures spontaneously and intensely and without any shame or the least sense of guilt, so long as they were disconnected with my own body. I thus detect another element in the shame which I had in being caught looking at myself in the glass in the hall. I must have been ashamed or afraid of my own body. Another memory, also of the hall, may help to explain

* In marrying Jane Catherine Venn, James Stephen had allied himself with the very heart of the Clapham Sect.

† Julian Morrell was the daughter of Ottoline and Philip Morrell; Garsington Manor was their house in Oxfordshire.

this. There was a slab outside the dining room door for standing dishes upon. Once when I was very small Gerald Duckworth lifted me onto this, and as I sat there he began to explore my body. I can remember the feel of his hand going under my clothes; going firmly and steadily lower and lower. I remember how I hoped that he would stop; how I stiffened and wriggled as his hand approached my private parts. But it did not stop. His hand explored my private parts too. I remember resenting, disliking it—what is the word for so dumb and mixed a feeling? It must have been strong, since I still recall it. This seems to show that a feeling about certain parts of the body; how they must not be touched; how it is wrong to allow them to be touched; must be instinctive. It proves that Virginia Stephen was not born on the 25th January 1882, but was born many thousands of years ago; and had from the very first to encounter instincts already acquired by thousands of ancestresses in the past.

And this throws light not merely on my own case, but upon the problem that I touched on the first page; why it is so difficult to give any account of the person to whom things happen. The person is evidently immensely complicated. Witness the incident of the looking-glass. Though I have done my best to explain why I was ashamed of looking at my own face I have only been able to discover some possible reasons; there may be others; I do not suppose that I have got at the truth; yet this is a simple incident; and it happened to me personally; and I have no motive for lying about it. In spite of all this, people write what they call 'lives' of other people; that is, they collect a number of events, and leave the person to whom it happened unknown. Let me add a dream; for it may refer to the incident of the looking-glass. I dreamt that I was looking in a glass when a horrible face—the face of an animal—suddenly showed over my shoulder. I cannot be sure if this was a dream, or if it happened. Was I looking in the glass one day when something in the back-ground moved, and seemed to me alive? I cannot be sure. But I have always remembered the other face in the glass, whether it was a dream or a fact, and that it frightened me.

These then are some of my first memories. But of course as an account of my life they are misleading, because the things one does not remember are as important; perhaps they are more important. If I could remember one whole day I should be able to describe, superficially at least, what life was like as a child. Unfortunately, one only remembers what is exceptional. And there seems to be no reason why one thing is exceptional and another not. Why have I forgotten so many things that must have been, one would have thought, more memorable than what I do remember? Why remember the hum of bees in the garden going down to the beach, and forget completely being thrown naked by father into the sea? (Mrs Swanwick says she saw that happen.)*

This leads to a digression, which perhaps may explain a little of my own psychology; even of other people's. Often when I have been writing one of my so-called novels I have been baffled by this same problem; that is, how to describe what I call in my private shorthand —"non-being". Every day includes much more non-being than being. Yesterday for example, Tuesday the 18th of April, was [as] it happened a good day; above the average in "being". It was fine; I enjoyed writing these first pages; my head was relieved of the pressure of writing about Roger; I walked over Mount Misery† and along the river; and save that the tide was out, the country, which I notice very closely always, was coloured and shaded as I like—there were the willows, I remember, all plumy and soft green and purple against the blue. I also read Chaucer with pleasure; and began a book—the memoirs of Madame de la Fayette—which interested me. These separate moments of being were however embedded in many more moments of non-being. I have already forgotten what Leonard and I talked about at lunch; and at tea; although it was a good day the goodness was embedded in a kind of nondescript cotton wool. This is always so. A great part of every day is not lived consciously. One walks, eats, sees things, deals with what has to be done; the broken vacuum cleaner; ordering dinner; writing orders to Mabel; washing; cooking dinner; bookbinding. When it is a bad day the proportion of non-being is much larger. I had a slight temperature last week; almost the whole day was non-being. The real novelist can somehow convey both sorts of being. I think Jane Austen can; and Trollope; perhaps Thackeray and Dickens and Tolstoy. I have never been able to do both. I tried—in *Night and Day*; and in *The Years*. But I will leave the literary side alone for the moment.

* Mrs Swanwick was the only daughter of Oswald and Eleanor Sickert. In her autobiography, *I Have Been Young* (London, 1935), she recalls having known Leslie Stephen at St Ives: "We watched with delight his naked babies running about the beach or being towed into the sea between his legs, and their beautiful mother."

† Two cottages on the down between Southease and Piddinghoe known locally as Mount Misery.

As a child then, my days, just as they do now, contained a large proportion of this cotton wool, this non-being. Week after week passed at St Ives and nothing made any dint upon me. Then, for no reason that I know about, there was a sudden violent shock; something happened so violently that I have remembered it all my life. I will give a few instances. The first: I was fighting with Thoby on the lawn. We were pommelling each other with our fists. Just as I raised my fist to hit him, I felt: why hurt another person? I dropped my hand instantly, and stood there, and let him beat me. I remember the feeling. It was a feeling of hopeless sadness. It was as if I became aware of something terrible; and of my own powerlessness. I slunk off alone, feeling horribly depressed. The second instance was also in the garden at St Ives. I was looking at the flower bed by the front door; "That is the whole", I said. I was looking at a plant with a spread of leaves; and it seemed suddenly plain that the flower itself was a part of the earth; that a ring enclosed what was the flower; and that was the real flower; part earth; part flower. It was a thought I put away as being likely to be very useful to me later. The third case was also at St Ives. Some people called Valpy had been staying at St Ives, and had left. We were waiting at dinner one night, when somehow I overheard my father or my mother say that Mr Valpy had killed himself. The next thing I remember is being in the garden at night and walking on the path by the apple tree. It seemed to me that the apple tree was connected with the horror of Mr Valpy's suicide. I could not pass it. I stood there looking at the grey-green creases of the bark—it was a moonlit night—in a trance of horror. I seemed to be dragged down, hopelessly, into some pit of absolute despair from which I could not escape. My body seemed paralysed.

These are three instances of exceptional moments. I often tell them over, or rather they come to the surface unexpectedly. But now that for the first time I have written them down, I realise something that I have never realised before. Two of these moments ended in a state of despair. The other ended, on the contrary, in a state of satisfaction. When I said about the flower "That is the whole," I felt that I had made a discovery. I felt that I had put away in my mind something that I should go back [to], to turn over and explore. It strikes me now that this was a profound difference. It was the difference in the first place between despair and satisfaction. This difference I think arose from the fact that I was quite unable to deal with the pain of discovering that people hurt each other; that a man I had seen had killed himself. The sense of horror held me powerless. But in the case of the flower I found a reason; and was thus able to deal with the sensation. I was not powerless. I was conscious—if only at a distance—that I should in time explain it. I do not know if I was older when I saw the flower than I was when I had the other two experiences. I only know that many of these exceptional moments brought with them a peculiar horror and a physical collapse; they seemed dominant; myself passive. This suggests that as one gets older one has a greater power through reason to provide an explanation; and that this explanation blunts the sledge-hammer force of the blow. I think this is true, because though I still have the peculiarity that I receive these sudden shocks, they are now always welcome; after the first surprise, I always feel instantly that they are particularly valuable. And so I go on to suppose that the shock-receiving capacity is what makes me a writer. I hazard the explanation that a shock is at once in my case followed by the desire to explain it. I feel that I have had a blow; but it is not, as I thought as a child, simply a blow from an enemy hidden behind the cotton wool of daily life; it is or will become a revelation of some order; it is a token of some real thing behind appearances; and I make it real by putting it into words. It is only by putting it into words that I make it whole; this wholeness means that it has lost its power to hurt me; it gives me, perhaps because by doing so I take away the pain, a great delight to put the severed parts together. Perhaps this is the strongest pleasure known to me. It is the rapture I get when in writing I seem to be discovering what belongs to what; making a scene come right; making a character come together. From this I reach what I might call a philosophy; at any rate it is a constant idea of mine; that behind the cotton wool is hidden a pattern; that we—I mean all human beings—are connected with this; that the whole world is a work of art; that we are parts of the work of art. *Hamlet* or a Beethoven quartet is the truth about this vast mass that we call the world. But there is no Shakespeare, there is no Beethoven; certainly and emphatically there is no God; we are the words; we are the music; we are the thing itself. And I see this when I have a shock.

This intuition of mine—it is so instinctive that it seems given to me, not made by me—has certainly given its scale to my life ever since I saw the flower in the bed by the front door at St Ives. If I were painting myself I should have to find some — rod, shall I say — something that would stand for the conception. It proves that one's life is not confined to one's body and what one says and does; one is living all the time in relation to certain background rods or conceptions. Mine is that there is a pattern hid behind the cotton wool. And this conception affects me every day. I prove this, now, by spending the morning writing, when I might be walking, running a shop, or learning to do something that will be useful if war comes. I feel that by writing I am doing what is far more necessary than anything else.

All artists I suppose feel something like this. It is one of the obscure elements in life that has never been much discussed. It is left out in almost all biographies and autobiographies, even of artists. Why did Dickens spend his entire life writing stories? What was his conception? I bring in Dickens partly because I am reading *Nicholas Nickleby* at the moment; also partly because it struck me, on my walk yesterday, that these moments of being of mine were scaffolding in the background; were the invisible and silent part of my life as a child. But in the foreground there were of course people; and these people were very like characters in Dickens. They were caricatures; they were very simple; they were immensely alive. They could be made with three strokes of the pen, if I could do it. Dickens owes his astonishing power to make characters alive to the fact that he saw them as a child sees them; as I saw Mr Wolstenholme; C. B. Clarke, and Mr Gibbs.

I name these three people because they all died when I was a child. Therefore they have never been altered. I see them exactly as I saw them then. Mr Wolstenholme was a very old gentleman who came every summer to stay with us. He was brown; he had a beard and very small eyes in fat cheeks; and he fitted into a brown wicker beehive chair as if it had been his nest. He used to sit in this beehive chair smoking and reading. He had only one characteristic — that when he ate plum tart he spurted the juice through his nose so that it made a purple stain on his grey moustache. This seemed enough to cause us perpetual delight. We called him 'The Woolly One'. By way of shading him a little I remember that we had to be kind to him because he was not happy at home; that he was very poor, yet once gave Thoby half a crown; that he had a son who was drowned in Australia; and I know too that he was a great mathematician. He never said a word all the time I knew him. But he still seems to me a complete character; and whenever I think of him I begin to laugh.

Mr Gibbs was perhaps less simple. He wore a tie ring; had a bald, benevolent head; was dry; neat; precise; and had folds of skin under his chin. He made father groan—"why can't you go—why can't you go?" And he gave Vanessa and myself two ermine skins, with slits down the middle out of which poured endless wealth—streams of silver. I also remember him lying in bed, dying; husky; in a night shirt; and showing us drawings by Retzsch.* The character of Mr Gibbs also seems to me complete and amuses me very much.

As for C. B. Clarke, he was an old botanist; and he said to my father "All you young botanists like Osmunda." He had an aunt aged eighty who went for a walking tour in the New Forest. That is all—that is all I have to say about these three old gentlemen. But how real they were! How we laughed at them! What an immense part they played in our lives!

One more caricature comes into my mind; though pity entered into this one. I am thinking of Justine Nonon. She was immensely old. Little hairs sprouted on her long bony chin. She was a hunch-back; and walked like a spider, feeling her way with her long dry fingers from one chair to another. Most of the time she sat in the arm-chair beside the fire. I used to sit on her knee; and her knee jogged up and down; and she sang in a hoarse cracked voice "Ron ron ron—et plon plon plon—" and then her knee gave and I was tumbled onto the floor. She was French; she had been with the Thackerays. She only came to us on visits. She lived by herself at Shepherd's Bush; and used to bring Adrian a glass jar of honey. I got the notion that she was extremely poor; and it made me un-comfortable that she brought this honey, because I felt she did it by way of making her visit acceptable. She said too: "I have come in my carriage and pair"—which meant the red omnibus. For this too I pitied her; also because she began to wheeze; and the nurses said she would not live much longer; and soon she died. That is all I know about her; but I remember her as if she were a completely real person, with nothing left out, like the three old men.

* Friedrich Retzsch (1779–1857), a German engraver widely known in Germany and England. The ts has 'Ketsch' which is obviously a typing error.

2nd May . . . I write the date, because I think that I have discovered a possible form for these notes. That is, to make them include the present—at least enough of the present to serve as platform to stand upon. It would be interesting to make the two people, I now, I then, come out in contrast. And further, this past is much affected by the present moment. What I write today I should not write in a year's time. But I cannot work this out; it had better be left to chance, as I write by fits and starts by way of a holiday from Roger. I have no energy at the moment to spend upon the horrid labour that it needs to make an orderly and expressed work of art; where one thing follows another and all are swept into a whole. Perhaps one day, relieved from making works of art, I will try to compose this.

But to continue—the three old men and the one old woman are complete, as I was saying, because they died when I was a child. They none of them lived on to be altered as I altered—as others, like the Stillmans or the Lushingtons, lived on and were added to and filled and left finally incomplete. The same thing applies to places. I cannot see Kensington Gardens as I saw it as a child because I saw it only two days ago—on a chill afternoon, all the cherry trees lurid in the cold yellow light of a hail storm. I know that it was very much larger in 1890 when I was seven than it is now. For one thing, it was not connected with Hyde Park. Now I walk from one to the other. We drive in our car; and leave it by the new kiosk. But then there was the Broad Walk, the Round Pond, and the Flower Walk. Then —I will try to get back to then—there were two gates, one opposite Gloucester Road, the other opposite Queen's Gate. At each gate sat an old woman. The Queen's Gate old woman was an elongated, emaciated figure with a goat-like face, yellow and pockmarked. She sold nuts and boot-laces, I think. And Kitty Maxse said of her: "Poor things, it's drink that makes them like that." She always sat, and wore a shawl and had to me a faint, obliterated, debased likeness to Granny; whose face was elongated too, but she wore a very soft shawl, like tapioca pudding, over her head, and it was fastened by an amethyst brooch set in pearls. The other old woman was round and squat. To her was attached a whole wobbling balloon of air-balls. She held this billowing, always moving, most desirable mass by one string. They glowed in my eyes always red and purple, like the flower my mother wore; and they were always billowing in the air. For a penny, she would detach one from the bellying soft mass, and I would dance away with it. She too wore a shawl and her face was puckered, as the air-balls puckered in the nursery if they survived to be taken home. I think Nurse and Sooney were on speaking terms with her; but I never heard what she said. Anemones, the blue and purple bunches that are now being sold, always bring back that quivering mound of air-balls outside the gate of Kensington Gardens.

Then we went up the Broad Walk. The Broad Walk had a peculiar property—when we took our first walk there after coming back from St Ives, we always abused it; it was not a hill at all, we said. By degrees as the weeks passed the hill became steeper and steeper until by the summer it was a hill again. The swamp—as we called the rather derelict ground behind the Flower Walk—had to Adrian and myself at least the glamour of the past on it. When Nessa and Thoby were very small, that is to say, it had been, they told us, a real swamp; they had found the skeleton of a dog there. And it must have been covered with reeds and full of pools, we thought, for we believed that the dog had been starved and drowned. In our day it had been drained, though it was still muddy. But it had a past always to us. And we compared it, of course, with Halestown bog* near St Ives. Halestown bog where the Osmunda grew; and those thick ferns with bulbous roots that had trees marked on them, if you cut them across. I brought some home every autumn to make into pen holders. It was natural always to compare Kensington Gardens with St Ives, always of course to the disadvantage of London. That was one of the pleasures of scrunching the shells with which now and then the Flower Walk was strewn. They had little ribs on them like the shells on the beach. On the other hand the crocodile tree was itself; and is still there—the tree on the Speke Monument path;† which has a great root exposed; and the root is polished, partly by the friction of our hands, for we used to scramble over it.

As we walked, to beguile the dulness [of] innumerable winter walks we made up stories, long long stories that were taken up at the same place and added to each in turn. There was the Jim Joe and Harry Hoe story; about three brothers who had herds of animals and adventures—I have forgotten what. But there again, the Jim Joe and Harry Hoe story was a London story; and inferior to the Talland House garden story about Beccage and Hollywinks; spirits

* Halse Town bog which the Stephens always called 'Halestown bog'.
† The red granite obelisk in Kensington Gardens dedicated to the memory of the explorer John Hanning Speke.

of evil who lived on the rubbish heap; and disappeared through a hole in the escallonia hedge—as I remember telling my mother and Mr Lowell.* Walks in Kensington Gardens were dull. Non-being made up a great proportion of our time in London. The walks—twice every day in Kensington Gardens—were so monotonous. Speaking for myself, non-being lay thick over those years. Past the thermometer we went—sometimes it was below the little freezing bar but not often save in the great 1894–5 winter when we skated every day; when I dropped my watch and the rough man gave it me; and asked for money; and a kind lady offered three coppers; and he said he would only take silver; and she shook her head and faded away—past the thermometer we went, past the gate-keeper in his green livery and his gold laced hat, up the Flower Walk, round the pond. We sailed boats of course. There was the great day when my Cornish lugger sailed perfectly to the middle of the pond and then with my eyes upon it, amazed, sank suddenly; "Did you see that?" my father cried, coming striding towards me. We had both seen it and both were amazed. To make the wonder complete, many weeks later in the spring, I was walking by the pond and a man in a flat-boat was dredging the pond of duckweed, and to my unspeakable excitement, up he brought my lugger in his dredging net; and I claimed it; and he gave it me, and I ran home with this marvellous story to tell. Then my mother made new sails; and my father rigged it, and I remember seeing him fixing the sails to the yard-arm after dinner; and how interested he became and said, with his little snort, half laughing, something like "Absurd—what fun it is doing this!"

I could collect a great many more floating incidents—scenes in Kensington Gardens; how if we had a penny we went to the white house near the palace and bought sweets from the smooth-faced, pink-cheeked woman in a grey cotton dress who used then to keep a sweet shop there; how on one day of the week we bought *Tit-Bits* and read the jokes—I liked the Correspondence best—sitting on the grass, breaking our chocolate into "Frys" as we called them, for a penny slab was divided into four; how we knocked into a lady racing our go-cart round a steep corner, and her sister scolded us violently; how we tied Shag to a railing, and some children told the Park Keeper that we were cruel—but the stories were not then very

* James Russell Lowell, the poet and critic, American Ambassador to the Court of St James 1880–85, and friend of Leslie Stephen, was Virginia's godfather.

exciting; though they helped to break up the eternal round of Kensington Gardens.

What then has remained interesting? Again those moments of being. Two I always remember. There was the moment of the puddle in the path; when for no reason I could discover, everything suddenly became unreal; I was suspended; I could not step across the puddle; I tried to touch something . . . the whole world became unreal. Next, the other moment when the idiot boy sprang up with his hand outstretched mewing, slit-eyed, red-rimmed; and without saying a word, with a sense of the horror in me, I poured into his hand a bag of Russian toffee. But it was not over, for that night in the bath the dumb horror came over me. Again I had that hopeless sadness; that collapse I have described before; as if I were passive under some sledge-hammer blow; exposed to a whole avalanche of meaning that had heaped itself up and discharged itself upon me, unprotected, with nothing to ward it off, so that I huddled up at my end of the bath, motionless. I could not explain it; I said nothing even to Nessa sponging herself at the other end.

Looking back, then, at Kensington Gardens, though I can recover incidents, many more than I have patience to describe, I cannot recover, save by fits and starts, the focus, the proportions of the external world. It seems to me that a child must have a curious focus; it sees an air-ball or a shell with extreme distinctness; I still see the air-balls, blue and purple, and the ribs on the shells; but these points are enclosed in vast empty spaces. How large for instance was the space beneath the nursery table! I see it still as a great black space with the table-cloth hanging down in folds on the outskirts in the distance; and myself roaming about there, and meeting Nessa. "Have black cats got tails?" she asked, and I said "NO", and was proud because she had asked me a question. Then we roamed off again into that vast space. The night nursery was vast too. In winter I would slip in before bed to take a look at the fire. I was very anxious to see that the fire was low, because it frightened me if it burnt after we went to bed. I dreaded that little flickering flame on the walls; but Adrian liked it; and to make a compromise, Nurse folded a towel over the fender; but I could not help opening my eyes, and there often was the flickering flame; and I looked and looked and could not sleep; and in order to have company, said "What did you say, Nessa?" although she was asleep, to wake her and to hear someone's voice. These were early fears; for later, when Thoby had gone to school, leaving Nessa to take his monkey Jacko to bed with her, no sooner was the door shut than we began story-telling. The story always began thus: "Clémont* dear child, said Mrs Dilke," and it went on to tell wild stories of the Dilke family† and Miss Rosalba the governess; how they dug under the floor and discovered sacks of gold; and held great feasts and ate fried eggs "with plenty of frizzling", for the wealth of the Dilkes in real life compared with our own moderate means impressed us. We noticed how many new clothes Mrs Dilke wore; how seldom my mother bought a new dress.

Many bright colours; many distinct sounds; some human beings, caricatures; comic; several violent moments of being, always including a circle of the scene which they cut out: and all surrounded by a vast space—that is a rough visual description of childhood. This is how I shape it; and how I see myself as a child, roaming about, in that space of time which lasted from 1882 to 1895. A great hall I could liken it to; with windows letting in strange lights; and murmurs and spaces of deep silence. But somehow into that picture must be brought, too, the sense of movement and change. Nothing remained stable long. One must get the feeling of everything approaching and then disappearing, getting large, getting small, passing at different rates of speed past the little creature; one must get the feeling that made her press on, the little creature driven on as she was by growth of her legs and arms, driven without her being able to stop it, or to change it, driven as a plant is driven up out of the earth, up until the stalk grows, the leaf grows, buds swell. That is what is indescribable, that is what makes all images too static, for no sooner has one said this was so, than it was past and altered. How immense must be the force of life which turns a baby, who can just distinguish a great blot of blue and purple on a black background, into the child who thirteen years later can feel all that I felt on May 5th 1895—now almost exactly to a day, forty-four years ago—when my mother died.

This shows that among the innumerable things left out in my sketch I have left out the most important—those instincts, affections,

* In a paper written by Vanessa Bell for the Memoir Club ("Notes on Virginia's Childhood, a Memoir", ed. Richard Schaubeck, Jr.: Frank Hallman; New York, 1974) 'Clémont' is spelled 'Clémenté'.

† Next door neighbours.

passions, attachments—there is no single word for them, for they changed month by month—which bound me, I suppose, from the first moment of consciousness to other people. If it were true, as I said above, that the things that ceased in childhood, are easy to describe because they are complete, then it should be easy to say what I felt for my mother, who died when I was thirteen. Thus I should be able to see her completely undisturbed by later impressions, as I saw Mr Gibbs and C. B. Clarke. But the theory, though true of them, breaks down completely with her. It breaks down in a curious way, which I will explain, for perhaps it may help to explain why I find it now so curiously difficult to describe both my feeling for her, and her herself.

Until I was in the forties—I could settle the date by seeing when I wrote *To the Lighthouse*, but am too casual here to bother to do it— the presence of my mother obsessed me.* I could hear her voice, see her, imagine what she would do or say as I went about my day's doings. She was one of the invisible presences who after all play so important a part in every life. This influence, by which I mean the consciousness of other groups impinging upon ourselves; public opinion; what other people say and think; all those magnets which attract us this way to be like that, or repel us the other and make us different from that; has never been analysed in any of those Lives which I so much enjoy reading, or very superficially.

Yet it is by such invisible presences that the "subject of this memoir" is tugged this way and that every day of his life; it is they that keep him in position. Consider what immense forces society brings to play upon each of us, how that society changes from decade to decade; and also from class to class; well, if we cannot analyse these invisible presences, we know very little of the subject of the memoir; and again how futile life-writing becomes. I see myself as a fish in a stream; deflected; held in place; but cannot describe the stream.

To return to the particular instance which should be more definite and more capable of description than for example the influence on me of the Cambridge Apostles,† or the influence of the

* *To the Lighthouse* was begun in 1925 and published in 1927 when VW was forty-five.

† The popular name for the semi-secret 'Cambridge Conversazione Society' which was founded in the 1820s. All the young men who formed the nucleus of 'old Bloomsbury' belonged to it, except Clive Bell and Thoby Stephen.

Galsworthy, Bennett, Wells school of fiction, or the influence of the Vote, or of the War—that is, the influence of my mother. It is perfectly true that she obsessed me, in spite of the fact that she died when I was thirteen, until I was forty-four. Then one day walking round Tavistock Square I made up, as I sometimes make up my books, *To the Lighthouse*; in a great, apparently involuntary, rush.* One thing burst into another. Blowing bubbles out of a pipe gives the feeling of the rapid crowd of ideas and scenes which blew out of my mind, so that my lips seemed syllabling of their own accord as I walked. What blew the bubbles? Why then? I have no notion. But I wrote the book very quickly; and when it was written, I ceased to be obsessed by my mother. I no longer hear her voice; I do not see her.

I suppose that I did for myself what psycho-analysts do for their patients. I expressed some very long felt and deeply felt emotion. And in expressing it I explained it and then laid it to rest. But what is the meaning of "explained" it? Why, because I described her and my feeling for her in that book, should my vision of her and my feeling for her become so much dimmer and weaker? Perhaps one of these days I shall hit on the reason; and if so, I will give it, but at the moment I will go on, describing what I can remember, for it may be true that what I remember of her now will weaken still further. (This note is made provisionally, in order to explain in part why it is now so difficult to give any clear description of her.)

Certainly there she was, in the very centre of that great Cathedral space which was childhood; there she was from the very first. My first memory is of her lap; the scratch of some beads on her dress comes back to me as I pressed my cheek against it. Then I see her in her white dressing gown on the balcony; and the passion flower with the purple star on its petals. Her voice is still faintly in my ears— decided, quick; and in particular the little drops with which her laugh ended—three diminishing ahs... "Ah—ah—ah..." I sometimes end a laugh that way myself. And I see her hands, like Adrian's, with the very individual square-tipped fingers, each finger with a waist to it, and the nail broadening out. (My own are the same size all the way, so that I can slip a ring over my thumb.) She had three rings; a diamond ring, an emerald ring, and an opal ring. My eyes used to fix themselves upon the lights in the opal as it moved across the page of the lesson book when she taught us, and I was glad

* 52 Tavistock Square was the London home of the Woolfs from 1924 to 1939.

that she left it to me (I gave it to Leonard). Also I hear the tinkle of
her bracelets, made of twisted silver, given her by Mr Lowell, as she
went about the house; especially as she came up at night to see if we
were asleep, holding a candle shaded; this is a distinct memory, for,
like all children, I lay awake sometimes and longed for her to come.
Then she told me to think of all the lovely things I could imagine.
Rainbows and bells . . . But besides these minute separate details,
how did I first become conscious of what was always there — her
astonishing beauty? Perhaps I never became conscious of it; I think
I accepted her beauty as the natural quality that a mother — she
seemed typical, universal, yet our own in particular — had by virtue
of being our mother. It was part of her calling. I do not think that I
separated her face from that general being; or from her whole body.
Certainly I have a vision of her now, as she came up the path by the
lawn at St Ives; slight, shapely — she held herself very straight. I was
playing. I stopped, about to speak to her. But she half turned from
us, and lowered her eyes. From that indescribably sad gesture I knew
that Philips, the man who had been crushed on the line and whom
she had been visiting, was dead. It's over, she seemed to say. I knew,
and was awed by the thought of death. At the same time I felt that
her gesture as a whole was lovely. Very early, through nurses or
casual visitors, I must have known that she was thought very beautiful. But that pride was snobbish, not a pure and private feeling: it
was mixed with pride in other people's admiration. It was related to
the more definitely snobbish pride caused in me by the nurses who
said one night talking together while we ate our supper: "They're
very well connected . . . ."

But apart from her beauty, if the two can be separated, what was
she herself like? Very quick; very direct; practical; and amusing, I
say at once offhand. She could be sharp, she disliked affectation. "If
you put your head on one side like that, you shan't come to the
party," I remember she said to me as we drew up in a carriage in
front of some house. Severe; with a background of knowledge that
made her sad. She had her own sorrow waiting behind her to dip
into privately. Once when she had set us to write exercises I looked
up from mine and watched her reading — the Bible perhaps; and,
struck by the gravity of her face, told myself that her first husband
had been a clergyman and that she was thinking, as she read what he
had read, of him. This was a fable on my part; but it shows that she
looked very sad when she was not talking.

But can I get any closer to her without drawing upon all those descriptions and anecdotes which after she was dead imposed themselves upon my view of her? Very quick; very definite; very upright; and behind the active, the sad, the silent. And of course she was central. I suspect the word "central" gets closest to the general feeling I had of living so completely in her atmosphere that one never got far enough away from her to see her as a person. (That is one reason why I see the Gibbses and the Beadles and the Clarkes so much more distinctly.) She was the whole thing; Talland House was full of her; Hyde Park Gate was full of her. I see now, though the sentence is hasty, feeble and inexpressive, why it was that it was impossible for her to leave a very private and particular impression upon a child. She was keeping what I call in my shorthand the panoply of life — that which we all lived in common — in being. I see now that she was living on such an extended surface that she had not time, nor strength, to concentrate, except for a moment if one were ill or in some child's crisis, upon me, or upon anyone — unless it were Adrian. Him she cherished separately; she called him 'My Joy'. The later view, the understanding that I now have of her position must have its say; and it shows me that a woman of forty with seven children, some of them needing grown-up attention, and four still in the nursery; and an eighth, Laura, an idiot, yet living with us; and a husband fifteen years her elder, difficult, exacting, dependent on her; I see now that a woman who had to keep all this in being and under control must have been a general presence rather than a particular person to a child of seven or eight. Can I remember ever being alone with her for more than a few minutes? Someone was always interrupting. When I think of her spontaneously she is always in a room full of people; Stella, George and Gerald are there; my father, sitting reading with one leg curled round the other, twisting his lock of hair; "Go and take the crumb out of his beard," she whispers to me; and off I trot. There are visitors, young men like Jack Hills who is in love with Stella; many young men, Cambridge friends of George's and Gerald's; old men, sitting round the tea table talking — father's friends, Henry James, Symonds,* (I see him peering up at me on the broad staircase at St Ives with his drawn yellow face and a tie made of a yellow cord

* John Addington Symonds, man of letters, was the father of Katherine who married the artist Charles Furse and Margaret (Madge) who married William Wyamar Vaughan.

with two plush balls on it); Stella's friends—the Lushingtons, the Stillmans; I see her at the head of the table underneath the engraving of Beatrice given her by an old governess and painted blue; I hear jokes; laughter; the clatter of voices; I am teased; I say something funny; she laughs; I am pleased; I blush furiously; she observes; someone laughs at Nessa for saying that Ida Milman is her B.F.; Mother says soothingly, tenderly, "Best friend, that means." I see her going to the town with her basket; and Arthur Davies goes with her; I see her knitting on the hall step while we play cricket; I see her stretching her arms out to Mrs Williams when the bailiffs took possession of their house and the Captain stood at the window bawling and shying jugs, basins, chamber pots onto the gravel— "Come to us, Mrs Williams"; "No, Mrs Stephen," sobbed Mrs Williams, "I will not leave my husband."—I see her writing at her table in London and the silver candlesticks, and the high carved chair with the claws and the pink seat; and the three-cornered brass ink pot; I wait in agony peeping surreptitiously behind the blind for her to come down the street, when she has been out late the lamps are lit and I am sure that she has been run over. (Once my father found me peeping; questioned me; and said rather anxiously but reprovingly, "You shouldn't be so nervous, Jinny.") And there is my last sight of her; she was dying; I came to kiss her and as I crept out of the room she said: "Hold yourself straight, my little Goat." ... What a jumble of things I can remember, if I let my mind run, about my mother; but they are all of her in company; of her surrounded; of her generalised; dispersed, omnipresent, of her as the creator of that crowded merry world which spun so gaily in the centre of my childhood. It is true that I enclosed that world in another made by my own temperament; it is true that from the beginning I had many adventures outside that world; and often went far from it; and kept much back from it; but there it always was, the common life of the family, very merry, very stirring, crowded with people; and she was the centre; it was herself. This was proved on May 5th 1895. For after that day there was nothing left of it. I leant out of the nursery window the morning she died. It was about six, I suppose. I saw Dr Seton walk away up the street with his head bent and his hands clasped behind his back. I saw the pigeons floating and settling. I got a feeling of calm, sadness, and finality. It was a beautiful blue spring morning, and very still. That brings back the feeling that everything had come to an end.

May 15th 1939. The drudgery of making a coherent life of Roger has once more become intolerable, and so I turn for a few day's respite to May 1895. The little platform of present time on which I stand is, so far as the weather is concerned, damp and chilly. I look up at my skylight—over the litter of *Athenaeum* articles, Fry letters— all strewn with the sand that comes from the house that is being pulled down next door—I look up and see, as if reflecting it, a sky the colour of dirty water. And the inner landscape is much of a piece. Last night Mark Gertler* dined here and denounced the vulgarity, the inferiority of what he called "literature"; compared with the integrity of painting. "For it always deals with Mr and Mrs Brown," —he said—with the personal, the trivial, that is; a criticism which has its sting and its chill, like the May sky. Yet if one could give a sense of my mother's personality one would have to be an artist. It would be as difficult to do that, as it should be done, as to paint a Cézanne.

One of the few things that is certain about her is that she married two very different men. If one looks at her not as a child, of seven or eight, but as a woman now older than she was when she died, there is something to take hold of in that fact. She was not so rubbed out and featureless, not so dominated by the beauty of her own face, as she has since become—and inevitably. For what reality can remain real of a person who died forty-four years ago† at the age of forty-nine, without leaving a book, or a picture, or any piece of work—apart from the three children who now survive and the memory of her that remains in their minds? There is the memory; but there is nothing to check that memory by; nothing to bring it to ground with.

There are however these two marriages; and they show that she was capable of falling in love with two very different men; one, to put it in a nutshell, the pink of propriety; the other, the pink of intellectuality. She could span them both. This must serve me by way of foot rule, in trying to measure her character.

The elements of that character, though, are formed in twilight. She was born, I think, in 1848;‡ I think in India; the daughter of Dr Jackson and his half-French wife. Not very much education

* The artist who committed suicide in this same year, 23 June 1939.
† VW mistakenly typed '43 years ago'.
‡ Julia was born in 1846, not in 1848.

came her way. An old governess—was she Mademoiselle Rose? did she give her the picture of Beatrice that hung in the dining room at Talland House?—taught her French, which she spoke with a very good accent; and she could play the piano and was musical. I remember that she kept De Quincey's *Opium Eater* on her table, one of her favourite books; and for a birthday present she chose all the works of Scott which her father gave her in the first edition—some remain; others are lost. For Scott she had a passion. She had an instinctive, not a trained mind. But her instinct, for books at least, seems to me to have been strong, and I liked it, for she gave a jump, I remember, when reading *Hamlet* aloud to her I misread 'sliver' 'silver'—she jumped as my father jumped at a false quantity when we read Virgil with him. She was her mother's favourite daughter of the three; and as her mother was an invalid even as a child she was used to nursing; to waiting on a sick bed. They had a house at Well Walk during the Crimean War; for there was an anecdote about watching the soldiers drill on the Heath. But her beauty at once came to the fore, even as a little girl; for there was another anecdote—how she could never be sent out alone, but must have Mary with her, to protect her from admiring looks: to keep her unconscious of that beauty—and she was, my father said, very little conscious of it. It was due to this beauty, I suspect, that she had that training which was much more important than any she had from governesses—the training of life at Little Holland House. She was a great deal at Little Holland House as a child, partly, I imagine, because she was acceptable to the painters, and the Prinseps—Aunt Sara and Uncle Thoby must have been proud of her.*

Little Holland House was her world then. But what was that world like? I think of it as a summer afternoon world. To my thinking Little Holland House is an old white country house, standing in a large garden. Long windows open onto the lawn. Through them comes a stream of ladies in crinolines and little straw hats; they are attended by gentlemen in peg-top trousers and whiskers. The date is round about 1860. It is a hot summer day. Tea tables with great bowls of strawberries and cream are scattered about the lawn. They

---

* Julia's Aunt Sara, one of the seven Pattle sisters, married Thoby Prinsep. They settled in Little Holland House, Kensington, where they entertained in a highly eccentric fashion an aristocracy of intellect in which the painters—Holman Hunt, Burne-Jones and above all, G. F. Watts who was long a resident—played a dominant role.

are "presided over" by some of the six lovely sisters;* who do not
wear crinolines, but are robed in splendid Venetian draperies; they
sit enthroned, and talk with foreign emphatic gestures — my mother
too gesticulated, throwing her hands out — to the eminent men
(afterwards to be made fun of by Lytton);† rulers of India, states-
men, poets, painters. My mother comes out of the window wearing
that striped silk dress buttoned at the throat with a flowing skirt that
appears in the photograph.‡ She is of course "a vision" as they used
to say; and there she stands, silent, with her plate of strawberries and
cream; or perhaps is told to take a party across the garden to
Signior's studio.§ The sound of music also comes from those long
low rooms where the great Watts pictures hang; Joachim playing
the violin; also the sound of a voice reading poetry — Uncle Thoby
would read his translations from the Persian poets. How easy it is to
fill in the picture with set pieces that I have gathered from memoirs
— to bring in Tennyson in his wideawake; Watts in his smock frock;
Ellen Terry dressed as a boy; Garibaldi in his red shirt — and Henry
Taylor turned from him to my mother — "the face of one fair girl
was more to me" — so he says in a poem. But if I turn to my mother,
how difficult it is to single her out as she really was; to imagine what
she was thinking, to put a single sentence into her mouth! I dream;
I make up pictures of a summer's afternoon.

But the dream is based upon one fact. Once when we were
children, my mother took us to Melbury Road; and when we came
to the street that had been built on the old garden she gave a little
spring forward, clapped her hands, and cried "That was where it
was!" as if a fairyland had disappeared. Thus I think it is true that
Little Holland House was a summer afternoon world to her. As a
fact too I know that she adored her Uncle Thoby. His walking stick,
with a hole in the top through which a tassel must have hung, a
beautiful eighteenth-century looking cane, always stood at the head
of her bed at Hyde Park Gate. She was a hero worshipper, simple,
uncritical, enthusiastic. She felt for Uncle Thoby, my father said,
much more than she felt for her own father — "old Dr Jackson";

* Although there were seven Pattle sisters, no one ever spoke of Julia
(Cameron) as beautiful. However, F. W. Maitland in *The Life and Letters of
Leslie Stephen* (London, 1906) makes the same error when referring to Maria
Pattle as "one of six sisters" (p. 317n).
† Strachey.
‡ Efforts to trace this photograph have been unsuccessful.
§ The studio of G. F. Watts.

"respectable"; but, for all his good looks and the amazing mane of white hair that stood out like a three-cornered hat round his head, he was a commonplace prosaic old man; boring people with his stories of a famous poison case in Calcutta; excluded from this poetical fairyland; and no doubt out of temper with it. My mother had no romance about him; but she derived from him, I suspect, the practicality, the shrewdness, which were among her qualities.

Little Holland House then was her education. She was taught there to take such part as girls did then in the lives of distinguished men; to pour out tea; to hand them their strawberries and cream; to listen devoutly, reverently to their wisdom; to accept the fact that Watts was the great painter; Tennyson the great poet; and to dance with the Prince of Wales. For the sisters, with the exception of my grandmother who was devout and spiritual, were worldly in the thoroughgoing Victorian way. Aunt Virginia, it is plain, put her own daughters, my mother's first cousins, through tortures compared with which the boot or the Chinese shoe is negligible, in order to marry one to the Duke of Bedford, the other to Lord Henry Somerset. (That is how we came to be, as the nurses said, so "well connected".) But here again I am dipping into memoirs, and leaving Julia Jackson, the real person, on one side. The only certainties I can lay hands on in those early years are that two men proposed to her (or to her parents on her behalf); one was Holman Hunt; the other Woolner, a sculptor.* Both proposals were made and refused when she was scarcely out of the nursery. I know too that she went once wearing a hat with grey feathers to a river party where Anny Thackeray† was; and Nun (that is Aunt Caroline, father's sister) saw her standing alone; and was amazed that she was not the centre of a bevy of admirers; "Where are they?" she asked Anny Thackeray; who said, "Oh they don't happen to be here today"—a little scene which makes me suspect that Julia aged seventeen or eighteen was aloof; and shed a certain silence round her by her very beauty.

That little scene is dated; she cannot have been more than

* Hunt and Thomas Woolner were founder members of the Pre-Raphaelite Brotherhood.

† Anne Thackeray was the elder daughter of the novelist W. M. Thackeray and sister of Leslie Stephen's first wife. She married her cousin, Richmond Ritchie.

eighteen; because she married when she was nineteen.* She was in Venice; met Herbert Duckworth; fell head over ears in love with him, he with her, and so they married. That is all I know, perhaps all that anyone now knows, of the most important thing that ever happened to her. How important it was is proved by the fact that when he died four years later she was "as unhappy as it is possible for a human being to be". That was her own saying; it came to me from Kitty Maxse. "I have been as unhappy and as happy as it is possible for a human being to be." Kitty remembered it, because though she was very intimate with my mother, this was the only time in all their friendship that she ever spoke of what she had felt for Herbert Duckworth.

What my mother was like when she was as happy as anyone can be, I have no notion. Not a sound or a scene has survived from those four years. They were well off; lived in Bryanston Square; he practised not very seriously at the Bar; (once they went on circuit; and a friend said to him, "I spent the whole morning in Court looking at a beautiful face"—Herbert's wife); George was born; then Stella; and Gerald was about to be born when Herbert Duckworth died. They were staying with the Vaughans at Upton;† he stretched to pick a fig for my mother; an abscess burst; and he died in a few hours. Those are the only facts I know about those four happy years.

If it were possible to know what Herbert himself was like, some ray of light might fall from him upon my mother. But, like all very handsome men who die tragically, he left not so much a character behind him as a legend. Youth and death shed a halo through which it is difficult to see a real face—a face one might see today in the street or here in my studio. To Aunt Mary—my mother's sister, likely thus to share some of her feelings—he was "Oh darling, a beam of light . . . like no one I have ever met . . . When Herbert Duckworth smiled . . . when Herbert Duckworth came into the room . . ." here she broke off, shook her head quickly from side to side and screwed her face up, as if he were ineffable; no words could describe him. And in this spasmodic way she gave an echo of what must have been my mother's feeling; only hers was much deeper, and stronger. He must have been to her the perfect man; heroic; handsome;

---

* She was twenty-one when she married Herbert Duckworth.

† Julia's sister, Adeline, married Henry Halford Vaughan. Upton Castle, in Pembrokeshire, was rented by the Vaughans.

magnanimous; "the great Achilles, whom we knew"—it seems natural to quote Tennyson—and also genial, lovable, simple, and also her husband; and her children's father. It was thus natural to her when she was a girl to love the simple, the genial, the normal ordinary type of man, in preference to the queer, the uncouth artistic, the intellectual, whom she had met and who had wished to marry her. Herbert was the perfect type of public school boy and English gentleman, my father said. She chose him; and how completely he satisfied her is proved by the collapse, the complete collapse into which she fell when he died. All her gaiety, all her sociability left her. She was as unhappy as it is possible for anyone to be. There is very little known of the years that were thus stamped. Only that saying, and Stella once told me that she used to lie upon his grave at Orchardleigh. As she was undemonstrative that seems a superlative expression of her grief.

What is known, and is much more remarkable, is that during those eight years spent, so far as she had time over from her children and house, 'doing good', nursing, visiting the poor, she lost her faith. This hurt her mother, a deeply religious woman, to whom she was devoted, and thus must have been a genuine conviction; something arrived at as the result of solitary and independent thinking. It proves that there was more in her than simplicity; enthusiasm; romance; and thus makes sense of her two incongruous choices: Herbert and my father. There was a complexity in her; great simplicity and directness combined with a sceptical, a serious spirit. Probably it was that combination that accounted for the great impression she made on people; the positive impression. Her character was sharpened by the mixture of simplicity and scepticism. She was sociable yet severe; very amusing; but very serious; extremely practical but with a depth in her . . . "She was a mixture of the Madonna and a woman of the world," is Miss Robins's description.*

The certain fact at any rate is that when at last she was left alone —"Oh the torture of never being left alone!" is a saying of hers, reported I forget by whom, that refers to her widowhood, and the fuss that friends and family made—when she was alone at last in Hyde Park Gate, she began to think out her position; and for this reason perhaps read something my father had written. She liked it (he says in the 'Mausoleum Book'), when she was not sure that she liked him. It is thus permissible to think of her sitting in the creeper-

* Elizabeth Robins, the actress, had been a friend of Julia's.

shaded drawing room at Hyde Park Gate in her widow's dress, alone, when the children had gone to bed, with a copy of the *Fortnightly*, trying to reason out the case for agnosticism. From that she would go on to think of Leslie Stephen, the gaunt bearded man who lived up the street, married to Minny Thackeray. He was in every way the opposite of Herbert Duckworth; but there was something in his mind that interested her. One evening she called on the Leslie Stephens, [and] found them sitting over the fire together; a happy married pair, with one child in the nursery, and another to be born soon. She sat talking; and then went home, envying them their happiness and comparing it with her own loneliness. Next day Minny died suddenly. And about two years later she married the gaunt bearded widower.*

"How did father ask you to marry him?" I once asked her, with my arm slipped in hers as we went down the twisted stairs into the dining room. She gave her little laugh, half surprised, half shocked. She did not answer. He asked her in a letter; and she refused him. Then one night when he had given up all thought of it, and had been dining with her, and asking her advice about a governess for Laura, she followed him to the door and said "I will try to be a good wife to you."

Perhaps there was pity in her love; certainly there was devout admiration for his mind; and so she spanned the two marriages with the two different men; and emerged from that corridor of the eight silent years to live fifteen years more;† to bear four children; and [to] die early on the morning of the 5th of May 1895. George took us down to say goodbye. My father staggered from the bedroom as we came. I stretched out my arms to stop him, but he brushed past me, crying out something I could not catch; distraught. And George led me in to kiss my mother, who had just died.

May 28th 1939. Led by George with towels wrapped round us and given each a drop of brandy in warm milk to drink, we were taken into the bedroom. I think candles were burning; and I think the sun was coming in. At any rate I remember the long looking-glass; with the drawers on either side; and the washstand; and the great bed on

* Minny died in 1875; Leslie Stephen married Julia in 1878.
† After her marriage to Leslie Stephen, Julia lived seventeen years.

which my mother lay. I remember very clearly how even as I was
taken to the bedside I noticed that one nurse was sobbing, and a
desire to laugh came over me, and I said to myself as I have often
done at moments of crisis since, "I feel nothing whatever". Then I
stooped and kissed my mother's face. It was still warm. She [had]
only died a moment before. Then we went upstairs into the day
nursery.

Perhaps it was the next evening that Stella took me into the
bedroom to kiss mother for the last time. She had been lying on her
side before. Now she was lying straight in the middle of her pillows.
Her face looked immeasurably distant, hollow and stern. When I
kissed her, it was like kissing cold iron. Whenever I touch cold iron
the feeling comes back to me—the feeling of my mother's face, iron
cold, and granulated. I started back. Then Stella stroked her cheek,
and undid a button on her nightgown. "She always liked to have it
like that," she said. When she came up to the nursery later she said
to me, "Forgive me. I saw you were afraid." She had noticed that I
had started. When Stella asked me to forgive her for having given
me that shock, I cried—we had been crying off and on all day—and
said, "When I see mother, I see a man sitting with her." Stella
looked at me as if I had frightened her. Did I say that in order to
attract attention to myself? Or was it true? I cannot be sure, for
certainly I had a great wish to draw attention to myself. But certainly it was true that when she said: "Forgive me," and thus made
me visualize my mother, I seemed to see a man sitting bent on the
edge of the bed.

"It's nice that she shouldn't be alone", Stella said after a moment's
pause.

Of course the atmosphere of those three or four days before the
funeral was so melodramatic, histrionic and unreal that any
hallucination was possible. We lived through them in hush, in
artificial light. Rooms were shut. People were creeping in and out.
People were coming to the door all the time. We were all sitting in
the drawing room round father's chair sobbing. The hall reeked of
flowers. They were piled on the hall table. The scent still brings
back those days of astonishing intensity. But I have one memory of
great beauty. A telegram had been sent to Thoby at Clifton. He was
to arrive in the evening at Paddington. George and Stella whispered
together in the hall, about who was to go and meet him. To my
relief, Stella overcame some objection on George's part, and said,

"But I think it would do her good to go"; and so I was taken in a cab with George and Nessa to meet Thoby at Paddington. It was sunset, and the great glass dome at the end of the station was blazing with light. It was glowing yellow and red and the iron girders made a pattern across it. I walked along the platform gazing with rapture at this magnificent blaze of colour, and the train slowly steamed into the station. It impressed and exalted me. It was so vast and so fiery red. The contrast of that blaze of magnificent light with the shrouded and curtained rooms at Hyde Park Gate was so intense. Also it was partly that my mother's death unveiled and intensified; made me suddenly develop perceptions, as if a burning glass had been laid over what was shaded and dormant. Of course this quickening was spasmodic. But it was surprising—as if something were becoming visible without any effort. To take another instance—I remember going into Kensington Gardens about that time. It was a hot spring evening, and we lay down—Nessa and I—in the long grass behind the Flower Walk. I had taken *The Golden Treasury* with me. I opened it and began to read some poem. And instantly and for the first time I understood the poem (which it was I forget). It was as if it became altogether intelligible; I had a feeling of transparency in words when they cease to be words and become so intensified that one seems to experience them; to foretell them as if they developed what one is already feeling. I was so astonished that I tried to explain the feeling. "One seems to understand what it's about", I said awkwardly. I suppose Nessa has forgotten; no one could have understood from what I said the queer feeling I had in the hot grass, that poetry was coming true. Nor does that give the feeling. It matches what I have sometimes felt when I write. The pen gets on the scent.

But though I remember so distinctly those two moments—the arch of glass burning at the end of Paddington Station and the poem I read in Kensington Gardens, those two clear moments are almost the only clear moments in the muffled dulness that then closed over us. With mother's death the merry, various family life which she had held in being shut for ever. In its place a dark cloud settled over us; we seemed to sit all together cooped up, sad, solemn, unreal, under a haze of heavy emotion. It seemed impossible to break through. It was not merely dull; it was unreal. A finger seemed laid on one's lips.

I see us now, all dressed in unbroken black, George and Gerald in

black trousers, Stella with real crape deep on her dress, Nessa and
myself with slightly modified crape, my father black from head to
foot—even the notepaper was so black bordered that only a little
space for writing remained—I see us emerging from Hyde Park Gate
on a fine summer afternoon and walking in procession hand in hand,
for we were always taking hands—I see us walking—I rather proud
of the solemn blackness and the impression it must make—into
Kensington Gardens; and how golden the laburnum shone. And
then we sat silent under the trees. The silence was stifling. A finger
was laid on our lips. One had always to think whether what one was
about to say was the right thing to say. It ought to be a help. But how
could one help? Father used to sit sunk in gloom. If he could be got
to talk—and that was part of our duty—it was about the past. It was
about "the old days". And when he talked, he ended with a groan.
He was getting deaf, and his groans were louder than he knew.
Indoors he would walk up and down the room, gesticulating, crying
that he had never told mother how he loved her. Then Stella would
fling her arms round him and protest. Often one would break in
upon a scene of this kind. And he would open his arms and call one
to him. We were his only hope, his only comfort, he would say. And
there kneeling on the floor one would try—perhaps only to cry.

Stella of course bore the brunt. She grew whiter and whiter in her
unbroken black dress. She would sit at her table with the black-
edged notepaper before her writing, answering letters of sympathy.
There was a photograph of mother in front of her; and sometimes
she would cry, as she wrote. As the summer wore on, visitors came,
sympathetic women, old friends. They were admitted to the back
drawing room, where father sat like the Queen in Shakespeare—
"here I and sorrow sit"—with the Virginia Creeper hanging a
curtain of green over the window, so that the room was like a green
cave. We in the front room sat crouched, hearing muffled voices,
ready for the visitor to emerge with tears on tear-stained cheeks. The
shrouded, cautious, dulled life took the place of all the chatter and
laughter of the summer. There were no more parties; no more young
men and women laughing. No more flashing visions of white summer
dresses and hansoms dashing off to private views and dinner parties,
none of that natural life and gaiety which my mother had created.
The grown-up world into which I would dash for a moment and
pick off some joke or little scene and dash back again upstairs to the
nursery was ended. There were none of those snatched moments

that were so amusing and for some reason so soothing and yet exciting when one ran downstairs to dinner arm in arm with mother; or chose the jewels she was to wear. There was none of that pride when one said something that amused her, or that she thought very remarkable. How excited I used to be when the 'Hyde Park Gate News' was laid on her plate on Monday morning, and she liked something I had written!* Never shall I forget my extremity of pleasure — it was like being a violin and being played upon — when I found that she had sent a story of mine to Madge Symonds; it was so imaginative, she said; it was about souls flying round and choosing bodies to be born into.

The tragedy of her death was not that it made one, now and then and very intensely, unhappy. It was that it made her unreal; and us solemn, and self-conscious. We were made to act parts that we did not feel; to fumble for words that we did not know. It obscured, it dulled. It made one hypocritical and immeshed in the conventions of sorrow. Many foolish and sentimental ideas came into being. Yet there was a struggle, for soon we revived, and there was a conflict between what we ought to be and what we were. Thoby put this into words. One day before he went back to school, he said: "It's silly going on like this . . . ", sobbing, sitting shrouded, he meant. I was shocked at his heartlessness; yet he was right, I know; and yet how could we escape?

It was Stella who lifted the canopy again. A little light crept in.

June 20th 1939. I was thinking as I crossed the Channel last night of Stella; in a very jerky disconnected way, with people quarrelling outside the door; the boat train arriving; chains clanking; and the steamer giving those sudden stertorous snorts. And as the first morning after a broken night is distracted and broken, instead of beginning Roger again, as I ought, I will write down some of my distracted and disconnected thoughts; to serve, should the time come, for notes.

How many people are there still able to think about Stella on the 20th June 1939? Very few. Jack died last Christmas; George and

* The 'Hyde Park Gate News' appeared weekly, as far as is known, from 9 February 1891 until April 1895. The paper was at first the joint venture of Virginia and Thoby but gradually it became almost entirely Virginia's responsibility. See QB, I, pp. 28–32.

Gerald a year or two ago; Kitty Maxse and Margaret Massingberd have been dead many years now. Susan Lushington and Lisa Stillman are still alive; but how they live and where, I know not. Perhaps thus I think of her less disconnectedly and more truly than anyone now living, save for Vanessa and Adrian; and perhaps old Sophie Farrell.* Of her childhood I know practically nothing. She was the only daughter of the handsome barrister Herbert Duckworth, but as he died when she was three or four, she did not remember him, or those years when her mother was as happy as anyone can be. I think, from stray anecdotes and from what I noticed myself, that when she came to consciousness as a child the unhappy years were at their height. That would account for some qualities in Stella. Her first memories were of a very sad widowed mother, who "went about doing good"—Stella wished to have that on the tombstone—visiting the slums, visiting too the Cancer Hospital in the Brompton Road. Our Quaker Aunt told me that this was her habit; for she said how one case there had "shocked her". Thus Stella as a child lived in the shade of that widowhood; saw that beautiful crape-veiled figure daily; and perhaps took then the ply that was so marked—that attitude of devotion, almost canine in its touching adoration, to her mother; that passive, suffering affection; and also that complete unquestioning dependence.

They were sun and moon to each other; my mother the positive and definite; Stella the reflecting and satellite. My mother was stern to her. All her devotion was given to George who was like his father; and her care was for Gerald, born posthumously and very delicate. Stella she treated severely; so much so that before their marriage my father ventured a protest. She replied that it might be true; she was hard on Stella because she felt Stella "part of myself". A pale silent child I imagine her; sensitive; modest; uncomplaining; adoring her mother, thinking only how she could help her, and without any ambition or even character of her own. And yet she had character. Very gentle, very honest, and in some way individual—so she made her own impression on people. Friends, like Kitty Maxse, the brilliant, the sparkling, loved her with a real laughing tenderness for her own sake. Her charm was great; it came partly from this modesty, from this honesty, from this perfectly simple

* Sophie Farrell was the Stephens' cook at 22 Hyde Park Gate and at 46 Gordon Square, Bloomsbury. After Vanessa's marriage she went with Virginia and Adrian to 29 Fitzroy Square and later to George Duckworth.

unostentatious unselfishness; it came too from her lack of pose, her lack of snobbery; and from the genuineness, from something that was—could I put my finger on it—perfectly herself, individual. This unnamed quality—the sensitiveness to real things—was queer in the sister of George and Gerald, who were so opaque and conventional; who had so innate a respect for the conventions and respectabilities. By some odd fling in her birth, she had escaped all taint of Duckworth philistinism; she had none of their shrewd middle-class complacency. Instead of their little brown eyes that were so greedy and twinkling, hers were very large and rather a pale blue. They were dreamy, candid eyes. She was without their instinctive worldliness. She was lovely too, in a far vaguer, less perfect way than my mother. She reminded me always of those large white flowers—elderblossom, cow parsley, that one sees in the fields in June. Perhaps my mother's laughing nickname—'Old Cow'—suggests the cow parsley. Or again, a white faint moon in a blue sky suggests her. Or those large white roses that have many petals and are semi-transparent. She had beautiful fair hair, growing in horns over her forehead; and no colour in her face at all. As for teaching—she had perhaps a governess; went to classes; was taught the violin by Arnold Dolmetsch and played in Mrs Marshall's orchestra. But there was a stoppage in her mind, a gentle impassivity about books and learning. As Jack told me after her death, she thought herself so stupid as to be almost wanting; and said that the rheumatic fever she had as a child had (I remember the word) 'touched' her. But again, what was remarkable considering the Duckworth strain—so boorish, so rustic, so philistine—is that however simple she was in brain, she was not, as George's sister might so well have been, a cheery ordinary English upper middle class girl with rosy cheeks and bright brown eyes. She was herself. She remains quite distinct in my mind. What is odd is that I cannot compare her either in character or face with anyone else. What she would have looked like now in a room full of other people I cannot imagine; or how she would have talked. I have never seen anyone who reminded me of her; and that is true too of my mother. They do not blend in the world of the living at all.

She was nineteen when I was six or seven; and as a girl could not then go about London alone, I used as a small child to be sent with her, as chaperone. Among my earliest memories is the memory of going out with her perhaps to shop, or to pay some call; and, the errand done, she would take me to a shop and give me a glass of milk and biscuits sprinkled with sugar on a marble table. And sometimes we went in hansoms. But she lived, of course, downstairs in the drawing room; pouring out tea; and there were many young men, it seemed when one dashed in for a second, sitting round her. Vaguely we knew that Arthur Studd was in love with her; and Ted Sanderson; and I think Richard Norton; and Jim Stephen.* That great figure with the deep voice and the wild eyes would come to the house looking for her, with his madness on him; and would burst into the nursery and spear the bread on his swordstick and at one time we were told to go out by the back door and if we met Jim we were to say that Stella was away.

19th July 1939. I was forced to break off again, and rather suspect that these breaks will be the end of this memoir.

I was thinking about Stella as we crossed the Channel a month ago. I have not given her a thought since. The past only comes back when the present runs so smoothly that it is like the sliding surface of a deep river. Then one sees through the surface to the depths. In those moments I find one of my greatest satisfactions, not that I am thinking of the past; but that it is then that I am living most fully in the present. For the present when backed by the past is a thousand times deeper than the present when it presses so close that you can feel nothing else, when the film on the camera reaches only the eye. But to feel the present sliding over the depths of the past, peace is necessary. The present must be smooth, habitual. For this reason—that it destroys the fullness of life—any break—like that of house moving—causes me extreme distress; it breaks; it shallows; it turns the depth into hard thin splinters. As I say to L[eonard]: "What's there real about this? Shall we ever live a real life again?" "At Monks House," he says. So I write this, taking a morning off from the word filing and fitting that my life of Roger means—I write this partly in order to recover my sense of the present by getting the past to shadow this broken surface. Let me then, like a child advancing with bare feet into a cold river, descend again into that stream.

. . . Jim Stephen was in love with Stella. He was mad then. He

* James Kenneth Stephen, second son of James Fitzjames Stephen, brother of Leslie.

was in the exalted stage of his madness. He would dash up in a
hansom; leave my father to pay it. The hansom had been driving
him about London all day. The man wanted perhaps a sovereign. It
was paid. For 'dear Jim' was a great favourite. Once, as I say, he
dashed up [to] the nursery and speared the bread. Another time, off
we went to his room in De Vere Gardens and he painted me on a
small bit of wood. He was a great painter for a time. I suppose
madness made him believe he was all powerful. Once he came in at
breakfast, "Savage* has just told me I'm in danger of dying or
going mad", he laughed. And soon he ran naked through Cambridge; was taken to an asylum; and died. This great mad figure
with his broad shoulders and very clean cut mouth, and the deep
voice and the powerful face — and the very blue eyes — this mad man
would recite poetry to us; "The Burial of Sir John Moore", I
remember; and he always brings to mind some tormented bull; and
also Achilles — Achilles on his pressed bed lolling roars out a deep
applause. He was in love with Stella — incongruously enough. And
we had orders to tell him, if we met him in the street, that she was
away, staying with the Lushingtons at Pyports. There was a great
mystery about love then.

Jim was one of her lovers. The other — that is, the most important
— was Jack Hills. It was at St Ives that she refused him; late one
night we heard her sobbing through the attic wall. He had gone at
once. A refusal in those days was catastrophic. It meant a complete
breach. Human relations, at least between the sexes, were carried on
as relations between countries are now — with ambassadors, and
treaties. The parties concerned met on the great occasion of the
proposal. If this were refused, a state of war was declared. That
explains why she cried so bitterly. For she had done something of
great practical as well as emotional importance. He went off at
once — to Norway to fish; later perhaps they met in a completely
formal way at parties. Negotiations were kept faintly alive through
my mother; an interpreter was necessary. All this procedure gave
love its solemnity. Feelings were banked up; silence interposed;
there was in every family a code, a religious code, that penetrated,
somehow or other, to the children. It was secret; but we guessed.

Thus, when my mother died, Stella was left without any negotiator, for my father did not fill the part. He must have come back — it

* Dr George Savage, later Sir George, was an old friend of the Stephen
family. He was also Virginia's specialist.

proves how deep the feeling was to admit such a return—the night before my mother died. It was desperate but not hopeless.*

June 8th 1940. I have just found this sheaf of notes, thrown away into my waste-paper basket. I had been tidying up; and had cast all my life of Roger into that large basket, and with it, these sheets too. Now I am correcting the final page proofs of Roger; and it was to refresh myself from that antlike meticulous labour that I determined to look for these pages. Shall I ever finish these notes—let alone make a book from them? The battle is at its crisis; every night the Germans fly over England; it comes closer to this house daily. If we are beaten then—however we solve that problem, and one solution is apparently suicide (so it was decided three nights ago in London among us)—book writing becomes doubtful. But I wish to go on, not to settle down in that dismal puddle.

Jack Hills, I was saying, came back the night before my mother died, which shows that though the negotiations had been broken off, there must have been a connection, or how could he have come that night of great crisis? We were in the back drawing room, and there was the tea tray, for we had a curious habit of drinking tea about nine o'clock. The silver hot water jug which I still possess—but it has a hole in it—had a handle that grew hot. Aunt Mary, summoned from Brighton, picked it up and put it down quickly.† "Only Mrs Stephen and Stella can manage that", said Jack Hills with the queer sad little smile that went with the little joke. And I remember that he said 'Stella'. And since he was there, that last night, the affair must have been in being—sufficiently so to make it possible for him to be with us in intimacy. That was the 4th May, 1895.

The next thing I remember is the night at Hindhead (August 22nd 1896)—the black and silver night of mysterious voices, the night when father packed us off to bed early; and we heard voices in

* The source of the ambiguity of this passage can be traced to an earlier ms version (A.5c, p. 4, l.22–p. 5, l.3) which reads: "Thus, when my mother died, Stella was left without any negotiator in this affair of marriage; & Jack Hills came to the house on a very queer footing. He must have come the night my mother died. For I remember the doctors had gone; it was desperate but not hopeless; it was after dinner; & Aunt Mary poured out coffee. (Stella being in the bedroom.)"

† Aunt Mary (née Jackson), Julia's elder sister who married Herbert Fisher and had seven sons and four daughters.

the garden; and saw Stella and Jack passing; and disappearing; and the tramp came; and Thoby countered him; and Nessa and I sat up in our bedroom waiting; and Stella never came; and at last in the early morning she came and told us that she was engaged; and I whispered, "Did mother know?" and she murmured, "Yes".

And next morning at breakfast there was excitement and emotion and gloom. Adrian cried; and Jack kissed him; and father said gently but seriously: "We must all be happy, because Stella is happy"—a command which, poor man, he could not himself obey.

But Jack Hills? He had been at Eton with George. He stands in my mind's picture gallery for a type—and a desirable type; the English country gentleman type, I might call it, by way of running a line round it; and I add, it is a type I have seldom been intimate with; perhaps no one is ever intimate with the country gentleman type; yet for nine years I was intimate with Jack Hills; a reason perhaps why we became so completely separate later; it was impossible to begin again formally after that intimacy. And the country gentleman came to the surface and separated us.

Can I quickly fill in that outline? To begin then, he was the son of a commonplace little round man—Judge Hills—'Buzzy' he was called in the family—and like a bluebottle, buzzing, I still remember him; short, jocular, in knickerbockers, giving us Russian toffee up at Corby. Buzzy had once written a sonnet that had been taken for Shakespeare's, and liked to make little facetious jokes with young ladies—I remember Susan Lushington "didn't know which way to look", she said, when he chaffed her about a husband—"I seemed to be sitting on a tripod and looking into the future", Buzzy said, having archly used the word husband when it should have been father—Buzzy lived chiefly in Egypt, and Mrs Hills—Anna her name was—lived mostly alone at Corby. She was a hard, worldly woman, tightly dressed in black satin in London; up at Corby, a county lady, collecting Chelsea enamel snuff boxes, with ambitions to be the friend of intellectual men. She detested women; she got on very well with Andrew Lang. He stayed there often; and she described a party when the local dentist came in a frock coat—"all the other men looking so picturesque in knickerbockers." And she said: "I was in mourning for nine people at Easter"; also, looking at horses in the paddock, "That makes the second pair"; also she stressed "under housemaid" to impress us that she had several; and dwelt on the noble descent of the Curwens, to whom they were related; and went weekly to Naworth with a wreath to lay on Christopher Howard's grave. It was handed in at the carriage; like a picnic basket—the weekly wreath. And I still see her in shiny black satin and feathered Victorian hat bending over the grave in Naworth burial ground; and Susan whispering in agitation "Suppose Lady Carlisle or one of them should come out and catch us!" These recollections spring from that dreary and terrifying week at Corby after Stella's death in the autumn of 1897. They leased Corby from the Howards; the lion stood with his tail perfectly straight on top of the roof. The river dashed through the grounds; and there I saw Jack catch a salmon; for the first time after those desperate months he looked triumphant; and worn as he [had] come to look, I was struck by his sudden exultation as the line tautened and he held the fish there in the river. We saw it afterwards in the game larder; and Mrs Hills asked: "Has he those little creatures on him?" It was a proof of freshness, I think, if you found lice on a salmon. Tuddenham, the keeper, who stood by us on the bank, said: "He's hooked him."

To return to Anna Hills. She hated women. But I doubt that she was sexually ambitious. I think all she wanted was to rule a little court of well brushed, mildly well-known males; in the decorous, snobbish Victorian manner. She was thankful, I remember she told us, that she had no daughters; and it was plain she detested having us two rather gawky girls to stay. "Your hair's parted awry", she said, fixing me with her little black eyes. Fortunately she had three sons; and they were sent to Eton and Oxford. She liked the soft sweet voiced Eustace with his drawl, and his pleasant manners, and his gentle ways, far the best. Jack and she were on very distant terms. Thus it was natural that when he was living alone in Ebury Street, very hard up, very hard worked, stammering, and lonely, that he came to my mother for sympathy. They were very intimate. Indeed Kitty Maxse said, discussing my mother and her masterful ways once: "For instance, how could Mrs Hills have liked it—Jack treating your mother as if she were his?" He was, roughly speaking, affectionate, honest, domestic, and a perfect gentleman. He was a real [countryman] too; not a fake; a passionate countryman. He rode very well; he fished very well; and there was too a vein of poetry in him. Once when we met years later he told me he read every book of new poetry that came out; and thought the young poets (then Siegfried Sassoon; Robert Graves; and de la Mare) every bit as good as the old. He read philosophy too; Nettleship, the Oxford philosopher, had been a kind of god to him. "He was like Christ", I remember his saying, in his emphatic sententious way, as he tried very laboriously to explain Nettleship's philosophy; he lent us the book; it was at Warboys that I remember him explaining Plato to me and Nessa and Marny Vaughan.* Gerald, who sat beneath the window, sneered later: "Well, how did the Sunday prayer meeting go off?" But he was not, compared with my own friends, anything but a simple, primitive-minded man. Unlike them, however—was it for this I liked him, yet could never be altogether at my ease with him?—he was an all-round man; without any gift that dominated, he did a great many different things. He was a Gunner. "I have heard of him standing on one foot, driving three horses", Ethel Dilke wrote when the engagement was public, "and I've no doubt he does other things as well." He was a good solicitor. Doggedly he worked his way high up into the firm of Roper and Whateley; of Whateley he used to tell many stories: "a disgusting man, but in some ways the ablest man I have ever known. He was a great fisherman—so they say. And I like his fishing books." Politics came later. He was also very deft with his hands. But as I heard my mother tell my father once, he was 'nothing out of the way' intellectually. His appearance was in keeping with this rough sketch. He had beautiful brown eyes, a nose with an obstinate knob at the end of it; curious wrinkles, like a dachshund's, round his retreating chin. (He was of course very fond of dogs.) He stammered, and his stammer made his very positive statements—"A duck must have water"—all the more positive when at last he got them out. We laughed at him and could imitate him as time went on. He was scrupulously clean; he washed all over ever so many times a day, and was scrupulously well dressed, as a Victorian city solicitor; also as a countryman. The word 'scrupulous' suggests itself when I think of Jack Hills. He was scrupulously honest, honourable, in the Eton and Balliol sense, but there was more to his scrupulosity than that. He it was who first spoke to me openly and deliberately about sex— in Fitzroy Square, with the green carpet and the red Chinese curtains.† He opened my eyes on purpose, as I think, to the part

* Margaret, one of the Vaughan cousins whom the young Stephens saw frequently.
† 29 Fitzroy Square, Bloomsbury, where Virginia and Adrian moved after Vanessa's marriage to Clive Bell in 1907.

played by sex in the life of the ordinary man. He shocked me a little, wholesomely. He told me that young men talked incessantly of women; and 'had' them incessantly. "But are they—" I hesitated for a word and then ventured "honourable?" He laughed, "of course—of course", he assured me. Sexual relations had nothing to do with honour. Having women was a mere trifle in a man's life, he explained, and made not a jot of difference to their honourableness—to their reputation with other men. I was incredibly, but only partially, innocent. I knew nothing about ordinary men's lives, and thought all men, like my father, loved one woman only, and were 'dishonourable' if unchaste, as much as women; yet, at the same time I had known since I was sixteen or so, all about sodomy, through reading Plato. That was Jack's honesty; and it differed from George's or Gerald's. Neither of them would have spoken to any girl as cleanly, humorously, openly, about sex. That quality penetrated to us as children, and he brought too, country life into our distinguished literary, book-loving world. He taught us to sugar trees; he gave us his copy of Morris's *Butterflies and Moths*,* over which I spent many hours, hunting up our catches among all those pictures of hearts and darts and setaceous Hebrew characters.†
For I had the post of name finder in our Entomological Society; and was scolded severely by Thoby, I remember, for slackness. At dinner one night Gerald disclosed, with his teasing and treacherous laughter, how we had a store of dying insects in old tooth-powder jars at the bottom of the well. Greatly to our relief instead of scolding and forbidding, mother and, I think, father recognised our mania; and put it on a legal basis; bought us nets and setting boards; and indeed she went with Walter Headlam‡ down to the St Ives public house and bought us rum. How strange a scene—my mother buying rum. She would go round the sugar after we were in bed.

But to return to Jack—when Stella accepted him, we approved,

* Francis Orpen Morris (1810–93) wrote popular books on natural history. He published *A History of British Butterflies* (London, 1853) and *A History of British Moths* in four volumes (1859–70) but no book with the title *Butterflies and Moths*.

† These are the vernacular names of common British moths. VW's ts has 'harts and darts and sequacious Hebrew characters'.

‡ Walter Headlam, Fellow of King's College, Cambridge, distinguished Hellenist and minor poet, was an old friend of the Stephen family with whom Virginia carried on a flirtation after the marriage of Vanessa. He died in 1908.

in our republic, which, though rapidly losing shape, was still in being after mother's death. The marriage would have been, I think, a very happy marriage. It should have borne many children. And still she might have been alive. Certainly he was passionately in love; she at first passively. And it was through that engagement that I had my first vision—so intense, so exciting, so rapturous was it that the word vision applies—my first vision then of love between man and woman. It was to me like a ruby; the love I detected that winter of their engagement, glowing, red, clear, intense. It gave me a conception of love; a standard of love; a sense that nothing in the whole world is so lyrical, so musical, as a young man and a young woman in their first love for each other. I connect it with respectable engagements; unofficial love never gives me the same feeling. "My Love's like a red, red rose, that's newly sprung in June"—that was the feeling they gave; the feeling that has always come back, when I hear of 'an engagement'; not when I hear of 'an affair'. It derives from Stella and Jack. It springs from the ecstasy I felt, in my covert, behind the folding doors of the Hyde Park Gate drawing room. I sat there, shielded, being half insane with shyness and nervousness; reading Fanny Burney's diary; and feeling come over me intermittent waves of very strong emotion—rage sometimes; how often I was enraged by father then!—love, or the reflection of love, too. It was bodiless; a light; an ecstasy. But also extraordinarily enduring. Once I came on a letter from him which she had slipped between the blotting paper—a sign of the lack of privacy in which we lived—and read it. "There is nothing sweeter in the whole world than our love", he wrote. I put the page down, not so much guiltily, at having pried; but in a quiver of ecstasy at the revelation. Still I cannot read words that give me that quiver twice over. If I get a letter that pleases me intensely, I never read it again. Why I wonder? For fear lest it shall dwindle? This colour, this incandescence, was in Stella's whole body. Her pallor became lit up, her eyes bluer. She had something of moonlight about her that winter, as she went about the house. "There's never been anything like it in the world", I said—or something like it—when she found me awake one night. And she laughed, tenderly, very gently, and kissed me and said, "Oh lots of people are in love as we are. You and Nessa will be one day", she said. Once she told me, "You must expect people to look at you both".

"Nessa", she said, "is much more beautiful than I ever was"—at twenty-six she spoke of her beauty as a thing of the past. She told Aunt Mary—I think I read this too, nefariously, in some letter in a blotting book, she could only be neat and tidy now; she was to float us on the life of love; to launch us out on the ordinary woman's life that promised such treasures. At some party, perhaps Nessa's first party, a party where she wore white and amethysts perhaps, a party where Desmond* remarked her 'like a Greek slave', she was certain that George Booth† had fallen in love, and feared, tenderly foreboding, yet proudly, and gladly, how the Booths would mind if Nessa rejected him. Had Stella lived, the recollection makes me reflect, how different 'coming out' and those Greek slave years and all their drudgery and tyranny and rebellion would have been!

For some reason Stella and Jack's engagement lasted all the months from July till April. It was a clumsy, cruel, unnecessary trial for them both. Looking back, it seems everything was done without care or consideration, clumsily, wantonly. I conceive that as the months of that long waiting time passed she slowly roused herself out of the numb, frozen state in which mother's death had left her. At first she found in Jack rest and support; a refuge from all the worries and responsibilities of 'the family', relief too from those glooms which father never controlled, and spent on her. Slowly she became more positive, less passive; and asserted Jack's rights; her desire too for her own house; her own husband; a life, a home of their own. At last the promise, apparently exacted by father, and tacitly accepted, that they were to live on with us after their marriage, an arrangement now incredible but then accepted, became intolerable; and she went up to father one night in his study; and told him so; and there was 'an explosion'.

As the engagement went on, father became indeed increasingly tyrannical. He didn't like the name 'Jack', I remember his saying; it sounded like the smack of a whip. He was jealous clearly. But in those days nothing was clear. He had his traditional pose; he was the lonely; the deserted; the old unhappy man. In fact he was possessive; hurt; a man jealous of the young man. There was every excuse, he would have said, had he been asked, for his explosions. And as by

* Desmond MacCarthy, who belonged to the inner circle of Bloomsbury from its earliest days.
† George Booth was the son of Charles Booth, author of *Life and Labour of the People in London*. The Booths were 'Hyde Park Gaters', as Adrian was later to call them.

this time he had entrenched himself away from all truth, in a world which it is almost impossible to describe, for I know no one now who could inhabit such a world—the engagement was incredibly involved, frustrated, and impeded. At last in April 1897 the marriage took place—conventionally, ceremoniously, with bells ringing, and company collected, and silver engraved wedding invitations, at St Mary Abbots. Nessa and I handed flowers to the guests; father marched up the aisle with Stella on his arm.

"He took it for granted that he was to give her away", George and Gerald grumbled. He ignored the fact that they had any claim. No one would have dared to take that privilege from him. It was somehow typical—his assumption; and his enjoyment of the attitude. They went to Italy; we to Brighton. One fortnight was the length of their honeymoon. And directly she came back she was taken ill. It was appendicitis; she was going to have a baby. And that was mismanaged too; and so, after three months of intermittent illness, she died—at 24 Hyde Park Gate, on July 27th, 1897.*

By the time I had that room,† when I was fifteen that is, "we four" —"us four" as we called ourselves—had become separate. That was symbolized by our separate rooms. Thoby was at Clifton, Adrian at Evelyns. Yet we were not so separate as brothers and sisters become at that age. Mother's death and Stella's death kept us, I suppose, together. We never spoke of either of them; I can remember the awkwardness with which Thoby avoided saying "Stella" when a ship called *Stella* sank. (I remember when Thoby died, that Adrian and I agreed to talk about him. "There are so many people that are dead now", we said.) But this silence was known to cover something. And if I were to describe myself, at fifteen, I should have to describe Nessa and Thoby; both in great detail; for they [were] as much my life as anything. Thoby was two years (about) older than I was.‡ He dominated us four. He was a clumsy little boy, very fat, bursting through his Norfolk jacket. He was not a fawning or ingratiating child, I imagine: Napoleonic, one of the Aunts described him as a baby, sitting on a rock with a fishing net, staring contemplatively.

* The A. 5a typescript ends here. The text now follows the A. 5d manuscript from p. 10.

† See above, p. 105: 'my covert, behind the folding doors of the Hyde Park Gate drawing room'. See also the Editor's Note.

‡ The material from p. 10, l. 21 (ms) to the end of p. 11 has been omitted.

"Those far away eyes"—someone said. He grew very quickly out of
nursery ways. I cannot remember him, as I can Adrian, appealing,
childish. Florence* called him her Blue Mouse: mother called him
her Benjamin. Thoby was a determined, resolute little boy: whose
rages were very thorough and formidable. I see him struggling with
Gerald; or so truculent with the nurses that father had to be sent
for. He was powerful in mind, mastering things rather than guessing
at them; not clever, but gifted. He had a natural, easy gift for
drawing. He would take a sheet of paper, hold it at an odd angle and
begin drawing a bird, at some queer place, so that I could not guess
how the bird would become a bird. He was not precocious: now and
then he won a prize, but failed to win an Eton scholarship. His
Latin and Greek were rough, the masters said; his essays showed
great intelligence. I remember his easy, vigorous, slovenly handwriting. School I think suited him; he went through what he went
through silently. Was he unhappy, bullied? He never said so. I
suspect he held his own, fairly easily, and would rather be among
boys than at home. Yet, there was his sensibility—though rough and
slovenly, according to reports, he it was who first told me—handing
it on as something worth knowing—about the Greeks. The day after
he came back from Evelyns the first time he was very shy; unfamiliar; yet affectionate, glad, in his queer speechless way, to be
home; and we went walking up and down stairs together, and he
told me the story of the Greeks: about Hector and Troy. I felt he was
shy of telling it; and so must keep walking up and down; and so we
kept on going upstairs and then downstairs, and he told me about the
Greeks, fitfully, excitedly. To do that, he had to break through the
schoolboy convention about 'work'. There was no such convention
about friends. He told me stories about the boys at Evelyns: then
about the Clifton boys: and in the same way about his Cambridge
friends. These stories went on and on every holidays. That was very
characteristic. He had a great power for admiring his friends, for
liking them. That I suppose was why he found school tolerable. Yet
he held his own. He was not easy to put upon. He did not expect to
win things, or care very much. I felt he had taken stock of his own
power; dominated his friends in his own way; and was sure he
would come into possession of his gifts all in good time. He could
enjoy their gifts to the full. He was always amused by them;
admired them; saw a great deal in them; and yet I think felt himself

* Probably Florence Fisher, his cousin, who married F. W. Maitland.

in his own way their equal. And would not let himself be put upon. This blend of mastery and sensibility, of friendliness and composure, gave him a great deal of character. He was amazingly reserved. Not a word of feeling was allowed to escape him. And yet under that strange awkward silence there would creep out a curious sympathy, a pride in us.*

I continue (22nd September 1940) on this wet day; and we think of the weather now as it affects invasion, as it affects raids on London — not as weather that we like or dislike privately. I continue, for I am at a twist in my novel.† I was writing about Thoby when I left off. And last night I tried to soothe myself to sleep (being in a pucker, as Clive would say, about the Anreps coming here) by thinking of St Ives.‡ I will write about St Ives; and so, fittingly though indirectly, lead up to Thoby again.

Father, I think, was on one of his walking tours, in 1881 it must have been, when he discovered St Ives. He must have seen Talland House, which belonged to the G.W.R.;§ and have found it to let. He must have seen the town, almost as it had been in the sixteenth century; and the bay as it had been since time began. It was the first year, I think I have heard, that the line from St Erth to St Ives was open. Until then St Ives was about eight miles from any railway. And I suppose, munching his sandwich perhaps up at Tregenna, he had thought this might do for a summer place for us — and worked out, with [his] usual caution, ways and means. I was about to be born; and though they wished to limit their family, my conception (birth 1882) showed that they were not going to succeed. Adrian was to follow (1883) — also against their intention. It proves the ease and amplitude of those days that a man to whom money was an obscene nightmare, yet thought it feasible to take a house on the very toenail, as he said, of England — so that every summer he would be

* p. 13 of the ms ends in mid-sentence about three-quarters of the way down the page: " . . . a pride in us, & a".

† She was now at work on *Between the Acts* which at this period is referred to as 'P.H.' in *A Writer's Diary*, for 'Poyntzet Hall' or 'Poyntz Hall'.

‡ VW was upset because she feared — mistakenly as it turned out — that Helen Anrep, the companion of Roger Fry until his death, was planning to move permanently to Rodmell with her son and daughter. 'Clive' is, of course, Clive Bell.

§ Great Western Railway.

faced with the expense of moving family, nurses, servants, from one end of England to the other. Yet he did it. The distance was a drawback; for it meant that we could only go to St Ives in the summer. Our country was canalised into two or two months and a half. Yet that made the country more intense. And, in retrospect, probably nothing that we had as children was quite so important to us as our summer in Cornwall. To go away to the end of England; to have our own house, our own garden—to have that bay, that sea, and the mount: Clodgy and Halestown bog; Carbis Bay; Lelant; Zennor, Trevail, the Gurnard's Head; to hear the waves breaking that first night behind the yellow blind; to sail in the lugger; to dig in the sands; to scramble over the rocks and see the anemones flourishing their antennae in the pools; now and then to find a small fish flapping there; to look up over the lesson book in the dining room and see the lights changing on the waves; to go down to the town and buy penny boxes of tintacks or whatever it might be at Lanham's: Mrs Lanham wore false curls all round her face: the servants said Mr Lanham had married her 'from an advertisement'; to smell all the fishy smells in the steep little streets; and see the innumerable cats; and the women on the raised steps outside the houses pouring pails of dirty water down the gutters; every day to have a great dish of Cornish cream, skinned with a yellow skin, handed round with plenty of brown sugar ... I could fill pages remembering one thing after another that made the summer at St Ives the best beginning to a life conceivable. When they took Talland House, my father and mother gave me, at any rate, something I think invaluable. Suppose I had only Surrey or Sussex or the Isle of Wight to think about when I think about my childhood.

The town was then much as it must have been in the sixteenth century: a scramble, a pyramid, of whitewashed granite houses, crusting the slope made in the hollow under the Island. It was built there for shelter—built for a few fishermen, when Cornwall was a country more remote from England than Spain is now. It was a steep little town. Many houses had stairs running up from the pavement to the door. The walls were thick blocks of granite, to stand the sea and gale, I suppose. They were splashed with a wash the colour of Cornish cream. There was nothing mellow about them. There was no red brick: there was no thatch; the eighteenth century had left no mark, as it has in the south. St Ives might have been built yesterday; or in the time of the Conqueror. It had no architecture; no conscious arrangement. The market place was a jagged cobbled open place; the Church was a granite church—of what age, I do not know.* It was a windy, noisy, fishy, vociferous, narrow-streeted town; the colour of a mussel or a limpet; like a bunch of rough shell fish, oysters or mussels, all crowded together.

Our house, Talland House, was outside the town; on the hill. [When it was built, for] whom it was built by the G.W.R., I do not know; some time in the forties [or] fifties I suppose; a square house, like a child's drawing of a house; remarkable only for its flat roof, and the railing with crossed bars of wood that ran round the roof. It had, when we came there, a perfect view—right across the Bay to Godrevy Lighthouse. It had, running down the hill, little lawns, surrounded by thick escallonia bushes, whose leaves one picked and pressed and smelt: it had so many corners and lawns that each was named: the coffee garden; the fountain; the cricket ground; the love corner, under the greenhouse; jackmanii grew there; on the seat under the jackmanii, Leo Maxse became engaged to Kitty Lushington (I thought I heard Paddy talking to his son, Thoby announced); the strawberry bed; the kitchen garden; the pond; and the big tree. All different places were crowded together in that one garden; for it was a large garden—two or three acres at most, I suppose.† You entered Talland House by a large wooden gate, the sound of whose latch clicking comes back: you went up the carriage drive, with its steep wall scattered with mesembryanthemums; and then came to the Lookout place on the right. This was a mound, grassy, unplanted, that jutted out over the garden wall. There one stood to look if the signal was down. If it were down, it was time to start for the station to meet the train from St Erth—the train that brought Mr Lowell, Mr Gibbs, the Stillmans, the Symondses, the Lushingtons. But that was entirely a grown-up affair—receiving friends. We never had friends to stay with us. Did we want them? I think 'us four' were completely self-sufficing. When once a girl called Elsie was brought over by Mrs Westlake from Zennor I "broomed her round the garden", the grown ups laughing and approving. They liked us to be independent.

* P. 16 of the ms continues: "There were none of those rows of respectable professional houses, with carved doors, & brass window long window panes with brass lined blinds."

† Lines 3–8 (to 'St Erth') of the ms have been omitted; VW partially deleted lines 3–4.

From the Lookout place one had then a perfectly open view of the Bay. Mr Symonds said it reminded him of the Bay of Naples. The bay was a large lap, many-curved, sand-edged, silver green with sandhills, flowing to the Lighthouse rocks at one end, which made two black stops, one of them with the black and white Lighthouse tower on it. At the other end, the Hayle river made a bar, like a vein across the sand, with the stakes marking the channel, on which the seagulls sat. This great flowing scoop of sea was always changing colour: deep blue; emerald; green; purple; silver. Ships were always steaming in or out: the Haines line, for the most part small steamers going to Cardiff for coal. In rough weather all sorts of tramp steamers came in for shelter—low ships, with a dip in the middle, painted a rusty red. Sometimes a great three-funnelled ship would anchor; and once some famous white yacht. Then there was a perpetual sailing of fishing boats from the Harbour—the luggers, with their sails rigged half across the mast; the rather heavy clumsy boats that went far out, deep sea fishing, and the lighter mackerel boats, that came racing back in the evening, rounding the Island and dropping their sails. Early in September we would cry one morning, "The pilchard boats are out!" The pilchard boats lay up on the beach most of the year. But regularly in early autumn they were hauled down by horses and lay at anchor near the shore, looking like black shoes, for each had a hood at one end, and a great coil of net at the other. There they lay week after week; waiting for the Huer up in the little white watch house at Carbis Bay to sight the pil-chards, and sound his horn. Then they would shoot the seine. But year after year the boats lay waiting. The pilchards it was said had been disturbed by the steam trawlers; they never came to St Ives Bay. Once though we heard the Huer—a long clear wail sounded. All the seines were shot. We could see the dotted circles of cork and the dark net beneath. But the great shoal of pilchards, visible under the water to the Huer on his height, passed out of the bay; and the seines were drawn in again. (It was only in 1905 when, after father's death, we four took a little lodging house at Carbis Bay, that the pilchards came; and we rowed out early one morning and the sea bubbled and spat with silver. I remember some stranger in the next boat shovelling an armful out of that bubbling mass into our boat. I remember writing an article, rejected I suppose, describing it.) All the years we were at St Ives the pilchards never came; and the pilchard boats drowsed in the bay and we used to swim out and hang

onto the edge; and see some old man lying under the brown tar-
paulin tent. It was a sight that made father gloomy. He had a great
respect for fishermen. He minded their poverty; and mother, of
course, went about, down in St Ives, starting her nursing association
—The Julia Prinsep Stephen Nursing Association was founded after
she died; and I think, Ka A.F.* told me, still exists.

Every year the Regatta took place in the bay. There was the
Judges' boat, with lines of little flags going from mast to mast. The
St Ives notables went on board. Then all the little boats came out. A
band played. We went onto the Malakoff and stood in the crowd and
listened to the blare of music wafted across the water; and then a gun
was fired and off went the boats, racing round the bay; or the
swimmers plunged. And we could see the little heads bobbing in the
water and the arms flashing. One year the beautiful curly headed
postman was second. "I let the other man win", he said, "because it
was his last chance." There were races for men, for boys; races for
luggers, for pleasure boats. It was very gay, with the flags flying and
the gun firing and the music of the St Ives Band coming from the
Regatta boat across the water. A crowd collected in the Malakoff—
that octagonal space at the end of the terrace, which had been built,
presumably, in the Crimean War, and was the only attempt that the
town made at being a watering place. It had no pier; no parade;
only this angular piece of ground with a few stone benches, upon
which retired fishermen would sit in their blue jerseys, smoking and
talking. Regatta Day—always a fine day—remains in my mind, and
makes me think, what with its little flags and its little boats and its
movement and the people dotted on the sand and on the water and
the music coming over the water, of a French picture.

In those days St Ives, save for a few painters, had no visitors. Its
customs were its own customs: in August there was the Regatta. Once
in every twelve years† the old men and women danced round Knills
Steeple and the couple who danced longest was given—a shilling?
half a crown? I forget—by the Mayor—Dr Nicholls, on that occasion, wearing a fur trimmed cloak. The town crier every now and
then walked along the front, swinging a muffin man's bell and
crying "Oyez! Oyez! Oyez!" What he cried, I do not know; except

---

* Ka Arnold-Forster *née* Katherine Cox, a 'Neo-Pagan', Fabian and
Newnhamite, who was involved in a rather stormy love affair with Rupert
Brooke.
  † This ceremony takes place every five, not every twelve, years.

on one occasion, when a visitor of ours had lost a brooch, and old Charlie Pearce cried it. He was blind, with a long, wasted face, grey eyes, like the eyes of a fish that has been boiled, and he wore a very battered top hat and a frock coat tightly buttoned round his thin body, and he shambled along, swinging his bell and crying "Oyez! Oyez! Oyez!" We knew him, as we knew so many St Ives characters, through the servants, through Sophie* for the most part. I remember Alice Curnow, who brought the laundry in a great covered basket; and Mrs Adams, the fishwoman, who brought the fish. The lobsters were alive, still blue, hobbling about in [the] basket, and she would put them on the kitchen table, and the great claws would open and close and pinch. Can I be remembering a fact when I remember a long thick fish wriggling on a hook in the larder, and Gerald beating it to death with a broom handle?

The kitchen, Sophie's kitchen, was directly beneath our night nursery. We would let down a basket on a string and dangle it over the kitchen window, at night while dinner was going on. If she were in a good temper, the basket would be drawn in and laden with something left from the grown-ups' dinner; but if she were in a bad temper, the basket would be jerked in and the string cut. I can remember the different sensations: drawing up the heavy basket; and feeling the jerk; and the lightness of the string.

Every afternoon we went for a walk. Later these walks became a penance—father must have one of us to walk with him—mother, too much obsessed with his health, his pleasure, was too willing, I think now, to offer us up for sacrifice on that altar, leaving thus a legacy of dependence on his side which became a terrible imposition after her death. In spite of that, St Ives was the country. How much better it would have been for him and for us if she had left him to walk alone; to overwork if he chose. His health was her fetish; she died of overwork easily at forty-nine: he found it very difficult to die of cancer at seventy-two.

But, after making that parenthesis, St Ives gave us all the same the pure delight which is before my eyes even at this moment. The lemon-coloured leaves on the elm trees, the round apples glowing red in the orchard and the rustle of the leaves make me pause to think how many other than human forces affect us. While I am writing this, the light changes; an apple becomes a vivid green. I respond—how? And then the little owl [makes] a chattering noise.

* Farrell.

Another response. St Ives, to cut short an obscure train of thought, about the other voice or voices and their connection with art, with religion: figuratively, I could snapshot what I mean by fancying myself afloat, [in an element] which is all the time responding to things we have no words for—exposed to some invisible ray: but instead of labouring here to express this, to analyse the third voice, to discover whether 'pure delights' are connected with art, or religion: whether I am telling the truth when I see myself perpetually taking the breath of these voices in my sails, and tacking this way and that, in daily life as I yield to them—instead of that, I note only this influence, suspect it to be of great importance, cannot find how to check its power on other people; and so erect a finger here, by way of signalling that here is a vein to work out later.

To return to St Ives. Tren Crom,* as father liked to call it, Trick Robin as we called it, was the regular Sunday walk. You could see both seas from it—on one side, St Michael's Mount, on the other, St Ives Bay. Like all the Cornish hills it was scattered with blocks of granite and in some holes were driven, as for gate posts. Others were piled up and logged. There was a Loggan rock on Tren Crom; onto which we scrambled; and a hollow in the rough lichened surface had been made, so they said, to hold the blood of victims. Little paths led between heather and ling to the top. Our legs were pricked and scratched as we climbed; and the gorse was yellow, sweet smelling, nutty. In Fairyland, as we called a wood, [with a wall round it], and great ferns growing higher than our heads.† I think of oak apples and acorns. It was very dark and silent: we walked on the wall, looking down into the great ferns, smelling acorns and oak apples. All the granite walls were tufted with moss, and little flowers. At Halestown bog, one jumped from hay to hay; and went squelching in. There the Osmunda grew, and the rare maidenhair fern; and one would pitch down, above one's knee, in the brown bog water. Perhaps every ten days we would go sailing. Thoby would be allowed to steer. He had to keep the sail filled with wind, and father said, "Show them you can bring her in, my boy", and setting his face, flushing with the effort, he sat there, bringing us round the point. Once the sea was full of pale jelly fish; differently coloured; like lamps, only with streaming tentacles. They stung if you touched them. We would be given fishing lines, baited

* Usually spelled as one word—Trencrom.
† This is a rare example in the memoirs of an incomplete sentence.

with gobbets cut from fish; and the line thrilled in one's fingers in the water; and then there was a tug; a curious exciting throb; one hauled in; up through the water came the white twisting fish; and it was a gurnard, or a mackerel. There it lay flapping its tail in the water on the floor. Once father said to me: "I don't like to see fish caught; so I shan't come; but you can go if you like." I think it was very admirably done. Not a rebuke, not a forbidding; simply a statement; about which I could think and decide for myself. It made me decide that I disliked fishing; though the passion I had for it—for the thrill and the tug—had been beyond words. The desire to fish faded, leaving no grudge. And from the memory of my own passion I am still able to construct the sporting passion. It is one of those invaluable seeds—for as it is impossible to have every experience, one must make do with seeds—germs of what might have been. I pigeon-hole 'fishing' thus with other momentary glimpses, like those glances I cast into basements when I walk in London streets.

Oak apples, ferns with little clusters of seeds on their backs, the Regatta, Charlie Pearce, the click of the garden gate, the ants swarming on the step, buying tintacks, sailing, the smell of Halestown bog, splits for tea in the farmhouse at Trevail, the floor of the sea changing. Mr Wolstenholme in his beehive chair, the spotted elm leaves on the lawn, the rooks cawing as they flew over the house in the morning, the escallonia leaves changing from green to grey, the arc in the air when the powder magazine exploded at Hayle, the boom of the buoy; these are for some reason uppermost in my mind, thinking of St Ives: an incongruous miscellaneous catalogue—little corks that mark a sunken net. And to pull that net, leaving its contents unsorted, to shore, I add: two or three years before mother's death (1892–3–4) we heard ominous hints that we might leave St Ives. The distance had become a drawback. George and Gerald had work in London. Expense, always threatening, became more pressing. Thoby's school bills. Education . . . * And then, just opposite the Lookout place, a board appeared. The ground was for sale. Next summer an hotel had risen in the middle of our view. My mother complained, the view was spoilt. A great square building, the colour of oatcake, stood there. And so, one October, a house

* "[And so, one October, a board with To Let upon it, appeared;]" which follows in the ms (p. 25) has been deleted because the thought is expanded in the next sentences. The brackets are VW's.

agent's board appeared on our lawn. For some reason it required painting. I was allowed to fill in some of the letters from a pot of paint. No tenants came. The danger was averted. And then mother died. And perhaps a month later, Gerald went down to St Ives: some people called Millie Dow wanted to take the house. Our lease was sold to them; and St Ives vanished for ever.

I recover then today (October 12th 1940: a milky* autumn day; London is being battered nightly) from these rapid notes only one actual picture of Thoby: steering us in round the point without letting the sail flap. I recover the picture of a schoolboy whose jacket was rather tight; whose arms were too long for their sleeves; whose eyes became bluer when he was thus on his mettle; his face flushed a little. He was feeling, rather earlier than most boys, the responsibility laid on him by father's pride in him; the burden, the glory of being a man. Why do I shirk the task, not so very hard to a professional like myself, of wafting this boy from the boat into my bed sitting room at Hyde Park Gate? Because I want to think of St Ives; because I have left out many other pictures of him there; because always round him like the dew that collects on a rough coat in autumn hangs the country; butterflies; birds; mud; horses; and finally, because I do not want to go into my room at Hyde Park Gate again. I shrink from the years 1897–1904 — the seven unhappy years. So many lives were free from our burden. Why should our lives have been so tortured and fretted? by two unnecessary blunders — the lash of a random unheeding flail that pointlessly and brutally killed the two people who should, normally and naturally, have made those years, not perhaps happy but normal and natural. Mother's death: Stella's death. I am not thinking of them. I am thinking of the stupid damage that their deaths inflicted. That is why I do not wish to bring Thoby out of the boat into my room.

Without their deaths, to hark back to an earlier train of thought, he would not have been so dumbly, yet genuinely, bound to us. If there is any good (I doubt it) in this mutilation [of] natural feelings, it is that it sensitizes—if to be aware of the insecurity of life; [to] remember something gone; to feel, now and then, as I felt for father when he made no claim, an odd fumbling fellowship—if it is a good thing to be at fifteen or sixteen or seventeen aware of this; to feel, by

* Doubtful reading.

fits and starts, this sort of profound feeling, this unchildish feeling—
if, if, if—. But was it good? Would it not have been better (if there is
any sense in using good and better when there is no possible judge)
to go on feeling at St Ives the rush and tumble of things? to go on
exploring and adventuring privately, while all the while the family
as a whole continued its solid rumbling progress, from year to year?
To be so surrounded would have given one perhaps a greater scope,
more variety. But at fifteen to have that protection removed, to be
tumbled out of the family shelter, to see cracks and gashes in that
fabric, to be cut by them, to see beyond them—was that good? Did
it give one an experience that even if it was painful, yet meant that
the gods (as I used to phrase it) were taking one seriously; and
giving one a job which they would not think it worthwhile giving,
say to Meg and Imogen Booth, say to Ida and Sylvia Milman? I
had my visual way of putting it. I would see (after Thoby's death)
two great grindstones (as I walked round Goode Tye*) and myself
between them. I would typify a contest between myself and "them"
—some invisible giant. I would reason, or fancy, that if life were
thus made to rear and kick, it was at any rate, the real thing. Nobody
could say I had been fobbed off with an unmeaning slip of the
precious matter. So I came to think of life as something of extreme
reality. And this, of course, increased my feeling of my own importance. Not in relation to human beings: in relation to the force
which had respected me sufficiently to make me feel what was
real.†

It seems to me therefore that our relation (mine and Thoby's)
was more serious than it would have been without those deaths. The
unspoken thought—something like what I have visualized—was
there, in him, in me; when he came into my back room at Hyde
Park Gate. It was behind our arguments. We were of course
naturally attracted to each other. Besides his brother's feeling, he
had, I think, an amused, surprised, questioning attitude towards me.
I was a year and a half younger than he. I was a girl. And he found
me reading Greek, writing an essay—the first, the only essay I ever
showed father, upon the Elizabethan voyagers—when he was
writing one for a prize at Trinity. A shell-less little creature, I think he
thought me; so sequestered, in the room at Hyde Park Gate, com-

* Goode Tye is a doubtful reading.
† The marginal note in the ms reads: "to make me wince: spin; ground
between grindstones".

pared with himself; a very simple, eager recipient of his school stories; without any experience of my own with which to cap his; but all the same, not passive; rather, on the contrary, bubbling, inquisitive, restless, carrying on my own contradicting, at any rate questioning. We had each branched out, after those early ramblings up and down stairs; to read on our own. He had consumed Shakespeare, somehow or other, by himself. He had possessed himself of it, in his large clumsy way, and our first arguments—about books, that is—were heated; because out he would come with his sweeping assertion that everything was in Shakespeare: somehow I felt he had it all in his grasp; at which I revolted. He swept down on me. How could I oppose that? Rather feebly I suppose; but still it was then my genuine feeling. A play was antipathetic. How did they begin? With some dull speech; about a hundred miles from anything that interested me. I opened [*Twelfth Night*] to prove this; I opened at "If music be the food of love, play on. . . ."* I was downed that time. That was, I had to admit, a good beginning. And I remember his pride, for it seemed like a pride he took in a friend, at Shakespeare's shuffling Falstaff off without a sign of sympathy. That large impartial sweep in Shakespeare delighted him. I mean the impartiality of a tree that sheds leaves; and so on. On the other hand, when Desdemona wakes again, he thought possibly Shakespeare was 'sentimental'. These are the only particular criticisms I remember—for he was not, as I was, a breaker off of single words or sentences—not a notetaker—he was much more casual and rough and ready and comprehensive. And so I felt that Shakespeare was to him his other world; the place where he got the measure of his daily world: where he took his bearings; in which he took his way freely from Shakespeare, upon what happened. I wonder if I am right in thinking that [Shakespeare] had worked itself into his mind, so that he was half thinking of Falstaff and Hal and Cordelia and the rest— in the third-class smoker on the Underground when there was some squabble between drunken men: and Thoby with his pipe in his mouth sat in the corner, surveyed it over the edge of a paper, motionless, with a look that stuck in my memory; a look of one equipped, unperturbed, knowing his place, relishing his inheritance and his part in life, aware of his competence, scenting the battle; already, in anticipation, a law maker; proud of being a man and playing his part among Shakespeare's men. Had he been put on, he

* The ms leaves a blank space for the title.

would have played his part most royally. The words Walter Lamb used of him were very fitting.*

So we argued. But how reserved we were! Brothers and sisters today talk quite freely about — oh everything. We never talked about ourselves even, so far as I can remember. I can recall no confidences; no compliments; no kisses; no emotional scenes. As for sex, he passed from childhood to boyhood and from boyhood to manhood under our eyes, without saying a single thing that could have shown us, by word of mouth, what he was feeling. Did other boys fall in love with him? Not he with them, I suspect. From Clive I learned later that Lytton's sodomy was to him one of the jokes: one of 'the Strache's' amiable absurdities, eccentricities. Yet beneath that silence — it may be kept cool and sweet, it may be given a depth, a seriousness, an emotional quality that speech destroys — dwelt, as I felt, great susceptibility; great sensibility; great pride and love; and all the beliefs and desires which had he been put on would have made him privately a lover, a husband, a father; and publicly a Judge for sure: Mr Justice Stephen he would have been today; with several books to his credit, I suppose: some on law; one or two on birds; and for a side line there would have been something about pictures; perhaps the Hogarth Press would have published a history of birds with illustrations; some essays on literature; and history; public matters; some attacks on abuses; and by this time he would have been a figure much liked, a typical Englishman? No, not that, for he was melancholy; original; not able to take the ordinary ambitions seriously. I suppose he would have been more a figure than a success.

The knell of those words of course comes in; and affects my memory of a time when we had no idea that our relationship was to end when he was twenty-six and I was twenty-four. This is one of the falsifications that one cannot guard against; save by noting it. At the time, when he argued with me in my room at Hyde Park Gate, I never saw him as I now see him, with all his promise ended. I thought, if I thought, simply of the moment: it was a moment in which we were both emerging from childhood; and every day, certainly every time he came back from Clifton or from Cambridge, more of him, more of me, had emerged. Those were days of dis-

* From the final speech of Fortinbras in *Hamlet*: "Let four captains/ Bear Hamlet like a soldier to the stage,/For he was likely, had he been put on,/To have proved most royal . . . ."

covery. Very exciting our discoveries were. I remember discovering one October day, when he was about to go to Cambridge for the first time, his beauty. He wore a Hill suit for the first time. That summer, I discovered that he smoked a pipe. I discovered Bell, 'the Strache', and Sydney-Turner.* But I am going too far ahead of myself in Hyde Park Gate. I will return to the year Stella died — 1897.

I could sum it all up in one scene. I always see when I think of the month after her death the certain leafless bush; a skeleton tree in the dark of a summer night. This tree stands outside a garden house. Inside I am sitting with Jack Hills. He grips my hand in his. He groans. "It tears one asunder" he groaned. He was in agony. He gripped my hand to make his agony endurable; as if he were in physical torture. "But you can't understand" he broke off. "Yes, I can", I murmured. Subconsciously I knew that he meant that his sexual desires tore him asunder, together with his anguish at her loss. Both were torturing him. And the tree, outside in the dark garden, was to me the emblem, the symbol, of the skeleton agony to which her death had reduced him; and us; everything. Either Vanessa or I would go off alone with Jack after dinner. He would come down every week-end — it was to Painswick. Every day one or other of us had a letter. "Poor boy, he looks very bad", father once muttered audibly. And Jack, overhearing, stammered some awkward sentence to prevent him from saying more. The leafless tree and Jack's agony — I always see them as if they were one and the same, when I think of that summer.

The leafless tree was a very painful element in our life. Trees don't remain leafless. They begin to have little red chill buds. By that image I would convey the discomfort and misery and the quarrels, the suppressed irritations, the sharp words, the insinuations — which as soon as family life started again in Hyde Park Gate began to cover over the fact that Stella's death had left us all to take up new relationships.

Another garden scene — this time at Fritham — comes back to me. George had taken my arm in his. Indoors father was playing whist with the others. George singled me out; and walked me off round the lawn. I cannot remember any phrase exactly. A mumbling comes back — his emotional pressure on my arm; as he — with much

* Clive Bell, Lytton Strachey and Saxon Sydney-Turner, Thoby's Trinity College friends who were to form part of the nucleus of Bloomsbury.

circumlocution and more emotion and some vague threat about its being against the law and as Stella was her sister, marriage was illegal—told me that people were saying that Vanessa was in love with Jack; and asked me to do what I could (this flattered me) to make her give up seeing him alone.* It was a pity that people should say such things. And I could tell her—I could persuade her. What I said to her I do not remember—only her rather bitter answer: "So you take their side too."

Then I realised that she had her side: if that were so, of course I was on her side, as I said, very confusedly. I wobbled at once from George's side to her side. But my vagueness and confusion show that I knew very little of the exact state of things. Presumably George had not asked my help till he had tried other means—for one thing, as Nessa told me later, [he] had spoken his fears to father who, much to his credit, said that she was to do as she liked: he would not interfere.

These scenes, by the way, are not altogether a literary device—a means of summing up and making innumerable details visible in one concrete picture. Details there were; still, if I stopped to think, I could collect a number. But, whatever the reason may be, I find that scene making is my natural way of marking the past. Always a scene has arranged itself: representative; enduring. This confirms me in my instinctive notion: (it will not bear arguing about; it is irrational) the sensation that we are sealed vessels afloat on what it is convenient to call reality; and at some moments, the sealing matter cracks; in floods reality; that is, these scenes—for why do they survive undamaged year after year unless they are made of something comparatively permanent? Is this liability to scenes the origin of my writing impulse? Are other people also scene makers? These are questions to which I have no answer. Perhaps sometime I will consider it more carefully. Obviously I have developed the faculty, because, in all the writing I have done, I have almost always had to make a scene, either when I am writing about a person; I must find a representative scene in their lives; or when I am writing about a book, I must find their poem, novel ... But this may not be the same faculty.

So that was one of the little red buds, or thorns, on the skeleton

* The phrase 'with much circumlocution ... illegal' is a marginal addition; a reworking of 'very emotionally and circuitously and ambiguously' which has been omitted from the text.

tree: Vanessa was in love with Jack; Jack was behaving selfishly; people were talking; and George and Gerald (to a lesser degree) were getting their hackles up. That is one of the aspects of death which is left out when people talk of the message of sorrow: they never mention its unbecoming side: its legacy of bitterness, bad temper, ill adjustment.

For some months that winter (1897–8) Jack stayed with us, until he took a house—* 14 Victoria Grove. It "had associations." I believe one of our Great Aunts—Aunt Louisa Bayley?—had lived there. Kitty and Leo† had lived there. There Jack went to live with the Scotchers—Mr and Mrs Scotchbrook. He came to grief through drink and she, as Flora Baker used to hint—for the ladies of the family adopted Jack and his interests as if he were an orphan—threatened to have another baby.

(November 17th.) But we never spoke, during those unhappy years, of these scenes. Thoby, I imagine, may have had some vague conception that something, as I think he would have put it, was up between Jack and Vanessa. But his general attitude was aloof, judicial, conventional. From his remote station, as a schoolboy, as an undergraduate, he felt generally‡ we should accept our place: if George wanted us to go to parties, why not? If father wanted us to walk with him, why not? Once, at Salisbury, when the Fishers were our neighbours, and Vanessa, detesting Aunt Mary, who had most viciously intervened, writing surreptitious letters addressed to Copes School, in the chronic warfare between Vanessa and Jack and Vanessa and George, refused to visit them and cut them in the street, he made one of his rare impressive statements: gruffly he said it was not right to treat Aunt Mary like that.

It thus came about that Nessa and I formed together a very close conspiracy. In that world of many men, coming and going, we formed our private nucleus. There we were, alone, with father all day. In the evening Adrian would come back from Westminster; then Jack from Lincoln's Inn; then Gerald from Dent's or Henrietta

* p. 34, ll.23–4 (ms) have been omitted.
† Maxse.
‡ In the ms 'allied by old ties' follows 'felt generally'—which is an interlinear insertion—and a partial deletion. It has been omitted here because it confuses the sense.

Street; then George from the Post Office or the Treasury; and Thoby would be at Clifton or at Cambridge. The staple day would be a day spent together. And therefore we made together a small world inside the big world. We had an alliance that was so knit together that everything (with the exception of Jack perhaps) was seen from the same angle; and took its shape from our own vantage point. Very soon after Stella's death we saw life as a struggle to get some kind of standing place for ourselves in this [illegible].* We were always battling for that which was always being interfered with, muffled up, snatched away. The most imminent obstacle and burden was of course father. How could we, to take a concrete case, arrange that he should be out when perhaps Kitty Maxse, perhaps Katie Thynne, came to tea?† How could we escape Mr Bryce?‡ Must I spend the afternoon walking round Kensington Gardens? Could we possibly arrange to take our friends straight up to the Studio (the day nursery)? Then, what could one talk about at luncheon? Could we avoid Brighton at Easter? Must we be in because Aunt Mary was coming?

Over the whole week of these evasions and propitiations brooded the horror of Wednesday. On that day the weekly books were shown him. If they were over eleven pounds, that lunch was a torture. The books were presented. Silence. He was putting on his glasses.§ He had read the figures. Down came his fist on the account book. There was a roar. His vein filled. His face flushed. Then he shouted "I am ruined." Then he beat his breast. He went through an extraordinary dramatization of self-pity, anger and despair. He was ruined—dying . . . tortured by the wanton extravagance of Vanessa and Sophie. "And you stand there like a block of stone. Don't you pity me? Haven't you a word to say to me?" and so on. Vanessa stood by his side absolutely dumb. He flung at her all the phrases— about shooting Niagara and so on—that came handy. She remained static. Another attitude was adopted. With a deep groan he picked up his pen and with ostentatiously trembling fingers wrote out the cheque. This was wearily tossed to Vanessa. Slowly and with many

* One illegible word followed by a full stop (ms, p. 36); then two illegible words, one above the other, followed by a full stop.
† Lady Katherine Thynne who married Lord Cromer.
‡ 'Bryce', a doubtful reading.
§ Deletion of material from "A roar." at bottom of ms, p. 36 to the end of p. 37.

groans the pen, the account book were put away. Then he sank into his chair and sat with his head on his breast. And then at last, after glancing at a book, he would look up and say half plaintively, "And what are you doing this afternoon, Ginny?"

Never have I felt such rage and such frustration. For not a word of my feeling could be expressed.

This, as far as I can describe it, is an unexaggerated account of a bad Wednesday. Even now I can find nothing to say of his behaviour save that it was brutal. If, instead of words, he had used a whip the brutality would have been no greater. How can one explain it? He had been indulged of course ever since he broke the flower pot and threw the fragments at his mother (whatever the truth of that story, it ran something like that). Delicacy excused that. Then as he grew older there was the genius legend to which I have already referred.* Men of genius are very ill to live with ... But there are certain qualifications to be noted. These scenes were never indulged in before men. Fred Maitland† for example resolutely refused to believe in them when Caroline Emelia (the Quaker sister) tried to insinuate that Leslie had a temper. If Thoby had presented those books or George, the explosion would have been suppressed. Why had he no shame in front of women? Partly of course because the woman was his slave — being the most typical of Victorians. But that does not explain the self-dramatization, the attitudinizing, the histrionic element, the breast beating, the groaning, which played so large a part, so disgusting a part in these scenes. His dependence upon women perhaps explains that. He needed always a woman to sympathize, to flatter, to console. Why? Because he was conscious of his failure as a philosopher, as a writer. But his creed made him ashamed to confess this need of sympathy to men. The attitude that his intellect made him adopt with men, made him the most modest, the most reasonable of men.‡ [illegible] Vanessa, on Wednesdays, was the recipient of much discontent that he had suppressed; and her refusal to accept her role, part slave, part angel of sympathy, exacerbated him so that he was probably unconscious of his own barbarous violence: and would have been horrified had anyone

* There is no such reference in the Monks House Papers.

† Frederic William Maitland wrote the authorized 'Life' of Leslie Stephen. He married Florence Fisher, one of Aunt Mary's daughters.

‡ Thus to Fred Maitland or to Herbert Fisher he was entirely without vanity, without conceit' was deleted by VW.

said straight out "You are a blackguard to treat a girl like that." I cannot conceive how he would have taken an honest expression of opinion. And the reason for that is to be found in the disparity, so obvious in his books, between his critical and his creative powers. Give him a thought to analyse, the thought of Mill, Bentham, Hobbes; and his is (so Maynard* has told me) acute, clear, concise: an admirable model of the Cambridge analy[tical spirit]. But give him life, a character, and he is so crude, so elementary, so conventional, that a child with a box of coloured chalks is as subtle a portrait painter as he is. To explain this, one would have to discuss the crippling effect of Cambridge; and its one-sided education; and to follow that by a discussion of the professional writer, in the nineteenth century; and the crippling effect of intensive brain work; and to illustrate that by his lack of any distracting interests—music, art, the theatre, travel; and one would have to discover how much of this intensification and narrowness was natural; how much imposed by circumstances. But the fact does seem to be that at the age of sixty-five he was almost completely isolated, imprisoned. Whole tracts of his sensibility had atrophied. He had so ignored, or refused to face, or disguised his own feelings, that not only had he no conception of what he himself did and said; he had no idea what other people felt. Hence the horror and the terror of these violent displays of rage. These were sinister, blind, animal, savage. He did not realise what he did. No one could enlighten him. He suffered. We suffered. There was no possibility of communication. Vanessa stood silent. He shouted.†

Here of course, from my distance of time, I perceive what one could not then see—the difference of age. Two different ages confronted each other in the drawing room at Hyde Park Gate: the Victorian age; and the Edwardian age. We were not his children, but his grandchildren. When we both felt that he was not only terrifying but also ridiculous we were looking at him with eyes that saw ahead of us something—something so easily seen now by every boy and girl of sixteen and eighteen that the sight is perfectly familiar. The cruel thing was that while we could see the future, we were completely in the power of the past. That bred a violent struggle. By nature, both Vanessa and I were explorers, revolutionists,

* John Maynard Keynes. 'analytical spirit' was partially deleted by VW but must be restored for the sense.

† 'shouted' is only partially legible.

reformers. But our surroundings were at least fifty years behind the times. Father himself was a typical Victorian: George and Gerald were unspeakably* conventional. So that while we fought against them as individuals we also fought against them in their public capacity. We were living say in 1910: they were living in 1860.

In 22 Hyde Park Gate round about 1900 there was to be found a complete model of Victorian society. If I had the power to lift out a month of life as we lived it about 1900 I could extract a section of Victorian life, like one of those cases with glass covers in which one is shown ants or bees going about their affairs. Our day would begin with family breakfast at 8.30. Adrian bolted his; and whichever of us, Vanessa or myself, was down, would see him off. Standing at the front door we would wave a hand till he disappeared round the Martins' bulging wall. This was a relic left us by Stella—a flutter of the dead hand which lay beneath the surface of family life. Father would eat his breakfast sighing and snorting. If no letters, "Everyone has forgotten me", he would groan. A long envelope from Barkers would mean of course a sudden roar. George and Gerald came down. Vanessa disappeared behind the curtain. Dinner ordered, she would dash for the red bus to take her to the Academy. If Gerald coincided, he would give her a lift in his daily hansom —the same hansom, generally; the cabman in summer wore a carnation. George having breakfasted more deliberately—sometimes he would persuade me to sit on, on the three-cornered chair, and tell me gossip from last night's party—he too would button on his frock coat and give his top hat a promise with the velvet glove and disappear—smart and debonair, in his ribbed socks and very small well polished shoes, to the Treasury. Left alone in the great house, with Father shut in his study at the top, the housemaid polishing brass rods, Shag asleep on his mat, and some maid doing bedrooms while Sophie I suppose took in joints and milk from tradespeople at the back door, I mounted to my room and spread my Liddell and Scott upon my table and sat down to make out Euripides or Sophocles for my bi-weekly lesson with Janet Case.†

From ten to one we escaped the pressure of Victorian society.

* Doubtful reading.
† In the margin is written 'Clara Pater', the sister of Walter Pater, who taught Virginia Greek and Latin before Miss Case. Miss Case, in addition to being a severe and thorough teacher, became a lifelong friend of Virginia's.

Vanessa, I suppose, under the eye of Val Prinsep* or Ouless† or
occasionally Sargent, painted from the life—she would bring home
now and then very careful pencil drawings of Hermes perhaps, and
spray them with fixative; or an oil head of a very histrionic looking
male nude. And for the same three hours I would be reading perhaps
Plato's *Republic*, or spelling out a Greek chorus. Our minds would
escape to the world which on this November morning of 1940 she
inhabits at Charleston and I in my garden room at Monks House.
Our clothes would not be much different. She wore a blue painting
smock; I perhaps a blouse and skirt. If our skirts were longer, that
would be the only difference. Forty years ago she was rather tidier,
rather better dressed than I. The change would come in the afternoon. About 4.30 Victorian society exerted its pressure. Then we
must be 'in'. For at 5 father must be given his tea. And we must be
better dressed and tidier, for Mrs Green was coming; Mrs H. Ward
was coming; or Florence Bishop; or C. B. Clarke; or . . . We would
have to sit at that table, either she or I, decently dressed, having
nothing better to do, ready to talk.

The pressure of society was now very strong. It created that
"manner" which we both still use. It is the manner in which when
the front door bell rang we used to receive whoever it might be—say
it was Ronny Norman. Suppose that Elsa Bell and Florence Bishop
and Mr Gibbs arrived at ten minute intervals. We would have to be
ready with small talk; ready to take father's trumpet and convey
whatever was likely to help; ready to take our part—in what? Not
argument; nor gossip. I suppose a very exacting—'not gossip'
exactly. The older visitor would be sacrificed to father: given a chair
beside him; entrusted with the end of the trumpet. Then Ronny
Norman would be boyish, hearty: Elsa Bell would be worldly;
Florence Bishop a little flighty. The conversation would be lighter
than now; more mannered; jokes would be laughed at; Sir Leslie
would give a groan; his health would be discussed; Ronny Norman
would say (if Florence Bishop got going with father) something
about an awfully jolly play or picture: I would plunge rather reck-
lessly, say with Eveline Godley, into talk about the Navy: Elsa Bell
would say that she expected her brothers to take off their hats if they
met her in the street; father would be irritated: Florence Bishop
would too and [would] withdraw her unlucky remark—that he

* Julia Stephen's cousin, son of Sarah and Thoby Prinsep.
† Walter William Ouless, R.A. (1848–1933).

looked well; Ronny Norman would ask him if he remembered Mill;
he would unbend—for he liked Ronny Norman—and say how he
had met Mill with his father in Chelsea.* "Oh dear, these old
stories . . . " he would say. Well, the talk had its little steeps and
waterfalls—its dangers: but it went something like that; and the
whole was enclosed in the Victorian manner. It may have been
natural for Ronny Norman, for Eveline Godley, for Miss Bishop. It
was not natural for Vanessa or myself. We learned it. We learned it
partly from memory: and mother had that manner: it was imposed
on us partly by the other side—if Ronny Norman said that, one had
to reply in the same style. Nobody ever broke the convention. If you
listened, as I did, it was like watching a game. One had to know the
rules.†

We both learned the rules of the Victorian game of manners so
thoroughly that we have never forgotten them. We still play the
game. It is useful; it has its beauty, for it is founded upon restraint,
sympathy, unselfishness—all civilised qualities. It is helpful in
making something seemly and human out of raw odds and ends.
But the Victorian manner is perhaps—I am not sure—a disadvantage in writing. When I re-read my old *Common Reader* articles I
detect it there. I lay the blame for their suavity, their politeness,
their sidelong approach, to my tea-table training. I see myself
handing plates of buns to shy young men and asking them, not
directly and simply about their poems and their novels, but whether
they like cream as well as sugar. On the other hand, this surface
manner allows one to say a great many things which would be
inaudible if one marched straight up and spoke out. It was when the
lights went up in the evening that society came into force. During
daylight one could wear overalls; work. There was the Academy for

* In the ms, VW refers to the guests around the tea-table by their initials,
but not consistently which would suggest that convenience rather than
a stylistic effect was her motive. Thus, the full names have been restored in
the text. P. 49 of the ms booklet which does not appear to belong to the
version of the text used here provides a fuller context for Miss Bishop's
remark. The first half-dozen lines read: "Florence Bishop had said that she
thought him looking remarkably well. This was an insult—a breach of the
code: it was essential that he shd receive sympathy. And so we must brush
up our talk with that."

† Omission of approximately 20 lines (from p. 45, l.5 of the ms) which are
reworked in the following paragraph. One sentence was not included in the
reworking, however. "The Victorian manner is useful now on meeting
strangers: on going to meetings in the village."

Nessa; my Liddell and Scott and the Greek choruses for me. But in the evening society had it all its own way. At 7.30 we went upstairs to dress. However cold or foggy it might be, we slipped off our day clothes and stood shivering in front of washing basins. Neck and arms had to be scrubbed, for we had to come into the drawing room at 8 o'clock in evening dress: arms and neck bare. Dress and hair-doing became far more important than pictures and Greek. I would stand in front of George's Chippendale glass trying to make myself not only tidy but presentable. On an allowance of fifty pounds it was difficult, even for the skilful, to be well dressed of an evening. For though a house dress could be made by Jane Bride, at a cost of a pound or two, a party dress cost perhaps fifteen guineas if made by Mrs Young. The house dress therefore might be, as on this particular night, made of a green stuff bought erratically at a furniture shop—Story's—because it was cheaper than dress stuff; also more adventurous. Down I came: in my green evening dress; all the lights were up in the drawing room; and there was George, in his black tie and evening jacket, in the chair by the fire. He fixed on me that extraordinary observant [illegible] gaze with which he always inspected clothes. He looked me up and down as if [I] were a horse turned into the ring. Then the sullen look came over him; a look in which one traced not merely aesthetic disapproval; but something that went deeper; morally, socially, he scented some kind of insurrection; of defiance of social standards. I was condemned from many more points of view than I can analyse as I stood there, conscious of those criticisms; and conscious too of fear, of shame and of despair— "Go and tear it up", he said at last, in that curiously rasping and peevish voice which expressed his serious displeasure at this infringement of a code that meant more to him than he would admit.

For he accepted Victorian society so implicitly that an archaeologist would find him of the greatest interest. Like a fossil he had taken every crease and wrinkle of the conventions of 1890–1900. He was made presumably of precisely the right material. He flowed into the mould without a doubt to mar the pattern. If father had graved on him certain large marks of the age—his belief that women must be pure and men strong—his hatred of impropriety—"Damn!" Gerald exclaimed once, and up flew his hands in protest—Rezia* smoked a cigarette after tea—"I won't have my drawing room

* Rasponi.

turned into a bar parlour!" he exclaimed. He smoothed out the
petty details of the Victorian code with his admirable intellect, his
respect for reason—no one was less snobbish than he was—no one
cared less for rank and luxury. George filled in the large marks with a
criss-cross, a spider's web, of the most minute details. No more
perfect fossil of Victorian society could exist. And so, while father
preserved the framework of 1860, George filled in the framework
with all kinds of minutely teethed saws; and the machine into which
we were inserted in 1900* therefore held us tight; and brought
innumerable teeth into play.

What kind of material was George made of? What can he have
been made of to take the pattern so completely? He had very little
brain, in the first place, and he had an abundance of emotion. He
was poured into a perfectly adapted body. He was extremely handsome, perfectly healthy; and as well set up as a young man could be.
Thus whenever he appeared, society opened its arms. It welcomed
him. It embraced him. He can never have met with any opposition,
either at Eton, or at Cambridge, or in London, from society: if
society is taken to mean the upper middle class world in a drawing
room in the evening. He was so without brains that he never strayed
beyond that circle. He was never rebuffed or criticized because he
never put himself into a position where he encountered criticism. In
addition he had something like a thousand a year. He could play his
part so far as clothes, guns, horses were needed. And as the world
accepted him, praised him and gave him all he wanted, he found it
impossible to imagine any defiance: he found defiance silly, foolish,
unwise, in fact, immoral. My green dress was no doubt obscurely a
criticism of himself. Gerald, I remember with gratitude, said good-
naturedly: "I don't agree. I like it." George was silent. Dinner was a
torture. And, to my discredit, I never wore that dress if George was
at home.†

He was thirty-six when I was twenty. He had a thousand pounds
a year and I had fifty. Those were reasons that made it difficult to
defy George that night. But there was another element in our relationship which affected me as I stood there that winter's night
exposed to his criticism in my green dress. I was not wholly conscious
of it then. But besides feeling his age and his power, I felt too another

---

* The first version of the latter half of this sentence—after '1900'—was not
deleted. It reads: 'was about as complete a specimen as could exist.'

† Ms pp. 50–51 have been omitted.

feeling which I later called the outsider's feeling. When exposed to George's scowling, I felt as a tramp or a gipsy must feel who stands at the flap of a tent and sees the circus going on inside. Victorian society was in full swing; George was the acrobat who jumped through hoops, and Vanessa and I beheld the spectacle. We had good seats at the show, but we were not allowed to take part in it. We applauded, we obeyed—that was all.

All our male relations were adepts at the game. They knew the rules and attached immense importance to them. Father laid enormous stress upon schoolmasters' reports, upon scholarships, triposes and fellowships. The Fishers, the male Fishers, took every prize, honour, degree. What, I asked myself the other day, would Herbert Fisher have been without Winchester, New College and the Cabinet? What would have been his shape had he not been stamped and moulded by the patriarchal machinery? Every one of our male relations was shot into that machine and came out at the other end, at the age of sixty or so, a Headmaster, an Admiral, a Cabinet Minister, a Judge. It is as impossible to think of them as natural human beings as it is to think of a plough horse galloping wild and unshod in the street.

George of course had failed to get admittance to that particular machine. He failed again and again to enter the diplomatic service. But there was another machine—society. He learned the rules of that game so well, he played it so cunningly, that he emerged at the age of sixty with a knighthood, with an aristocratic wife, with a sinecure, a country house and three sons. Somehow, in ways so indefinite that one cannot name them, I felt, at twenty, that George no less than Herbert Fisher was obeying the laws of patriarchal society. He was in the swim; going through hoops; doing the required act. I could feel his adherence; he accepted the convention; he believed. A belief which is commonly accepted, as his was by all his friends, has an atmosphere of authority: it impresses even the outsider. It seems right, natural, taken for granted. When on [Sunday night, the BBC plays] "God Save the King", I feel a current [of] belief; but I criticise my own instinctive emotion. George never questioned his belief in the old tune that society played. He rose and took his hat off, not only without questioning; but with complete acceptance and approval.

These perceptions gave my attitude to George a queer twist. I must obey, because he had force, of age, of wealth, of tradition, behind him. But even while I obeyed I asked, "How could anyone believe what he believed?" There was a spectator in me who, while I squirmed at his criticism and deferred to it, yet remained cool, critical, observant. It fascinated me—the spectacle of George flying through those invisible hoops, so seriously, with such unquestioning belief. In a satirical moment I wrote a sketch of his career which his career followed almost to the letter.*

But unfortunately though we could sit passive and watch the Victorian males go through their intellectual hoops, George's hoops —his social triumphs—needed our help. Here of course his motives were—indeed they always were—mixed. We had to be brought out: to go into society. And he naturally played the part that mother would have played in taking us. But also we had to go where he wished us to go, to accept the invitations he thought desirable. Here the other motive came in—his desire to make us accept his views: his desire to make us pay our tribute to his own faith. And so, when the London season began, several times a week we would go upstairs after dinner, after the post had come, tea had been drunk and father had gone up to his study—and change into those long satin dresses for which Sally Young would charge fifteen guineas. We added white gloves, white slippers and a row of pearls or [an] amethyst round our necks. The cab would be called; and off we would drive along the silver paved streets, for wood pavement became silver in the dry summer nights, to the house where there was an awning, perhaps a strip of red carpet, and a little cluster of gaping passers by.

Now society exerted its full pressure, about 11 o'clock say, on a June night in 1900. I remember the dazed, elated, frozen feeling: as the lights beat on me, going upstairs; the unreality; the excitement; the paralysis. Can I recover anything further? At the Savoy I remember a dinner before the opera. It was *The Ring* and we were dining in full daylight. George had placed Mrs J. Chamberlain opposite the window, a failure in tact for which he reproached himself afterwards. For she had just passed her prime. I sat next a youth whom I now identify as Eddie Marsh. On that occasion I thought he was Richard Marsh; I vaguely connected him with novel writing. I recover only: "What is your father writing now?" he asked, and then I floundered, struck out wildly this way and that like a beginner on the ice.

* Ms pp. 55 (from l.3) and 56 have been omitted.

At Mrs Chamberlain's* I sat next a chubby official youth. We discussed oratory. "Our host", he said, "is generally supposed to be a good speaker." And then I see myself floundering again—stressing a theory that the crime of merrymaking is worse than theft. Silence falls. I felt myself struggling like a fly in glue. I felt that if one said things one thought, anything beyond the usual patter, glue stuck to one's feet. On the threshold of a ballroom, I remember Geoffrey Young primly telling me: "It is very good of you to come." Had I asserted that I hated dancing? He left me. At Trinity Ball, I remember galloping round the room with—I have forgotten the name. At Lady Sligo's I remember pressing some youth to tell me facts about the Garter. Meanwhile George was proposing to Flora Russell.† At the Lyulph Stanleys I remember failing to secure a partner. Elena Rathbone‡ introduced me to a girl. I remember the humiliation of standing, unasked, against a wall. I remember of these parties humiliation—I could not dance; frustration—I could not get young men to talk; and also, for happily that good friend has never deserted me—the scene as a spectacle to be described later. And some moments of elation: some moments of lyrical ecstasy. But the pressure of society in 1900 almost forbade any natural feeling. Perhaps I was too young. Perhaps I was wrongly adjusted. At any rate I never met a man or a woman with whom I struck up any real relationship. All the same there was the excitement of clothes, of lights, of society, in short; and the queerness, the strangeness of being alone, on my own, for a moment, with some complete stranger: he in white waistcoat and gloves, I in white satin and gloves. A more unreal relationship cannot be imagined; but there was a thrill in the unreality. For when I was once more in my own room I would see it small and untidy: I would ride the waves of the party still: I would lie in bed, tossing up and down on the things I had said, heard and done. And next morning I would still be thinking, as I read my Sophocles, of the party.

If that had been all, these parties would have slid off us easily enough. But there was George. To him a party was a very serious matter. We were not merely enjoying ourselves. We were made to

* VW has written 'Mrs Cⁿ'.

† Flora Russell was a niece of the Duke of Bedford. The engagement was brief. She died unmarried.

‡ Elena Rathbone who later married Bruce Richmond, editor of the *Times Literary Supplement*.

feel that every party was an examination, a test: a matter of the greatest importance; it led to success; it led to failure. What did success lead to? The only success he valued—social success. Failure led to the only failure—dowdiness, eccentricity. He held these beliefs implicitly. But he held them confusedly. You could never challenge him directly. "But if I hate parties why should I go to them?" He would wrinkle all those lines piteously. "You're too young to have an opinion. Besides, I love you. I hate going alone. I must have you with me." Here he would snatch Vanessa in his arms. Duty and emotion were indistinguishably mixed. And the ghosts of Stella and Mother presided over these scenes.

Hence these parties became wrangles, became efforts, became often humiliations. Vaguely, he felt that we criticised the whole conception. This angered him. In his anger he upbraided us with selfishness, with narrowness. He complained to his circle of enamoured dowagers. He invoked their help. He lavished clothes, jewels. He acted, in public, the role of the good brother. He acted with success. How could we resist his wishes—how could we cherish other desires? Society in those days was a very competent machine. It was convinced that girls must be changed into married women. It had no doubts, no mercy; no understanding of any other wish; of any other gift. Nothing was taken seriously. Even Beatrice Thynne* would say to me, when I told her I wished to write, "I'll ask Alice to invite you to meet Andrew Lang."† I protested, I did not mean that. She snapped I was silly. That was the way to get on. How strange it was to think that somewhere, there was a world where people did not go to parties—where they perhaps discussed pictures—books—philosophy—But it was not our world.‡

The division in our life was curious. Downstairs there was pure convention: upstairs pure intellect. But there was no connection between them. Father's deafness had cut off any ties that he would have had, naturally, with the younger generation of writers. Yet he kept his own attitude perfectly distinct. No one cared less for convention. No one respected intellect more. Thus I would go from the

* Lady Beatrice Thynne, daughter of the Marchioness of Bath and sister of Katherine and Alice.

† Andrew Lang (1844–1912) was a journalist and man of letters who wrote on an immense variety of subjects. He was a poet, novelist, historian, Greek scholar, anthropologist and the author of well-known collections of fairy tales.

‡ Ms p. 61, from l.9, has been omitted.

drawing room and George's gossip—"Mrs William Grenfell asked me to stay ... And I said, on the whole I thought I couldn't. She was taken by surprise "—to father's study to fetch a [new book]. There I would find him, swinging in his rocking chair, pipe in mouth. Slowly he would realise my presence. Rising, he would go to the shelves, put the book back and very kindly ask me what had I made of it? Perhaps I was reading Johnson. For some time we would talk and then, feeling soothed, stimulated, full of love for this un-worldly, very distinguished, lonely man, I would go down to the drawing room again and hear George's patter. There was no connection.

Nor indeed was there any close connection between ourselves and the world of intellect. The great figures were of course on the horizon: Meredith, Henry James, Henry Sidgwick, Symonds, Haldane, Watts, Burne-Jones: they were figures in the background. But the kind of memory I have of them is of figures only, looming very large, but very far away.

I remember looking down at J. A. Symonds from the landing at Talland House; and noting his nerve-drawn white face; and the tie that was a cord with two yellow blobs of plush. I remember Watts, in his frilled shirt and grey dressing gown: and Meredith, invoking a damsel in a purple petticoat—a flower. I remember Meredith's voice; and the irony with which he said "a book of mine". I remember not what they said, but the atmosphere surrounding them. I remember the ceremony of being taken to see them and the way in which both father and mother conveyed that a visit to Meredith was something altogether out of the way. Both shared a reverence for genius. The reverence impressed me. And the eccentricity, the individuality: how Meredith dropped rounds of lemon into his tea. How Watts had bowls of whipped cream and minced meat; how Lowell had a long knitted purse, with rings round it, and sixpences always came from the slit. What I received was some general impress of strength, of oddity. What they said I have forgotten. But I remember the roll of Meredith's voice. I remember the hesitation and qualification, the humming and hawing of Henry James' voice. So that no doubt I was supplied very early with a vision of greatness and great men. Greatness still seems to me booming, eccentric, set apart; something that we are led up to by our parents and is now entirely extinct.

There they were, on the verge of the drawing room, these great men : while, round the tea table, George and Gerald and Jack talked of the Post Office, the publishing office, and the Law Courts. And I, sitting by the table, was quite unable to make any connection. There were so many different worlds : but they were distant from me. I could not make them cohere ; nor feel myself in touch with them. And I spent many hours of my youth restlessly comparing them. No doubt the distraction and the differences were of use ; as a means of education ; as a way of showing one the contraries. For no sooner had I settled down to my Greek than I would be called off to hear George's case ; then from that I would be told to come up to the study to read German ; and then the gay world of Kitty Maxse would impinge.

THE MEMOIR CLUB CONTRIBUTIONS

(Editor's Note)

The three selections that follow were written by Virginia Woolf to be read aloud to the Memoir Club which had been formed in March 1920. It represented a re-grouping of 'Old Bloomsbury' which had dispersed during the war. According to Leonard Woolf, the thirteen original members of the Memoir Club corresponded exactly to the group of friends known to each other as 'Old Bloomsbury' and to the outside world, more simply, as 'Bloomsbury'.* He includes the following: Vanessa and Clive Bell, Virginia and himself, Desmond and Molly MacCarthy, Adrian Stephen, John Maynard Keynes, E. M. Forster, Roger Fry, Duncan Grant, Saxon Sydney-Turner and Lytton Strachey. Quentin Bell, in his book on Bloomsbury, does not mention Adrian Stephen and Saxon Sydney-Turner in the list of original members of the Memoir Club but adds that had it been formed in 1913 it would probably have included not only these two but 'Gerald Shove perhaps and H. T. J. Norton'.† Such a discrepancy calls attention to an important fact, perhaps one of the few indisputable facts about Bloomsbury, and that is that the vagueness which characterizes its outer limits extends, although to a lesser degree, to its innermost circle.

The group met periodically to dine, to read memoirs and to enjoy each other's company. They agreed at the start upon 'absolute frankness' and this comes through in the memoirs that follow but, as Leonard Woolf warns, 'absolute frankness, even among the most intimate, tends to be relative frankness', and there is a hint of that too.‡ In each of the selections there is an author playing to her audience: familiar but not exactly intimate, reminiscent but never sentimental, clever and often facetious, gambolling over surface oddities rather than probing — thoughtfully, hesitantly — the nature of memory and consciousness, of self and reality, as in "A Sketch of the Past".

---

* *Beginning Again: An Autobiography of the Years 1911 to 1918* (The Hogarth Press; London, 1964), p. 22.

† *Bloomsbury* (Weidenfeld and Nicolson; London, 1968), pp. 14–15.

‡ *Downhill All the Way: An Autobiography of the Years 1919 to 1939* (The Hogarth Press; London, 1967), p. 114.

22 HYDE PARK GATE

"22 Hyde Park Gate", although written almost twenty years before "A Sketch of the Past", takes up the narrative of the Stephens not much beyond the point where the latter ends, that is, after Stella's death but before the death of Leslie Stephen in 1904 and the move of the remaining Stephens to Bloomsbury. In his role as elder brother, George Duckworth undertook, on his own initiative, to chaperone first Vanessa's, and then Virginia's, launching into 'Society'. Needless to say, it was not, in either case, a successful launch.

In the entry for 26 May 1921 in *A Writer's Diary*, Virginia Woolf refers to a conversation she had had on the 25th with Maynard Keynes. "The best thing you ever did, he said, was your Memoir on George. You should pretend to write about real people and make it all up. I was dashed of course (and Oh dear what nonsense—for if George is my climax I'm a mere scribbler)."* The memoir must have been presented to the Memoir Club some time between its formation in March 1920 and 25 May 1921, the date of the conversation with Keynes.†

The present text brings together two typescripts: MH/A.14 and MH/A.15. A.14 consists of twenty-one pages typed by Virginia Woolf with a great many corrections in pen and pencil. The pages have been erratically numbered, suggesting that the typescript may have passed through several stages of revision. A.15 consists of fifteen pages typed by Virginia Woolf, with more than her customary care;‡ yet, on the last page, the line of type slopes off the page, in mid-sentence. There are no written corrections. A.15 is without doubt a revision of pages 1–11 of A.14 for it incorporates the pen and pencil

---

* (The Hogarth Press; London, 1959), p. 35.

† No minutes of the meetings of the Memoir Club are known to have survived.

‡ VW wrote to Ethel Smyth on 2 February 1932: "I'll copy out an old memoir that tumbled out of a box when I was looking for something else, that I wrote ten years ago about our doings with George Duckworth when we were so to speak virgins. It might amuse you: but it needs copying such a mess it's in." (Berg Collection)

corrections on these pages. The text below follows the A.15 typescript as far as it goes and then continues with the A.14 typescript
where it joins A.15 in mid-sentence (p. 11, l. 19). Although A.15s
is clearly more finished stylistically than A.14, the difference
between the two texts is not substantial. The copious written corrections of A.14 indicate considerable reworking, although there is little
doubt that many further changes would have been made had
Virginia Woolf completed the A.15 version.

22 *Hyde Park Gate*

As I have said, the drawing room at Hyde Park Gate was divided by black folding doors picked out with thin lines of raspberry red. We were still much under the influence of Titian. Mounds of plush, Watts' portraits, busts shrined in crimson velvet, enriched the gloom of a room naturally dark and thickly shaded in summer by showers of Virginia Creeper.

But it is of the folding doors that I wish to speak. How could family life have been carried on without them? As soon dispense with water-closets or bathrooms as with folding doors in a family of nine men and women, one of whom into the bargain was an idiot. Suddenly there would be a crisis—a servant dismissed, a lover rejected, pass books opened, or poor Mrs Tyndall who had lately poisoned her husband by mistake come for consolation. On one side of the door Cousin Adeline, Duchess of Bedford, perhaps would be on her knees—the Duke had died tragically at Woburn; Mrs Dolmetsch would be telling how she had found her husband in bed with the parlour-maid or Lisa Stillman would be sobbing that Walter Headlam had chalked her nose with a billiard cue—"which", she cried, "is what comes of smoking a pipe before gentlemen"— and my mother had much ado to persuade her that life had still to be faced, and the flower of virginity was still unplucked in spite of a chalk mark on the nose.

Though dark and agitated on one side, the other side of the door, especially on Sunday afternoons, was cheerful enough. There round the oval tea table with its pink china shell full of spice buns would be found old General Beadle, talking of the Indian Mutiny; or Mr Haldane, or Sir Frederick Pollock—talking of all things under the sun; or old C. B. Clarke, whose name is given to three excessively rare Himalayan ferns; and Professor Wolstenholme, capable, if you interrupted him, of spouting two columns of tea not unmixed with sultanas through his nostrils; after which he would relapse into a drowsy ursine torpor, the result of eating opium to which he had been driven by the unkindness of his wife and the untimely death of his son Oliver who was eaten, somewhere off the coast of Coromandel, by a shark. These gentlemen came and came again; and they were often reinforced by Mr Frederick Gibbs, sometime tutor to the

Prince of Wales, whose imperturbable common sense and fund of information about the colonies in general and Canada in particular were a perpetual irritation to my father who used to wonder whether a brain fever at college in the year 1863 had not something to do with it. These old gentlemen were generally to be found, eating very slowly, staying very late and making themselves agreeable at Christmas-time with curious presents of Indian silver work, and hand bags made from the skin of the ornithorhynchus—as I seem to remember.

The tea table however was also fertilized by a ravishing stream of female beauty—the three Miss Lushingtons, the three Miss Stillmans, and the three Miss Montgomeries—all triplets, all ravishing, but of the nine the paragon for wit, grace, charm and distinction was undoubtedly the lovely Kitty Lushington—now Mrs Leo Maxse. (Their engagement under the jackmanii in the Love Corner at St Ives was my first introduction to the passion of love.)* At the time I speak of she was in process of disengaging herself from Lord Morpeth, and had, I suspect, to explain her motives to my mother, a martinet in such matters, for first promising to marry a man and then breaking it off. My mother believed that all men required an infinity of care. She laid all the blame, I feel sure, upon Kitty. At any rate I have a picture of her as she issued from the secret side of the folding doors bearing on her delicate pink cheeks two perfectly formed pear-shaped crystal tears. They neither fell nor in the least dimmed the lustre of her eyes. She at once became the life and soul of the tea table—perhaps Leo Maxse was there—perhaps Ronny Norman—perhaps Esmé Howard—perhaps Arthur Studd, for the gentlemen were not all old, or all professors by any means—and when my father groaned beneath his breath but very audibly, "Oh Gibbs, what a bore you are!" it was Kitty whom my mother instantly threw into the breach. "Kitty wants to tell you how much she loved your lecture", my mother would cry, and Kitty still with the tears on her cheeks would improvise with the utmost gallantry some compliment or opinion which pacified my father who was extremely sensitive to female charm and largely depended upon female praise. Repenting of his irritation he would press poor Gibbs

---

* In describing the love between Stella and Jack Hills she wrote: "And it was through that engagement that I had my first vision—so intense, so exciting, so rapturous was it that the word vision applies—my first vision then of love between man and woman." See p. 105.

warmly by the hand and beg him to come soon again — which needless to say, poor Gibbs did.

And then there would come dancing into the room rubbing his hands, wrinkling his forehead, the most remarkable figure, as I sometimes think, that our household contained. I have alluded to a grisly relic of another age which we used to disinter from the nursery wardrobe — Herbert Duckworth's wig. (Herbert Duckworth had been a barrister.) Herbert Duckworth's son — George Herbert — was by no means grisly. His hair curled naturally in dark crisp ringlets; he was six foot high; he had been in the Eton Eleven; he was now cramming at Scoones' in the hope of passing the Foreign Office examination. When Miss Willett of Brighton saw him 'throwing off his ulster' in the middle of her drawing room she was moved to write an Ode Comparing George Duckworth to the Hermes of Praxiteles — which Ode my mother kept in her writing table drawer, along with a little Italian medal that George had won for saving a peasant from drowning. Miss Willett was reminded of the Hermes; but if you looked at him closely you noticed that one of his ears was pointed; and the other round; you also noticed that though he had the curls of a God and the ears of a faun he had unmistakably the eyes of a pig. So strange a compound can seldom have existed. And in the days I speak of, God, faun and pig were all in all alive, all in opposition, and in their conflicts producing the most astonishing eruptions.

To begin with the God — well, he was only a plaster cast perhaps of Miss Willett's Hermes, but I cannot deny that the benign figure of George Duckworth teaching his small half-brothers and sisters by the hour on a strip of coco-nut matting to play forward with a perfectly straight bat had something Christlike about it. He was certainly Christian rather than Pagan in his divinity, for it soon became clear that this particular forward stroke to be applied to every ball indifferently, was a symbol of moral rectitude, and that one could neither slog nor bowl a sneak without paltering rather dangerously (as poor Gerald Duckworth used to do) with the ideals of a sportsman and an English gentleman. Then, he would run miles to fetch cushions; he was always shutting doors and opening windows; it was always George who said the tactful thing, and broke bad news, and braved my father's irritation, and read aloud to us when we had the whooping cough, and remembered the birthdays of aunts, and sent turtle soup to the invalids, and attended funerals, and took children to the pantomime—oh yes, whatever else George might be he was certainly a saint.

But then there was the faun. Now this animal was at once sportive and demonstrative and thus often at variance with the self-sacrificing nature of the God. It was quite a common thing to come into the drawing room and find George on his knees with his arms extended, addressing my mother, who might be adding up the weekly books, in tones of fervent adoration. Perhaps he had been staying with the Chamberlains for the week-end. But he lavished caresses, endearments, enquiries and embraces as if, after forty years in the Australian bush, he had at last returned to the home of his youth and found an aged mother still alive to welcome him. Meanwhile we gathered round—the dinner bell had already rung—awkward, but appreciative. Few families, we felt, could exhibit such a scene as this. Tears rushed to his eyes with equal abandonment. For example when he had a tooth out he flung himself into the cook's arms in a paroxysm of weeping. When Judith Blunt refused him he sat at the head of the table sobbing loudly, but continuing to eat. He cried when he was vaccinated. He was fond of sending telegrams which began "My darling mother" and went on to say that he would be dining out. (I copied this style of his, I regret to say, with disastrous results on one celebrated occasion. "She is an angel" I wired, on hearing that Flora Russell had accepted him, and signed my nickname 'Goat'. "She is an aged Goat" was the version that arrived, at Islay, and had something to do, George said, with Flora's reluctance to ally herself with the Stephen family.) But all this exuberance of emotion was felt to be wholly to George's credit. It proved not only how deep and warm his feelings were, but how marvellously he had kept the open heart and simple manners of a child.

But when nature refused him two pointed ears and gave him only one she knew, I think, what she was about. In his wildest paroxysms of emotion, when he bellowed with grief, or danced round the room, leaping like a kid, and flung himself on his knees before the Dowager Lady Carnarvon there was always something self conscious, a little uneasy about him, as though he were not quite sure of the effect—as though the sprightly faun had somehow been hobbled together with a timid and conventional old sheep.

It is true that he was abnormally stupid. He passed the simplest examinations with incredible difficulty. For years he was crammed by Mr Scoones; and again and again he failed to pass the Foreign

Office examination. He had existed all his life upon jobs found for him by his friends. His small brown eyes seemed perpetually to be boring into something too hard for them to penetrate. But when one compares them to the eyes of a pig, one is alluding not merely to their stupidity, or to their greed—George, I have been told, had the reputation of being the greediest young man in London ball-rooms—but to something obstinate and pertinacious in their expression as if the pig were grouting for truffles with his snout and would by sheer persistency succeed in unearthing them. Never shall I forget the pertinacity with which he learnt "Love in the Valley" by heart in order to impress Flora Russell; or the determination with which he mastered the first volume of *Middlemarch* for the same purpose; and how immensely he was relieved when he left the second volume in a train and got my father, whose set was ruined, to declare that in his opinion one volume of *Middlemarch* was enough. Had his obstinacy been directed solely to self-improvement there would have been no call for us to complain. I myself might even have been of use to him. But it gradually became clear that he was muddling out a scheme, a plan of campaign, a system of life—I scarcely know what to call it —and then we had every reason to feel the earth tremble beneath our feet and the heavens darken. For George Duckworth had become after my mother's death, for all practical purposes, the head of the family. My father was deaf, eccentric, absorbed in his work, and entirely shut off from the world. The management of affairs fell upon George. It was usually said that he was father and mother, sister and brother in one—and all the old ladies of Kensington and Belgravia added with one accord that Heaven had blessed those poor Stephen girls beyond belief, and it remained for them to prove that they were worthy of such devotion.

But what was George Duckworth thinking and what was there alarming in the sight of him as he sat in the red leather arm-chair after dinner, mechanically stroking the dachshund Schuster, and lugubriously glancing at the pages of George Eliot? Well, he might be thinking about the crest on the post office notepaper, and how nice it would look picked out in red (he was now Austen Chamberlain's private secretary) or he might be thinking how the Duchess of St Albans had given up using fish knives at dinner; or how Mrs Grenfell had asked him to stay and he had created as he thought a good impression by refusing; at the same time he was revolving in the slow whirlpool of his brain schemes of the utmost thoughtfulness—

plans for sending us for treats; for providing us with riding lessons; for finding jobs for some of poor Augusta Croft's innumerable penniless children. But the alarming thing was that he looked not merely muddled and emotional but obstinate. He looked as if he had made up his mind about something and would refuse to budge an inch. At the time it was extremely difficult to say what he had made up his mind to, but after the lapse of many years I think it may be said brutally and baldly, that George had made up his mind to rise in the social scale. He had a curious inborn reverence for the British aristocracy; the beauty of our great aunts had allied us in the middle of the nineteenth century with, I think I am right in saying, two dukes and quite a number of earls and countesses. They naturally showed no particular wish to remember the connection but George did his best to live up to it. His reverence for the symbols of greatness now that he was attached to a Cabinet Minister had fuller scope. His talk was all of ivory buttons that the coachmen of Cabinet Ministers wear in their coats; of having the entrée at Court; of baronies descending in the female line; of countesses secreting the diamonds of Marie Antoinette in black boxes under their beds. His secret dreams as he sat in the red leather chair stroking Schuster were all of marrying a wife with diamonds, and having a coachman with a button, and having the entrée at Court. But the danger was that his dreams were secret even to himself. Had you told him—and I think Vanessa did once—that he was a snob, he would have burst into tears. What he liked, he explained, was to know 'nice people'; Lady Jeune was nice; so were Lady Sligo, Lady Carnarvon and Lady Leitrim. Poor Mrs Clifford, on the other hand, was not; nor was old Mr Wolstenholme; of all our old friends, Kitty Maxse, who might have been Lady Morpeth, came nearest to his ideal. It was not a question of birth or wealth; it was—and then if you pressed him further he would seize you in his arms and cry out that he refused to argue with those he loved. "Kiss me, kiss me, you beloved", he would vociferate; and the argument was drowned in kisses. Everything was drowned in kisses. He lived in the thickest emotional haze, and as his passions increased and his desires became more vehement—he lived, Jack Hills assured me, in complete chastity until his marriage—one felt like an unfortunate minnow shut up in the same tank with an unwieldy and turbulent whale.

Nothing stood in the way of his advancement. He was a bachelor of prepossessing appearance though inclined to fat, aged about thirty years, with an independent income of something over a thousand a year. As private secretary to Austen Chamberlain he was as a matter of course invited to all the great parties of all the great peers. Hostesses had no time to remember, if they had ever known, that the Duckworths had made their money in cotton, or coal, not a hundred years ago, and did not really rank, as George made out, among the ancient families of Somersetshire. For I have it on the best authority that when the original Duckworth acquired Orchard-leigh about the year 1810 he filled it with casts from the Greek to which he had attached not merely fig leaves for the Gods but aprons for the Goddesses — much to the amusement of the Lords of Longleat who never forgot that old Duckworth had sold cotton by the yard and probably bought his aprons cheap. George, as I say, could have mounted alone to the highest pinnacles of London society. His mantelpiece was a gallery of invitation cards from every house in London. Why then did he insist upon cumbering himself with a couple of half-sisters who were more than likely to drag him down? It is probably useless to enquire. George's mind swam and steamed like a cauldron of rich Irish stew. He believed that aristocratic society was possessed of all the virtues and all the graces. He believed that his family had been entrusted to his care. He believed that it was his sacred duty — but when he reached that point his emotions over-came him; he began to sob; he flung himself on his knees; he seized Vanessa in his arms; he implored her in the name of her mother, of her grandmother, by all that was sacred in the female sex and holy in the traditions of our family to accept Lady Arthur Russell's invitation to dinner, to spend the week-end with the Chamberlains at Highbury.

I cannot conceal my own opinion that Vanessa was to blame; not indeed that she could help herself, but if, I sometimes think, she had been born with one shoulder higher than another, with a limp, with a squint, with a large mole on her left cheek, both our lives would have been changed for the better. As it was, George had a good deal of reason on his side. It was plain that Vanessa in her white satin dress made by Mrs Young, wearing a single flawless amethyst round her neck, and a blue enamel butterfly in her hair — the gifts, of course, of George himself — beautiful, motherless, aged only eighteen, was a touching spectacle, an ornament for any dinner table, a potential peeress, anything might be made of such precious material as she was — outwardly at least; and to be seen hovering round her, providing her with jewels, and Arab horses, and expensive clothes, whispering encouragement, lavishing embraces which were not entirely concealed from the eyes of strangers, redounded to the credit of George himself and invested his figure with a pathos which it would not otherwise have had in the eyes of the dowagers of Mayfair. Unfortunately, what was inside Vanessa did not altogether correspond with what was outside. Underneath the necklaces and the enamel butterflies was one passionate desire—for paint and turpentine, for turpentine and paint. But poor George was no psychologist. His perceptions were obtuse. He never saw within. He was completely at a loss when Vanessa said she did not wish to stay with the Chamberlains at Highbury; and would not dine with Lady Arthur Russell—a rude, tyrannical old woman, with a bloodstained complexion and the manners of a turkey cock. He argued, he wept, he complained to Aunt Mary Fisher, who said that she could not believe her ears. Every battery was turned upon Vanessa. She was told that she was selfish, unwomanly, callous and incredibly ungrateful considering the treasures of affection that had been lavished upon her—the Arab horse she rode and the slabs of bright blue enamel which she wore.* Still she persisted. She did not wish to dine with Lady Arthur Russell. As the season wore on, every morning brought its card of invitation for Mr Duckworth and Miss Stephen; and every evening witnessed a battle between them. For the first year or so George, I suppose, was usually the victor. Off they went, in the hansom cab of those days and late at night Vanessa would come into my room complaining that she had been dragged from party to party, where she knew no one, and had been bored to death by the civilities of young men from the Foreign Office and the condescensions of old ladies of title. The more Vanessa resisted, the more George's natural obstinacy persisted. At last there was a crisis. Lady Arthur Russell was giving a series of select parties on Thursday evenings in South Audley Street. Vanessa had sat through one entire evening without opening her lips. George insisted that she must go next week and make amends, or he said, "Lady Arthur will never ask you to her house again." They argued until it was getting too late to dress. At last Vanessa, more in desperation than in concession, rushed upstairs, flung on her clothes and announced

* The A.15 revision of A.14, pp. 1–11, ends in the middle of this sentence. From this point the text follows the less revised A.14 ts.

that she was ready to go. Off they went. What happened in the cab
will never be known. But whenever they reached 2 South Audley
Street—and they reached it several times in the course of the
evening—one or the other was incapable of getting out. George
refused to enter with Vanessa in such a passion; and Vanessa refused
to enter with George in tears. So the cabman had to be told to drive
once more round the Park. Whether they ever managed to alight I
do not know.

But next morning as I was sitting spelling out my Greek George
came into my room carrying in his hand a small velvet box. He
presented me with the jewel it contained—a Jews' harp made of
enamel with a pinkish blob of matter swinging in the centre which I
regret to say only fetched a few shillings when I sold it the other day.
But his face showed that he had come upon a different errand. His
face was sallow and scored with innumerable wrinkles, for his skin
was as loose and flexible as a pug dog's, and he would express his
anguish in the most poignant manner by puckering lines, folds, and
creases from forehead to chin. His manner was stern. His bearing
rigid. If Miss Willett of Brighton could have seen him then she
would certainly have compared him to Christ on the cross. After
giving me the Jews' harp he stood before the fire in complete
silence. Then, as I expected, he began to tell me his version of the
preceding night—wrinkling his forehead more than ever, but
speaking with a restraint that was at once bitter and manly. Never,
never again, he said, would he ask Vanessa to go out with him. He
had seen a look in her eyes which positively frightened him. It should
never be said of him that he made her do what she did not wish to
do. Here he quivered, but checked himself. Then he went on to say
that he had only done what he knew my mother would have wished
him to do. His two sisters were the most precious things that remained to him. His home had always meant more to him—more
than he could say, and here he became agitated, struggled for composure, and then burst into a statement which was at once dark and
extremely lurid. We were driving Gerald from the house, he cried—
when a young man was not happy at home—he himself had always
been content—but if his sisters—if Vanessa refused to go out with
him—if he could not bring his friends to the house—in short, it was
clear that the chaste, the immaculate George Duckworth would be
forced into the arms of whores. Needless to say he did not put it like
that; and I could only conjure up in my virgin consciousness, dimly

irradiated by having read the "Symposium" with Miss Case, horrible visions of the vices to which young men were driven whose sisters did not make them happy at home. So we went on talking for an hour or two. The end of it was that he begged me, and I agreed, to go a few nights later to the Dowager Marchioness of Sligo's ball. I had already been to May Week at Cambridge, and my recollections of gallopading round the room with Hawtrey, or sitting on the stairs and quizzing the dancers with Clive,* were such as to make me wonder why Vanessa found dances in London so utterly detestable. A few nights later I discovered for myself. After two hours of standing about in Lady Sligo's ball-room, of waiting to be introduced to strange young men, of dancing a round with Conrad Russell or with Esmé Howard, of dancing very badly, of being left without a partner, of being told by George that I looked lovely but must hold myself upright, I retired to an ante-room and hoped that a curtain concealed me. For some time it did. At length old Lady Sligo discovered me, judged the situation for herself and being a kind old peeress with a face like a rubicund sow's carried me off to the dining room, cut me a large slice of iced cake, and left me to devour it by myself in a corner.

On that occasion George was lenient. We left about two o'clock, and on the way home he praised me warmly, and assured me that I only needed practice to be a great social success. A few days later he told me that the Dowager Countess of Carnarvon particularly wished to make my acquaintance, and had invited me to dinner. As we drove across the Park he stroked my hand, and told me how he hoped that I should make friends with Elsie—for so both he and Vanessa had called her for some time at her own request—how I must not be frightened—how though she had been vice-reine of Canada and vice-reine of Ireland she was simplicity itself—always since the death of her husband dressed in black—refused to wear any of her jewels though she had inherited the diamonds of Marie Antoinette—and was the one woman, he said, with a man's sense of honour. The portrait he drew was of great distinction and bereavement. There would also be present her sister, Mrs Popham of Littlecote, a lady also of distinction and also bereaved, for her husband, Dick Popham of Littlecote, came of an ancient unhappy race, cursed in the reign of Henry the Eighth, since which time the property had never descended from father to son. Sure enough Mary

* Ralph Hawtrey and Clive Bell.

Popham was childless, and Dick Popham was in a lunatic asylum. I felt that I was approaching a house of grandeur and desolation, and was not a little impressed. But I could see nothing alarming either in Elsie Carnarvon or in Mrs Popham of Littlecote. They were a couple of spare prim little women, soberly dressed in high black dresses, with grey hair strained off their foreheads, rather prominent blue eyes, and slightly protruding front teeth. We sat down to dinner.

The conversation was mild and kindly. Indeed I soon felt that I could not only reply to their questions—was I fond of painting?—was I fond of reading?—did I help my father in his work?—but could initiate remarks of my own. George had always complained of Vanessa's silence. I would prove that I could talk. So off I started. Heaven knows what devil prompted me—or why to Lady Carnarvon and Mrs Popham of Littlecote of all people in the world I, a chit of eighteen, should have chosen to discourse upon the need of expressing the emotions! That, I said, was the great lack of modern life. The ancients, I said, discussed everything in common. Had Lady Carnarvon ever read the dialogues of Plato? "We—both men and women—" once launched it was difficult to stop, nor was I sure that my audacity was not holding them spell-bound with admiration. I felt that I was earning George's gratitude for ever. Suddenly a twitch, a shiver, a convulsion of amazing expressiveness, shook the Countess by my side; her diamonds, of which she wore a chaste selection,* flashed in my eyes; and stopping, I saw George Duckworth blushing crimson on the other side of the table. I realised that I had committed some unspeakable impropriety. Lady Carnarvon and Mrs Popham began at once to talk of something entirely different; and directly dinner was over George, pretending to help me on with my cloak, whispered in my ear in a voice of agony, "They're not used to young women saying anything—." And then as if to apologize to Lady Carnarvon for my ill breeding, I saw him withdraw with her behind a pillar in the hall, and though Mrs Popham of Littlecote tried to attract my attention to a fine specimen of Moorish metal work which hung on the wall, we both distinctly heard them kiss. But the evening was not over. Lady Carnarvon had taken tickets for the French actors, who were then appearing in some play whose name I have forgotten. We had stalls of course, and filed soberly to our places in the very centre of the crowded theatre. The

* Cf. p. 151, ll.31-3.

curtain went up. Snubbed, shy, indignant, and uncomfortable, I paid little attention to the play. But after a time I noticed that Lady Carnarvon on one side of me, and Mrs Popham on the other, were both agitated by the same sort of convulsive twitching which had taken them at dinner. What could be the matter? They were positively squirming in their seats. I looked at the stage. The hero and heroine were pouring forth a flood of voluble French which I could not disentangle. Then they stopped. To my great astonishment the lady leapt over the back of a sofa; the gentleman followed her. Round and round the stage they dashed, the lady shrieking, the man groaning and grunting in pursuit. It was a fine piece of realistic acting. As the pursuit continued, the ladies beside me held to the arms of their stalls with claws of iron. Suddenly, the actress dropped exhausted upon the sofa, and the man with a howl of gratification, loosening his clothes quite visibly, leapt on top of her. The curtain fell. Lady Carnarvon, Mrs Popham of Littlecote and George Duckworth rose simultaneously. Not a word was said. Out we filed. And as our procession made its way down the stalls I saw Arthur Cane leap up in his seat like a jack-in-the-box, amazed and considerably amused that George Duckworth and Lady Carnarvon of all people should have taken a girl of eighteen to see the French actors copulate upon the stage.

The brougham was waiting, and Mrs Popham of Littlecote, without speaking a word or even looking at me, immediately secreted herself inside it. Nor could Lady Carnarvon bring herself to face me. She took my hand, and said in a tremulous voice—her elderly cheeks were flushed with emotion—"I do hope, Miss Stephen, that the evening has not tired you very much." Then she stepped into the carriage, and the two bereaved ladies returned to Bruton Street. George meanwhile had secured a cab. He was much confused, and yet very angry. I could see that my remarks at dinner upon the dialogues of Plato rankled bitterly in his mind. And he told the cabman to go, not back to Hyde Park Gate as I hoped, but on to Melbury Road.

"It's quite early still", he said in his most huffy manner as he sat down. "And I think you want a little practice in how to behave to strangers.* It's not your fault of course, but you have been out much less than most girls of your age." So it appeared that my education

* There are three to four short illegible words written above 'how to behave' which is itself an interlinear correction; 'in' is a doubtful reading.

was to be continued, and that I was about to have another lesson in the art of behaviour at the house of Mrs Holman Hunt. She was giving a large evening party. Melbury Road was lined with hansoms, four-wheelers, hired flies, and an occasional carriage drawn by a couple of respectable family horses. "A very *dritte* crowd", said George disdainfully as we took our place in the queue. Indeed all our old family friends were gathered together in the Moorish Hall,* and directly I came in I recognised the Stillmans, the Lushingtons, the Montgomeries, the Morrises, the Burne-Joneses—Mr Gibbs, Professor Wolstenholme and General Beadle would certainly have been there too had they not all been sleeping for many years beneath the sod. The effect of the Moorish Hall, after Bruton Street, was garish, a little eccentric, and certainly very dowdy. The ladies were intense and untidy; the gentlemen had fine foreheads and short evening trousers, in some cases revealing a pair of bright red Pre-Raphaelite socks. George stepped among them like a Prince in disguise. I soon attached myself to a little covey of Kensington ladies who were being conveyed by Gladys Holman Hunt across the Moorish Hall to the studio. There we found old Holman Hunt himself dressed in a long Jaeger dressing gown, holding forth to a large gathering about the ideas which had inspired him in painting "The Light of the World", a copy of which stood upon an easel. He sipped cocoa and stroked his flowing beard as he talked, and we sipped cocoa and shifted our shawls—for the room was chilly—as we listened. Occasionally some of us strayed off to examine with reverent murmurs other bright pictures upon other easels, but the tone of the assembly was devout, high-minded, and to me after the tremendous experiences of the evening, soothingly and almost childishly simple. George was never lacking in respect for old men of recognised genius, and he now advanced with his opera hat pressed beneath his arm; drew his feet together, and made a profound bow over Holman Hunt's hand. Holman Hunt had no notion who he was, or indeed who any of us were; but went on sipping his cocoa, stroking his beard, and explaining what ideas had inspired him in painting "The Light of the World", until we left.

At last—at last—the evening was over.

* VW appears to have confused the Moorish Hall in nearby Leighton House with the Moorish decorations in Hunt's house. For a description of the latter, see *My Grandmothers and I* (London, 1960) by Diana Holman-Hunt.

I went up to my room, took off my beautiful white satin dress, and unfastened the three pink carnations which had been pinned to my breast by the Jews' harp. Was it really possible that tomorrow I should open my Greek dictionary and go on spelling out the dialogues of Plato with Miss Case? I felt I knew much more about the dialogues of Plato than Miss Case could ever do. I felt old and experienced and disillusioned and angry, amused and excited, full of mystery, alarm and bewilderment. In a confused whirlpool of sensation I stood slipping off my petticoats, withdrew my long white gloves, and hung my white silk stockings over the back of a chair. Many different things were whirling round in my mind—diamonds and countesses, copulations, the dialogues of Plato, Mad Dick Popham and "The Light of the World". Ah, how pleasant it would be to stretch out in bed, fall asleep and forget them all!

Sleep had almost come to me. The room was dark. The house silent. Then, creaking stealthily, the door opened; treading gingerly, someone entered. "Who?" I cried. "Don't be frightened", George whispered. "And don't turn on the light, oh beloved. Beloved—" and he flung himself on my bed, and took me in his arms.

Yes, the old ladies of Kensington and Belgravia never knew that George Duckworth was not only father and mother, brother and sister to those poor Stephen girls; he was their lover also.

OLD BLOOMSBURY

(*Editor's Note*)

"Old Bloomsbury" followed "22 Hyde Park Gate" as Virginia Woolf's contribution to the Memoir Club and was probably delivered within a year of the latter, that is, near the end of 1921 or in 1922.* It takes up where "22 Hyde Park Gate" ends, at "the height of the season of 1903", but it passes quickly over the move from Hyde Park Gate after Leslie Stephen's death to the establishment of the Stephens at 46 Gordon Square, Bloomsbury.

In viewing the origins of 'Old Bloomsbury' from the angle of Hyde Park Gate, Virginia Woolf is giving an account which would, in some respects at least, differ from that given by one who had passed through Cambridge on the way to Bloomsbury; just as the accounts of those who belonged to the Cambridge 'Apostles' do not in every respect accord with that of Clive Bell, for example, who did not belong.† The many versions of where it all started and when—at Cambridge with the 'Midnight Society' or the 'Apostles' in 1899, with 'Thursday evenings' at Gordon Square in 1905, or in the district of Bloomsbury about 1912, as Leonard Woolf suggests‡—merely underline once again the vagueness of the limits of Bloomsbury.

The throwing open of windows which flooded with fresh air and light the dark, cramped, heavily upholstered upper middle class Victorian world in which many of the 'Bloomsberries' had spent their youth, did not happen all at once, as this memoir makes clear. Virginia Woolf conveys—albeit with the emphasis other than where it might have been placed by one of the painters of the group, say Vanessa Bell or Roger Fry—the drama and the humour of certain critical events in the development of pre-war Bloomsbury.

The present text (Library reference number MH/A.16) is based on thirty-seven pages typed by Virginia Woolf with corrections in pen and pencil. The beginning of the last paragraph, however, comes from a one page mutilated and corrected typescript which was separated from A.16 and is now in the Berg Collection. The

---

* Quentin Bell writes "that it was read to the Memoir Club (in about 1922)." (QB, I, pp. 124–5n.)

† *Old Friends* (Chatto and Windus; London, 1956), p. 129.

‡ *Beginning Again*, pp. 21–22.

curator has generously given permission for this fragment to be included here. The typescript is erratically paginated in overlapping groups; the quality of the typing is poor; and the corrections are sometimes lengthy and often difficult to decipher.

Old Bloomsbury

At Molly's command I have had to write a memoir of Old Bloomsbury — of Bloomsbury from 1904 to 1914.* Naturally I see Bloomsbury only from my own angle — not from yours. For this I must ask you to make allowances. From my angle then, one approaches Bloomsbury through Hyde Park Gate — that little irregular cul-de-sac which lies next to Queen's Gate and opposite to Kensington Gardens. And we must look for a moment at that very tall house on the left hand side near the bottom which begins by being stucco and ends by being red brick; which is so high and yet — as I can say now that we have sold it — so rickety that it seems as if a very high wind would topple it over.

I was undressing at the top of that house when my last memoir ended, in my bedroom at the back. My white satin dress was on the floor. The faint smell of kid gloves was in the air. My necklace of seed-pearls was tangled with hairpins on the dressing table. I had just come back from a party — from a series of parties indeed, for it was a memorable night in the height of the season of 1903. I had dined with Lady Carnarvon in Bruton Street; I had seen George undoubtedly kiss her among the pillars in the hall; I had talked much too much — about my emotions on hearing music — at dinner; Lady Carnarvon, Mrs Popham, George and myself had then gone to the most indecent French play I have ever seen. We had risen like a flock of partridges at the end of the first act. Mrs Popham's withered cheeks had burnt crimson. Elsie's grey locks had streamed in the wind. We had parted, with great embarrassment on their side, on the pavement, and Elsie had said she did hope I wasn't tired — which meant, I felt, she hoped I wouldn't lose my virginity or something like that. And then we had gone on — George and I in a hansom together to another party, for George said, to my intense shame, I had talked much too much and I must really learn how to behave — we had gone on to the Holman Hunts, where "The Light of the World" had just come back from its mission to the chief cities of the British Empire, and Mr Edward Clifford, Mrs Russell Barrington, Mrs Freshfield and I know not what distinguished old

* Molly MacCarthy, wife of Desmond, was an original member of the Memoir Club and secretary when this paper was presented.

159

gentlemen with black ribbons attached to their eyeglasses and elderly ladies with curious vertebrae showing through their real but rather ragged old lace had talked in hushed voices of the master's art while the master himself sat in a skull cap drinking, in spite of the June night, hot cocoa from a mug.

It was long past midnight that I got into bed and sat reading a page or two of *Marius the Epicurean* for which I had then a passion. There would be a tap at the door; the light would be turned out and George would fling himself on my bed, cuddling and kissing and otherwise embracing me in order, as he told Dr Savage later, to comfort me for the fatal illness of my father—who was dying three or four storeys lower down of cancer.

But it is the house that I would ask you to imagine for a moment for, though Hyde Park Gate seems now so distant from Bloomsbury, its shadow falls across it. 46 Gordon Square could never have meant what it did had not 22 Hyde Park Gate preceded it.* It was a house of innumerable small oddly shaped rooms built to accommodate not one family but three. For besides the three Duckworths and the four Stephens there was also Thackeray's grand-daughter, a vacant-eyed girl whose idiocy was becoming daily more obvious, who could hardly read, who would throw the scissors into the fire, who was tongue-tied and stammered and yet had to appear at table with the rest of us.† To house the lot of us, now a storey would be thrown out on top, now a dining room flung out at bottom. My mother, I believe, sketched what she wanted on a sheet of notepaper to save the architect's fees. These three families had poured all their possessions into this one house. One never knew when one rummaged in the many dark cupboards and wardrobes whether one would disinter Herbert Duckworth's barrister's wig, my father's clergyman's collar, or a sheet scribbled over with drawings by Thackeray which we afterwards sold to Pierpont Morgan for a considerable sum.‡ Old letters filled dozens of black tin boxes. One opened them and got a terrific whiff of the past. There were chests of heavy family plate. There were hoards of china and glass. Eleven

---

* When Leslie Stephen died in 1904 the four Stephens moved from 22 Hyde Park Gate to 46 Gordon Square, Bloomsbury.

† Laura Stephen; she died in an asylum in York in 1945.

‡ In a letter to Violet Dickinson (22 July 1906), Virginia writes: "Thoby made £1000. *one thousand pounds* by selling 10 pages of Thackerays Lord Bateman. George sold it to Pierpont Morgan." (*Letters*, I, No. 279.)

people aged between eight and sixty lived there, and were waited upon by seven servants, while various old women and lame men did odd jobs with rakes and pails by day.

The house was dark because the street was so narrow that one could see Mrs Redgrave washing her neck in her bedroom across the way; also because my mother who had been brought up in the Watts-Venetian-Little Holland House tradition had covered the furniture in red velvet and painted the woodwork black with thin gold lines upon it. The house was also completely quiet. Save for an occasional hansom or butcher's cart nothing ever passed the door. One heard footsteps tapping down the street before we saw a top hat or a bonnet; one almost always knew who it was that passed; it might be Sir Arthur Clay; the Muir Mackenzies or the white-nosed Miss or the red-nosed Mrs Redgrave. Here then seventeen or eighteen people lived in small bedrooms with one bathroom and three water-closets between them. Here the four of us were born; here my grandmother died; here my mother died; here my father died; here Stella became engaged to Jack Hills* and two doors further down the street after three months of marriage she died too. When I look back upon that house it seems to me so crowded with scenes of family life, grotesque, comic and tragic; with the violent emotions of youth, revolt, despair, intoxicating happiness, immense boredom, with parties of the famous and the dull; with rages again, George and Gerald; with love scenes with Jack Hills; with passionate affection for my father alternating with passionate hatred of him, all tingling and vibrating in an atmosphere of youthful bewilderment and curiosity—that I feel suffocated by the recollection. The place seemed tangled and matted with emotion. I could write the history of every mark and scratch in my room, I wrote later. The walls and the rooms had in sober truth been built to our shape. We had permeated the whole vast fabric—it has since been made into an hotel—with our family history. It seemed as if the house and the family which had lived in it, thrown† together as they were by so many deaths, so many emotions, so many traditions, must endure for ever. And then suddenly in one night both vanished.

When I recovered from the illness which was not unnaturally the result of all these emotions and complications, 22 Hyde Park Gate no

* Stella and Jack *became* engaged at Hindhead but Stella, of course, lived at Hyde Park Gate during the engagement.

† 'thrown' is a doubtful reading.

longer existed.* While I had lain in bed at the Dickinsons' house at Welwyn thinking that the birds were singing Greek choruses and that King Edward was using the foulest possible language among Ozzie Dickinson's azaleas, Vanessa had wound up Hyde Park Gate once and for all. She had sold; she had burnt; she had sorted; she had torn up. Sometimes I believe she had actually to get men with hammers to batter down—so wedged into each other had the walls and the cabinets become. But now all the rooms stood empty. Furniture vans had carted off all the different belongings.† For not only had the furniture been dispersed. The family which had seemed equally wedged together had broken apart too. George had married Lady Margaret. Gerald had taken a bachelor flat in Berkeley Street. Laura had been finally incarcerated with a doctor in an asylum; Jack Hills had entered on a political career. The four of us were therefore left alone. And Vanessa—looking at a map of London and seeing how far apart they were—had decided that we should leave Kensington and start life afresh in Bloomsbury.

It was thus that 46 Gordon Square came into existence. When one sees it today, Gordon Square is not one of the most romantic of the Bloomsbury squares. It has neither the distinction of Fitzroy Square nor the majesty of Mecklenburgh Square. It is prosperous middle class and thoroughly mid-Victorian. But I can assure you that in October 1904 it was the most beautiful, the most exciting, the most romantic place in the world. To begin with it was astonishing to stand at the drawing room window and look into all those trees; the tree which shoots its branches up into the air and lets them fall in a shower; the tree which glistens after rain like the body of a seal— instead of looking at old Mrs Redgrave washing her neck across the way. The light and the air after the rich red gloom of Hyde Park Gate were a revelation. Things one had never seen in the darkness there—Watts pictures, Dutch cabinets, blue china—shone out for the first time in the drawing room at Gordon Square. After the muffled silence of Hyde Park Gate the roar of traffic was positively

* This was Virginia's second serious mental breakdown which began in May 1904. She spent almost three months at Burnham Wood, Welwyn, where she made her first attempt at suicide. She was cared for by Violet Dickinson, a family friend of the Duckworths, who, since 1902, had been Virginia's most intimate friend. Ozzie is Violet's brother.

† In this sentence and the following the additions in the ms, in both pen and pencil are confusing and incomplete and therefore have not been included.

alarming. Odd characters, sinister, strange, prowled and slunk past our windows. But what was even more exhilarating was the extraordinary increase of space. At Hyde Park Gate one had only a bedroom in which to read or see one's friends. Here Vanessa and I each had a sitting room; there was the large double drawing room; and a study on the ground floor. To make it all newer and fresher, the house had been completely done up. Needless to say the Watts-Venetian tradition of red plush and black paint had been reversed; we had entered the Sargent-Furse era; white and green chintzes were everywhere; and instead of Morris wall-papers with their intricate patterns we decorated our walls with washes of plain distemper. We were full of experiments and reforms. We were going to do without table napkins, we were to have [large supplies of] Bromo instead; we were going to paint; to write; to have coffee after dinner instead of tea at nine o'clock. Everything was going to be new; everything was going to be different. Everything was on trial.

We were, it appears, extremely social. For some months in the winter of 1904–05 I kept a diary from which I find that we were for ever lunching and dining out and loitering about the book shops — "Bloomsbury is ever so much more interesting than Kensington", I wrote — or going to a concert or visiting a picture gallery and coming home to find the drawing room full of the oddest collections of people. "Cousin Henry Prinsep, Miss Millais, Ozzie Dickinson and Victor Marshall all came this afternoon and stayed late, so that we had only just time to rush off to a Mr Rutter's lecture on Impressionism at the Grafton Gallery ... Lady Hylton, V. Dickinson and E. Coltman came to tea. We lunched with the Shaw Stewarts and met an art critic called Nicholls. Sir Hugh seemed nice but there isn't much in him ... I lunched with the Protheroes and met the Bertrand Russells. It was very amusing. Thoby and I dined with the Cecils and went on to the St Loe Stracheys where we knew a great many people ... I called for Nessa and Thoby at Mrs Flower's and we went on to a dance at the Hobhouses'. Nessa was in a state of great misery today waiting for Mr Tonks who came at one to criticise her pictures. He is a man with a cold bony face, prominent eyes and a look of serenity and boredom. Meg Booth and Sir Fred Pollock came to tea ... " So it goes on; but among all these short records of parties, of how the chintzes came home and how we went to the Zoo and how we went to *Peter Pan*, there are a few entries which bear on Bloomsbury. On Thursday March 2nd 1905 Violet

Dickinson brought a clergyman's wife to tea and Sydney-Turner and Strachey came after dinner and we talked till twelve. On Wednesday the 8th of March: "Margaret* sent round her new motor car this afternoon and we took Violet to pay a series of calls, but we, of course, forgot our cards. Then I went on to the Waterloo Road and lectured (a class of working men and women) on the Greek Myths.† Home and found Bell, and we talked about the nature of good till almost one!"

On the 16th [of] March Miss Power and Miss Malone dined with us. Sydney-Turner and Gerald came in after dinner—the first of our Thursday evenings. On the 23rd [of] March nine people came to our evening and stayed till one.

A few days later I went to Spain, and the duty which I laid on myself of recording every sight and sound, every wave and hill, sickened me with diary writing so that I stopped—with this last entry: May the 11th—"Our evening: gay Bell, D. MacCarthy and Gerald—who shocked the cultured."

So my diary ends just as it might have become interesting. Yet I think it is clear even in this brief record in which every sort of doing is piled up higgledy-piggledy that these few meetings of Bloomsbury in its infancy differed from the rest. These are the only occasions when I do not merely say I had met so and so and thought him long-faced like Reginald Smith or pompous like Moorsom, or quite easy to get on with, but nothing much in him, like Sir Hugh Shaw Stewart. I say we talked to Strachey and Sydney-Turner. I add with a note of exclamation that we talked with Bell about the nature of good till one! And I did not use notes of exclamation often—and once more indeed—when I say that I smoked a cigarette with Beatrice Thynne!‡

These Thursday evening parties were, as far as I am concerned, the germ from which sprang all that has since come to be called—in newspapers, in novels, in Germany, in France—even, I daresay, in Turkey and Timbuktu—by the name of Bloomsbury. They deserve to be recorded and described. Yet how difficult—how

* Lady Margaret Duckworth.
† Virginia lectured at Morley College which was then located in the Waterloo Road from 1905 to the end of 1907.
‡ The first half of the next page in the ts was deleted by VW; some of the material appears elsewhere. This deletion together with the irregular pagination points to the existence of another, possibly incomplete, version of the present text.

impossible. Talk—even the talk which had such tremendous results upon the lives and characters of the two Miss Stephens—even talk of this interest and importance is as elusive as smoke. It flies up the chimney and is gone.

In the first place it is not true to say that when the door opened and with a curious hesitation and self-effacement Turner* or Strachey glided in—that they were complete strangers to us. We had met them—and Bell, Woolf, Hilton Young† and others—in Cambridge at May Week before my father died. But what was of much greater importance, we had heard of them from Thoby. Thoby possessed a great power of romanticizing his friends. Even when he was a little boy at a private school there was always some astonishing fellow, whose amazing character and exploits he would describe hour after hour when he came home for the holidays. These stories had the greatest fascination for me. I thought about Pilkington or Sidney Irwin or the Woolly Bear whom I never saw in the flesh as if they were characters in Shakespeare. I made up stories about them myself. It was a kind of saga that went on year after year. And now just as I had heard of Radcliffe, Stuart, or whoever it might be, I began to hear of Bell, Strachey, Turner, Woolf. We talked of them by the hour, rambling about the country or sitting over the fire in my bedroom.

"There's an astonishing fellow called Bell", Thoby would begin directly he came back. "He's a sort of mixture between Shelley and a sporting country squire."

At this of course I pricked up my ears and began to ask endless questions. We were walking over a moor somewhere, I remember. I got a fantastic impression that this man Bell was a kind of Sun God—with straw in his hair. He was an [illegible] of innocence and enthusiasm. Bell had never opened a book till he came to Cambridge, Thoby said. Then he suddenly discovered Shelley and Keats and went nearly mad with excitement. He did nothing but spout poetry and write poetry. Yet he was a perfect horseman—a gift which Thoby enormously admired—and kept two or three hunters up at Cambridge.

* Saxon Sydney-Turner.
† Edward Hilton Young whose father had been a friend of Leslie Stephen was perhaps Virginia's most conventionally respectable suitor. He was President of the Union at Cambridge and when he moved to London he became a regular visitor on Thursday evenings at both Gordon and Fitzroy Squares.

"And is Bell a great poet?" I asked.

No, Thoby wouldn't go so far as to say that; but it was quite on the cards that Strachey was. And so we discussed Strachey—or 'the Strache', as Thoby called him. Strachey at once became as singular, as fascinating as Bell. But it was in quite a different way. 'The Strache' was the essence of culture. In fact I think his culture a little alarmed Thoby. He had French pictures in his rooms. He had a passion for Pope. He was exotic, extreme in every way—Thoby described him—so long, so thin that his thigh was no thicker than Thoby's arm. Once he burst into Thoby's rooms, cried out, "Do you hear the music of the spheres?" and fell in a faint. Once in the midst of a dead silence, he piped up—and Thoby could imitate his voice perfectly—"Let's all write Sonnets to Robertson."* He was a prodigy of wit. Even the tutors and the dons would come and listen to him. "Whatever they give you, Strachey," Dr Jackson had said when Strachey was in for some examination, "it won't be good enough." And then Thoby, leaving me enormously impressed and rather dazed, would switch off to tell me about another astonishing fellow—a man who trembled perpetually all over. He was as eccentric, as remarkable in his way as Bell and Strachey in theirs. He was a Jew. When I asked why he trembled, Thoby somehow made me feel that it was part of his nature—he was so violent, so savage; he so despised the whole human race. "And after all," Thoby said, "it is a pretty feeble affair, isn't it?" Nobody was much good after twenty-five, he said. But most people, I gathered, rather rubbed along, and came to terms with things. Woolf did not and Thoby thought it sublime. One night he dreamt he was throttling a man and he dreamt with such violence that when he woke up he had pulled his own thumb out of joint. I was of course inspired with the deepest interest in that violent trembling misanthropic Jew who had already shaken his fist at civilisation and was about to disappear into the tropics so that we should none of us ever see him again.†
And then perhaps the talk got upon Sydney-Turner. According to Thoby, Sydney-Turner was an absolute prodigy of learning. He had

* A. J. Robertson, a freshman at Trinity at the same time as Bell, Woolf, Strachey, Sydney-Turner and Thoby Stephen. Clive Bell remembered him as a founding member of the Midnight Society which he considered the nucleus of the Bloomsbury Group. However, he adds that Robertson disclaimed the honour. (*Old Friends*, p. 129.)

† Leonard Woolf was a civil servant in Ceylon from 1904 to 1911.

the whole of Greek literature by heart. There was practically
nothing in any language that was any good that he had not read. He
was very silent and thin and odd. He never came out by day. But
late at night if he saw one's lamp burning he would come and tap at
the window like a moth. At about three in the morning he would
begin to talk. His talk was then of astonishing brilliance. When
later I complained to Thoby that I had met Turner and had not
found him brilliant Thoby severely supposed that by brilliance
I meant wit; he on the contrary meant truth. Sydney-Turner
was the most brilliant talker he knew because he always spoke the
truth.

Naturally then, when the bell rang and these astonishing fellows
came in, Vanessa and I were in a twitter of excitement. It was late at
night; the room was full of smoke; buns, coffee and whisky were
strewn about; we were not wearing white satin or seed-pearls; we
were not dressed at all.* Thoby went to open the door; in came
Sydney-Turner; in came Bell; in came Strachey.

They came in hesitatingly, self-effacingly, and folded themselves
up quietly [in] the corners of sofas. For a long time they said
nothing. None of our old conversational openings seemed to do.
Vanessa and Thoby and Clive, if Clive were there—for Clive† was
always ready to sacrifice himself in the cause of talk—would start
different subjects. But they were almost always answered in the
negative. "No", was the most frequent reply. "No, I haven't seen
it"; "No, I haven't been there." Or simply, "I don't know." The
conversation languished in a way that would have been impossible
in the drawing room at Hyde Park Gate. Yet the silence was
difficult, not dull. It seemed as if the standard of what was worth
saying had risen so high that it was better not to break it unworthily.
We sat and looked at the ground. Then at last Vanessa, having said
perhaps that she had been to some picture show, incautiously used
the word "beauty". At that, one of the young men would lift his
head slowly and say, "It depends what you mean by beauty." At
once all our ears were pricked. It was as if the bull had at last been
turned into the ring.

The bull might be 'beauty', might be 'good', might be 'reality'.
Whatever it was, it was some abstract question that now drew out

* Two or three illegible words are written in the margin.
† To accommodate the interlinear correction which is set off by dashes it
was necessary to delete: (for Clive) 'differed in many ways from the others'.

all our forces. Never have I listened so intently to each step and half-step in an argument. Never have I been at such pains to sharpen and launch my own little dart. And then what joy it was when one's contribution was accepted.* No praise has pleased me more than Saxon's saying—and was not Saxon infallible after all?—that he thought I had argued my case very cleverly. And what strange cases those were! I remember trying to persuade Hawtrey† that there is such a thing as atmosphere in literature. Hawtrey challenged me to prove it by pointing out in any book any one word which had this quality apart from its meaning. I went and fetched *Diana of the Crossways*. The argument, whether it was about atmosphere or the nature of truth, was always tossed into the middle of the party. Now Hawtrey would say something; now Vanessa; now Saxon; now Clive; now Thoby. It filled me with wonder to watch those who were finally left in the argument piling stone upon stone, cautiously, accurately, long after it had completely soared above my sight. But if one could not say anything, one could listen. One had glimpses of something miraculous happening high up in the air. Often we would still be sitting in a circle at two or three in the morning. Still Saxon would be taking his pipe from his mouth as if to speak, and putting it back again without having spoken. At last, rumpling his hair back, he would pronounce very shortly some absolutely final summing up. The marvellous edifice was complete, one could stumble off to bed feeling that something very important had happened. It had been proved that beauty was—or beauty was not—for I have never been quite sure which—part of a picture.

From such discussions Vanessa and I got probably much the same pleasure that undergraduates get when they meet friends of their own for the first time. In the world of the Booths and the Maxses we were not asked to use our brains much. Here we used nothing else. And part of the charm of those Thursday evenings was that they were astonishingly abstract. It was not only that Moore's book‡ had set us all discussing philosophy, art, religion; it was that the atmo-sphere—if in spite of Hawtrey I may use that word—was abstract

* 'When after a silence, some one said' has been pencilled in above a deleted line of type following 'accepted', leaving the sentence incomplete. It has therefore been deleted.

† Ralph Hawtrey, educated at Trinity College, Cambridge, as a mathe-matician, was a member of the 'Apostles' at the same time as Woolf, Strachey and Sydney-Turner. He later became well known as an economist.

‡ G. E. Moore's *Principia Ethica* (1903).

in the extreme. The young men I have named had no 'manners' in the Hyde Park Gate sense. They criticised our arguments as severely as their own. They never seemed to notice how we were dressed or if we were nice looking or not. All that tremendous encumbrance of appearance and behaviour which George had piled upon our first years vanished completely. One had no longer to endure that terrible inquisition after a party—and be told, "You looked lovely." Or, "You did look plain." Or, "You must really learn to do your hair." Or, "Do try not to look so bored when you dance." Or, "You did make a conquest", or, "You were a failure." All this seemed to have no meaning or existence in the world of Bell, Strachey, Hawtrey and Sydney-Turner. In that world the only comment as we stretched ourselves after our guests had gone, was, "I must say you made your point rather well"; "I think you were talking rather through your hat." It was an immense simplification. And for my part it went deeper than this. The atmosphere of Hyde Park Gate had been full of love and marriage. George's engagement to Flora Russell, Stella's to Jack Hills, Gerald's innumerable flirtations were all discussed either in private or openly with the greatest interest. Vanessa was already supposed to have attracted Austen Chamberlain. My Aunt Mary Fisher, poking about as usual in nooks and corners, had discovered that there were six drawings of him in Vanessa's sketchbook and [had] come to her own conclusions. George rather suspected that Charles Trevelyan was in love with her. But at Gordon Square love was never mentioned. Love had no existence. So lightly was it treated that for years I believed that Desmond had married an old Miss Cornish, aged about sixty, with snow-white hair. One never took the trouble to find out. It seemed incredible that any of these young men should want to marry us or that we should want to marry them. Secretly I felt that marriage was a very low down affair, but that if one practised it, one practised it— it is a serious confession I know—with young men who had been in the Eton Eleven and dressed for dinner. When I looked round the room at 46 I thought—if you will excuse me for saying so—that I had never seen young men so dingy, so lacking in physical splendour as Thoby's friends. Kitty Maxse who came in once or twice sighed afterwards, "I've no doubt they're very nice but, oh darling, how awful they do look!" Henry James, on seeing Lytton and Saxon at Rye, exclaimed to Mrs Prothero, "Deplorable! Deplorable! How could Vanessa and Virginia have picked up such friends? How could

Leslie's daughters have taken up with young men like that?" But it was precisely this lack of physical splendour, this shabbiness! that was in my eyes a proof of their superiority. More than that, it was, in some obscure way, reassuring; for it meant that things could go on like this, in abstract argument, without dressing for dinner, and never revert to the ways, which I had come to think so distasteful, at Hyde Park Gate.

I was wrong. One afternoon that first summer Vanessa said to Adrian and me and I watched her, stretching her arms above her head with a gesture that was at once reluctant and yielding, in the great looking-glass as she said it — "Of course, I can see that we shall all marry. It's bound to happen" — and as she said it I could feel a horrible necessity impending over us; a fate would descend and snatch us apart just as we had achieved freedom and happiness. She, I felt, was already aware of some claim, some need which I resented and tried to ignore. A few weeks later indeed Clive proposed to her. "Yes," said Thoby grimly when I murmured something to him very shyly about Clive's proposal, "That's the worst of Thursday evenings!" And her marriage in the beginning of 1907 was in fact the end of them. With that, the first chapter of Old Bloomsbury came to an end. It had been very austere, very exciting, of immense importance. A small concentrated world dwelling inside the much larger and looser world of dances and dinners had come into exis-tence. It had already begun to colour that world and still I think colours the much more gregarious Bloomsbury which succeeded it.

But it could not have gone on. Even if Vanessa had not married, even if Thoby had lived,* change was inevitable. We could not have gone on discussing the nature of beauty in the abstract for ever. The young men, as we used to call them, were changing from the general to the particular. They had ceased to be Mr Turner, Mr Strachey, Mr Bell. They had become Saxon, Lytton, Clive. Then too one was beginning to criticise, to distinguish, to compare. Those old flam-boyant portraits were being revised. One could see that Walter Lamb whom Thoby had compared to a Greek boy playing a flute in a vineyard was in fact rather bald, and rather dull; one could wish that Saxon could be induced either to go or to say something perhaps that was not strictly true; one could even doubt, when *Euphrosyne* was published, whether as many of the poems in that

* Thoby Stephen died in November 1906 of typhoid fever.

famous book were sure of immortality as Thoby made out.* But
there was something else that made for a change though I at least
did not know what it was. Perhaps if I read you a passage from
another diary which I kept intermittently for a month or two in the
year 1909 you will guess what it was. I am describing a tea-party in
James Strachey's rooms at Cambridge.†

"His rooms," I wrote, "though they are lodgings, are discreet and
dim. French pastels hang upon the walls and there are cases of old
books. The three young men—Norton,‡ Brooke and James Strachey
—sat in deep chairs; and gazed with soft intent eyes into the fire.
Mr Norton knew that he must talk; he and I talked laboriously. The
others were silent. I should like to account for this silence, but time
presses and I am puzzled. For the truth is that these young men are
evidently respectable; they are not only able but their views seem to
me honest and simple. They lack all padding; so that one has con-
victions to disagree with if one disagrees. Yet we had nothing to say
to each other and I was conscious that not only my remarks but my
presence was criticised. They wished for the truth and doubted if I
could speak it or be it. I thought this courageous of them but un-
sympathetic. I admired the atmosphere—was it more?—and felt
in some respects at ease in it. Yet why should intellect and character
be so barren? It seems as if the highest efforts of the most intelligent
people produce a negative result; one cannot honestly be anything."

There is a great change there from what I should have written
two or three years earlier. In part, of course, the change was due to
circumstances; I lived alone with Adrian now in Fitzroy Square;
and we were the most incompatible of people.§ We drove each other
perpetually into frenzies of irritation or into the depths of gloom. We
still went to a great many parties: but the combination of the two
worlds which I think was so [illegible] was far more difficult. I could

---

* A volume of poems privately published in 1905 to which Bell, Strachey,
Sydney-Turner, Woolf, Walter Lamb and others contributed. Walter Lamb,
elder brother of the painter Henry Lamb, was also at Trinity College,
Cambridge.

† James Strachey was the younger brother of Lytton who became the
translator and general editor of the standard English edition of Freud.

‡ H. T. J. Norton, a Cambridge mathematician, associated with the
inner circle of pre-war Bloomsbury; Rupert Brooke, the poet, who died in
1915.

§ Adrian and Virginia moved to 29 Fitzroy Square after Vanessa's
marriage to Clive Bell.

not reconcile the two. True, we still had Thursday evenings as before. But they were always strained and often ended in dismal failure. Adrian stalked off to his room, I to mine, in complete silence. But there was more in it than that. What it was I was not altogether certain. I knew theoretically, from books, much more than I knew practically from life. I knew that there were buggers in Plato's Greece; I suspected—it was not a question one could just ask Thoby —that there were buggers in Dr Butler's Trinity [College], Cambridge; but it never occurred to me that there were buggers even now in the Stephens' sitting room at Gordon Square. It never struck me that the abstractness, the simplicity which had been so great a relief after Hyde Park Gate were largely due to the fact that the majority of the young men who came there were not attracted by young women. I did not realise that love, far from being a thing they never mentioned, was in fact a thing which they seldom ceased to discuss. Now I had begun to be puzzled. Those long sittings, those long silences, those long arguments—they still went on in Fitzroy Square as they had done in Gordon Square. But now I found them of the most perplexing nature. They still excited me much more than any men I met with in the outer world of dinners and dances—and yet I was, dared I say it or think it even?—intolerably bored. Why, I asked, had we nothing to say to each other? Why were the most gifted of people also the most barren? Why were the most stimulating of friendships also the most deadening? Why was it all so negative? Why did these young men make one feel that one could not honestly be anything? The answer to all my questions was, obviously —as you will have guessed—that there was no physical attraction between us.

The society of buggers has many advantages—if you are a woman. It is simple, it is honest, it makes one feel, as I noted, in some respects at one's ease. But it has this drawback—with buggers one cannot, as nurses say, show off. Something is always suppressed, held down. Yet this showing off, which is not copulating, necessarily, nor altogether being in love, is one of the great delights, one of the chief necessities of life. Only then does all effort cease; one ceases to he honest, one ceases to be clever. One fizzes up into some absurd delightful effervescence of soda water or champagne through which one sees the world tinged with all the colours of the rainbow. It is significant of what I had come to desire that I went straight—on almost the next page of my diary indeed—from the dim and discreet rooms of James Strachey at Cambridge to dine with Lady Ottoline Morrell at Bedford Square.* Her rooms, I noted without drawing any inferences, seemed to me instantly full of "lustre and illusion".

So one changed. But these changes of mine were part of a much bigger change. The headquarters of Bloomsbury have always been in Gordon Square. Now that Vanessa and Clive were married, now that Clive had shocked the Maxses, the Booths, the Cecils, the Protheroes, irretrievably, now that the house was done up once more, now that they were giving little parties with their beautiful brown table linen and their lovely eighteenth-century silver, Bloomsbury rapidly lost the monastic character it had had in Chapter One; the character of Chapter Two was superficially at least to be very different.

Another scene has always lived in my memory—I do not know if I invented it or not—as the best illustration of Bloomsbury Chapter Two. It was a spring evening. Vanessa and I were sitting in the drawing room. The drawing room had greatly changed its character since 1904. The Sargent-Furse age was over. The age of Augustus John was dawning. His "Pyramus" filled one entire wall. The Watts' portraits of my father and my mother were hung downstairs if they were hung at all. Clive had hidden all the match boxes because their blue and yellow swore with the prevailing colour scheme. At any moment Clive might come in and he and I should begin to argue— amicably, impersonally at first; soon we should be hurling abuse at each other and pacing up and down the room. Vanessa sat silent and did something mysterious with her needle or her scissors. I talked, egotistically, excitedly, about my own affairs no doubt. Suddenly the door opened and the long and sinister figure of Mr Lytton Strachey stood on the threshold. He pointed his finger at a stain on Vanessa's white dress.

"Semen?" he said.

Can one really say it? I thought and we burst out laughing. With that one word all barriers of reticence and reserve went down. A flood of the sacred fluid seemed to overwhelm us. Sex permeated our

* Lady Ottoline Morrell was the daughter of General Arthur Bentinck and Lady Bolsover. She rebelled against her upper class, philistine background and in marrying Philip Morrell, who later became a Liberal member of Parliament, she was able to make an escape. She entertained a wide circle of distinguished people, including many artists and writers, at 44 Bedford Square in London, at Garsington Manor in Oxfordshire and, after the war, at 10 Gower Street in London.

conversation. The word bugger was never far from our lips. We discussed copulation with the same excitement and openness that we
had discussed the nature of good. It is strange to think how reticent,
how reserved we had been and for how long. It seems a marvel now
that so late as the year 1908 or 9 Clive had blushed and I had blushed
too when I asked him to let me pass to go to the lavatory on the
French Express. I never dreamt of asking Vanessa to tell me what
happened on her wedding night. Thoby and Adrian would have died
rather than discuss the love affairs of undergraduates. When all
intellectual questions had been debated so freely, sex was ignored.
Now a flood of light poured in upon that department too. We had
known everything but we had never talked. Now we talked of
nothing else. We listened with rapt interest to the love affairs of the
buggers. We followed the ups and downs of their chequered his-
tories; Vanessa sympathetically; I—had I not written in 1905,
women are so much more amusing than men*—frivolously,
laughingly. "Norton tells me", Vanessa would say, "that James is in
utter despair. Rupert has been twice to bed with Hobhouse" and I
would cap her stories with some equally thrilling piece of gossip;
about a divine undergraduate with a head like a Greek God—but
alas his teeth were bad—called George Mallory.

All this had the result that the old sentimental views of marriage
in which we were brought up were revolutionized. I should be sorry
to tell you how old I was before I saw that there is nothing shocking
in a man's having a mistress, or in a woman's being one. Perhaps the
fidelity of our parents was not the only or inevitably the highest form
of married life. Perhaps indeed that fidelity was not so strict as one
had supposed. "Of course Kitty Maxse has two or three lovers",
said Clive—Kitty Maxse, the chaste, the exquisite, the devoted!
Again, the whole aspect of life was changed.

So there was now nothing that one could not say, nothing that one
could not do, at 46 Gordon Square. It was, I think, a great advance
in civilisation. It may be true that the loves of buggers are not—at
least if one is of the other persuasion—of enthralling interest or para-
mount importance. But the fact that they can be mentioned openly
leads to the fact that no one minds if they are practised privately.
Thus many customs and beliefs were revised. Indeed the future of
Bloomsbury was to prove that many variations can be played on the

* The first (deleted) version of the phrase set off by dashes was: 'it is one
of the differences between us'.

theme of sex, and with such happy results that my father himself
might have hesitated before he thundered out the one word which
he thought fit to apply to a bugger or an adulterer; which was
Blackguard!

Here I come to a question which I must leave to some other
memoir writer to discuss—that is to say, if we take it for granted that
Bloomsbury exists, what are the qualities that admit one to it, what
are the qualities that expel one from it? Now at any rate between
1910 and 1914 many new members were admitted. It must have
been in 1910 I suppose that Clive one evening rushed upstairs in a
state of the highest excitement. He had just had one of the most
interesting conversations of his life. It was with Roger Fry. They had
been discussing the theory of art for hours. He thought Roger Fry
the most interesting person he had met since Cambridge days. So
Roger appeared. He appeared, I seem to think, in a large ulster
coat, every pocket of which was stuffed with a book, a paint box or
something intriguing; special tips which he had bought from a little
man in a back street; he had canvases under his arms; his hair flew;
his eyes glowed. He had more knowledge and experience than the
rest of us put together. [His mind seemed hooked on to life] by an
extraordinary number of attachments. We started talking about
*Marie-Claire.**And at once we were all launched into a terrific
argument about literature; adjectives?† associations? overtones?
We had down Milton; we re-read Wordsworth. We had to think the
whole thing over again. The old skeleton arguments of primitive
Bloomsbury about art and beauty put on flesh and blood. There was
always some new idea afoot; always some new picture standing on a
chair to be looked at, some new poet fished out from obscurity and
stood in the light of day. Odd people wandered through 46;
Rothenstein, Sickert, Yeats, Tonks—Tonks who could, I suppose,
make Vanessa miserable no more. And sometimes one began to meet
a queer faun-like figure, hitching his clothes up, blinking his eyes,
stumbling oddly over the long words in his sentences. A year or two
before, Adrian and I had been standing in front of a certain gold and
black picture in the Louvre when a voice said: "Are you Adrian
Stephen? I'm Duncan Grant." Duncan now began to haunt the
purlieus of Bloomsbury. How he lived I do not know. He was

* An autobiographical novel by Marguerite Audoux, a seamstress. It was
widely acclaimed when it was published in 1910 in France.
† Three or four illegible words were written in pen above 'adjectives'.

penniless. Uncle Trevor* indeed said he was mad. He lived in a studio in Fitzroy Square with an old drunken charwoman called Filmer and a clergyman who frightened girls in the street by making faces at them. Duncan was on the best of terms with both. He was rigged out by his friends in clothes which seemed always to be falling to the floor. He borrowed old china from us to paint; and my father's old trousers to go to parties in. He broke the china and he ruined the trousers by jumping into the Cam to rescue a child who was swept into the river by the rope of Walter Lamb's barge, the 'Aholibah'. Our cook Sophie called him "that Mr Grant" and complained that he had been taking things again as if he were a rat in her larder. But she succumbed to his charm. He seemed to be vaguely tossing about in the breeze; but he always alighted exactly where he meant to.

And once at least Morgan flitted through Bloomsbury lodging for a moment in Fitzroy Square on his way even then to catch a train.† He carried, I think, the same black bag with the same brass label on it that is now in the hall outside at this moment. I felt as if a butterfly —by preference a pale blue butterfly—had settled on the sofa; if one raised a finger or made a movement the butterfly would be off. He talked of Italy and the Working Men's College. And I listened— with the deepest curiosity, for he was the only novelist I knew— except Henry James and George Meredith; the only one anyhow who wrote about people like ourselves. But I was too much afraid of raising my hand and making the butterfly fly away to say much. I used to watch him from behind a hedge as he flitted through Gordon Square, erratic, irregular, with his bag, on his way to catch a train.

These, with Maynard—very truculent, I felt, very formidable, like a portrait of Tolstoy as a young man to look at, able to rend any argument that came his way with a blow of his paw, yet concealing, as the novelists say, a kind and even simple heart under that im- mensely impressive armour of intellect—and Norton; Norton who was the essence of all I meant by Cambridge; so able; so honest; so ugly; so dry; Norton with whom I spent a whole night once talking and with whom I went at dawn to Covent Garden, whom I still see in memory scowling in his pince-nez—yellow and severe against a bank of roses and carnations—these I think were the chief figures in Bloomsbury before the war.

But here again it becomes necessary to ask—where does Blooms-

* Trevor Grant, uncle of both Duncan Grant and Lytton Strachey.
† E. M. Forster.

bury end? What is Bloomsbury? Does it for instance include Bedford
Square? Before the war, I think we should most of us have said
'Yes'. When the history of Bloomsbury is written—and what better
subject could there be for Lytton's next book?—there will have to be
a chapter, even if it is only in the appendix, devoted to Ottoline.
Her first appearance among us was, I think, in 1908 or 9. I find from
my diary that I dined with her on March the 30th 1909—I think for
the first time. But a few weeks before this, she had swooped down
upon one of my own Thursday evenings with Philip, Augustus
John and Dorelia in tow: she had written the next morning to ask
me to give her the names and addresses of all "my wonderful
friends". This was followed by an invitation to come to Bedford
Square any Thursday about ten o'clock and bring any one I liked.
I took Rupert Brooke. Soon we were all swept into that extraordinary
whirlpool where such odd sticks and straws were brought momentarily together. There was Augustus John, very sinister in a black
stock and a velvet coat; Winston Churchill, very rubicund, all gold
lace and medals, on his way to Buckingham Palace; Raymond
Asquith crackling with epigrams; Francis Dodd telling me most
graphically how he and Aunt Susie* had killed bugs: she held the
lamp; he a basin of paraffin; bugs crossed the ceiling in an incessant
stream. There was Lord Henry Bentinck at one end of the sofa and
perhaps Nina Lamb at the other. There was Philip fresh from the
House of Commons humming and hawing on the hearth-rug. There
was Gilbert Cannan who was said to be in love with Ottoline. There
was Bertie Russell, whom she was said to be in love with. Above all,
there was Ottoline herself.

"Lady Ottoline", I wrote in my diary, "is a great lady who has
become discontented with her own class and is trying to find what
she wants among artists and writers. For this reason, as if they were
inspired with something divine, she approaches them in a definite
way and they see her as a disembodied spirit escaping from her
world into one where she can never take root. She is remarkable to
look at if not beautiful. Like most passive people she is very careful
and elaborate in her surroundings. She takes the utmost pains to
set off her beauty as though it were some rare object picked up in a
dusky Florentine back street. It always seems possible that the rich

---

* Aunt Susie (Isabel Dacre) was a close friend of Francis Dodd, etcher,
painter and later Royal Academician.

American women who finger her Persian cloak and call it 'very good' may go on to finger her face and call it a fine work in the late renaissance style; the brow and eyes magnificent, the chin perhaps restored. The pallor of her cheeks, the way she has of drawing back her head and looking at you blankly gives her the appearance of a marble Medusa. She is curiously passive." And then I go on to exclaim rather rhapsodically that the whole place was full of "lustre and illusion".

When indeed one remembers that drawing room full of people, the pale yellows and pinks of the brocades, the Italian chairs, the Persian rugs, the embroideries, the tassels, the scent, the pomegranates, the pugs, the pot-pourri and Ottoline bearing down upon one from afar in her white shawl with the great scarlet flowers on it and sweeping one away out of the large room and the crowd into a little room with her alone, where she plied one with questions that were so intimate and so intense, about life and one's friends, and made one sign one's name in a little scented book—it was only last week that I signed my name in another little scented book in Gower Street—I think my excitement may be excused.*

Indeed lustre and illusion tinged Bloomsbury during those last years before the war. We were not so austere; we were not so exalted. There were quarrels and intrigues. Ottoline may have been a Medusa; but she was not a passive Medusa. She had a great gift for drawing people under. Even Middleton Murry, it is said, was pulled down by her among the vegetables at Garsington. And by this time we were far from drab. Thursday evenings with their silences and their arguments were a thing of the past. Their place was taken by parties of a very different sort. The Post-Impressionist movement had cast—not its shadow—but its bunch of variegated lights upon us. We bought poinsettias made of scarlet plush; we made dresses of the printed cotton that is specially loved by negroes; we dressed ourselves up as Gauguin pictures and careered round Crosby Hall.† Mrs Whitehead was scandalized.‡ She said that

* Presumably Ottoline kept a visitor's book at 10 Gower Street, where the Morrells moved after the war, as she had done at Bedford Square. The paragraph that follows—up to 'The Post-Impressionist movement'—is from the mutilated fragment in the Berg Collection.

† At the Ball to celebrate the end of the Second Post-Impressionist Exhibition (1912).

‡ The wife of Alfred North Whitehead, Cambridge philosopher and mathematician.

Vanessa and I were practically naked. My mother's ghost was invoked once more—by Violet Dickinson—to deplore the fact that I had taken a house in Brunswick Square and had asked young men to share it.* George Duckworth came all the way from Charles Street to beg Vanessa to make me give up the idea and was not comforted perhaps when she replied that after all the Foundling Hospital was handy. Stories began to circulate about parties at which we all undressed in public. Logan Pearsall Smith told Ethel Sands that he knew for a fact that Maynard had copulated with Vanessa on a sofa in the middle of the drawing room. It was a heartless, immoral, cynical society it was said; we were abandoned women and our friends were the most worthless of young men.

Yet in spite of Logan, in spite of Mrs Whitehead, in spite of Vanessa and Maynard and what they did on the sofa at Brunswick Square, Old Bloomsbury still survives. If you seek a proof—look around.

---

* Virginia shared 38 Brunswick Square with Adrian, Maynard Keynes, Duncan Grant and Leonard Woolf, 1911–12.

AM I A SNOB?

(*Editor's Note*)

Virginia Woolf wrote "Am I a Snob?" when she was at the height of her fame and near the end of the career that was being so painstakingly prepared when the first memoir in this collection was written. It was read to the Memoir Club some time between 27 October 1936—the date of Virginia Woolf's last visit to Sibyl Colefax at Argyll House—and February of the following year.

In "A Sketch of the Past", Virginia Woolf noted the curious division in her life at Hyde Park Gate: "Downstairs there was pure convention; upstairs pure intellect." After the first years in Bloomsbury the world of 'convention'—the world of George Duckworth, of Kitty Maxse—had clearly given way to the world of intellect. Humiliation, frustration and sheer boredom had marked many of her early encounters with the '*beau monde*' and yet some aspects of 'society' never ceased to fascinate her: the bright lights, the people talking, the strip of red carpet rolled out on the pavement.

The text that follows is based on thirty-two variously sized leaves dry-welded to form a booklet. The Library reference number is MH/A.17. The typing is by Virginia Woolf, with corrections in pen and pencil. The letters from Margot Oxford and Sibyl Colefax which are incorporated into the present text appear in the booklet on separate sheets preceding the pages for which they were intended. The typing is, however, clearly Virginia Woolf's and it is unlikely that the letters included are other than rather freely interpreted recollections of the originals.

The quality of the typing is poor even by Virginia Woolf's none too stringent standards; punctuation and spelling errors abound. Yet the thought flows smoothly and there are few corrections or additions involving more than a sentence; there are some pages with no corrections at all.

It is probable that this typescript was the text read to the Memoir Club although, according to Quentin Bell, it is unlikely that Virginia Woolf would have kept very closely to the text.

Am I a Snob?

Molly* has very unfairly, I think, laid upon me the burden of providing a memoir tonight. We all forgive Molly everything of course because of her insidious, her devastating charm. But it is unfair. It is not my turn; I am not the oldest of you. I am not the most widely lived or the most richly memoried. Maynard, Desmond, Clive and Leonard all live stirring and active lives; all constantly brush up against the great; all constantly affect the course of history one way or another. It is for them to unlock the doors of their treasure-houses and to set before us those gilt and gleaming objects which repose within. Who am I that I should be asked to read a memoir? A mere scribbler; what's worse, a mere dabbler in dreams; one who is not fish, flesh, fowl or good red herring. My memoirs, which are always private, and at their best only about proposals of marriage, seductions by half-brothers, encounters with Ottoline and so on, must soon run dry. Nobody now asks me to marry them; for many years nobody has attempted to seduce me. Prime Ministers never consult me. Twice I have been to Hendon, but each time the aeroplane refused to mount into the air. I have visited most of the capitals of Europe, it is true; I can speak a kind of dog French and mongrel Italian; but so ignorant am I, so badly educated, that if you ask me the simplest question—for instance, where is Guatemala?— I am forced to turn the conversation.

Yet Molly has asked me to write a paper. What can it be about? That is the question I asked myself, and it seemed to me, as I sat brooding, that the time has come when we old fogies—we ignorant and private living old fogies—must face this question—what are our memoirs to be about, if the Memoir Club is to go on meeting, and if half the members are people like myself to whom nothing ever happens? Dare I suggest that the time has come when we must interpret Molly's commands rather liberally, and instead of sweeping the lamp of memory over the adventures and excitement of real life, must turn that beam inwards and describe ourselves?

Am I speaking for myself only when I say that though nothing worth calling an adventure has befallen me since I last occupied this thorny and prominent chair I still seem to myself a subject of

* MacCarthy. See p. 159n.

inexhaustible and fascinating anxiety?—a volcano in perpetual eruption? Am I alone in my egotism when I say that never does the pale light of dawn filter through the blinds of 52 Tavistock Square but I open my eyes and exclaim, "Good God! Here I am again!"— not always with pleasure, often with pain; sometimes with a spasm of acute disgust—but always, always with interest?

Myself then might be the subject of this paper; but there are drawbacks. It would run to so many volumes—that single subject—that those of us who have hair; those whose hair is still capable of growth —would find it tickling their toes before I had done. I must break off one tiny fragment of this vast subject; I must give one brief glance at one small corner of this universe—which still to me seems as trackless and tiger-haunted as that other upon which is written— where I know not—the word Guatemala; I must, I say, choose one aspect only; and ask one question only; and this is it—Am I a snob?

As I try to answer it, I may perhaps turn up a memory or two; I may perhaps revive certain of your own memories; at any rate, I will try to give you facts; and though of course I shall not tell the whole truth, perhaps I shall tell enough to set you guessing. But in order to answer that question, I must begin by asking—what is a snob? And since I have no skill in analysis—since my education was neglected—I shall take the obvious course of trying to find some object against which I can measure myself: with which to compare myself. Desmond, for instance. Naturally I take Desmond first. Is he a snob?

He ought to be. He was educated at Eton, then went to Cambridge. We all know the old tag about grateful science adoring the aristocracy. But whatever Eton and Cambridge did to encourage snobbery in him, nature did far more. She gave him all the gifts that a grateful aristocracy adores in science; a golden tongue; perfect manners; complete self-possession; boundless curiosity, mixed with sympathy; he can also sit a horse and shoot a pheasant at a pinch. As for poverty, since Desmond has never minded how he dresses, no one else has ever given the matter a thought. So here then, undoubtedly, is my pattern; let me compare my case with his.

We were standing, when I thought this, at a window in the drawing room at Tavistock Square. Desmond had lunched with us; we had spent the afternoon talking; suddenly he remembered that he was dining somewhere. But where? "Now where am I dining?" he said and took out his pocket book. Something distracted his attention for a moment, and I looked over his shoulder. Hastily, furtively, I ran my eye over his engagements. Monday Lady Bessborough 8:30. Tuesday Lady Ancaster 8:30. Wednesday Dora Sanger seven sharp. Thursday Lady Salisbury ten o'clock. Friday lunch Wolves and dine Lord Revelstoke. White waistcoat. White waistcoat was twice underlined. Years later I discovered the reason—he was to meet our king, our late lamented George. Well, he glanced at his engagements; shut the book and made off. Not a word did he say about the peerage. He never brought the conversation round to Revelstoke; white waistcoats were unmentioned. "No," I said to myself with a keen pang of disappointment as he shut the door, "Desmond, alas, is not a snob."

I must seek another pattern. Take Maynard now. He too was at Eton and at Cambridge. Since then he has been concerned in so many great affairs that were he to rattle his engagements under our noses we should be fairly deafened with the clink of coronets and dazed with the glitter of diamonds. But are we deafened? Are we dazed? Alas, no. Dominated, I suspect by the iron rod of old Cambridge, dominated too by that moral sense which grows stronger in Maynard the older he gets, that stern desire to preserve our generation in its integrity, and to protect the younger generation from its folly, Maynard never boasts. It is for me to inform you that he lunched today with the Prime Minister. Poor old Baldwin with the tears running down his cheeks marched him up and down—up and down beneath the celebrated pictures of Pitt and Peel. "If only", he kept on saying, "you would take a seat in the Cabinet, Keynes; or a peerage, Keynes . . . " It is for me to tell you that story. Maynard never mentioned it. Pigs, plays, pictures—he will talk of them all. But never of Prime Ministers and peerages. Alas and alas— Maynard is not a snob. I am foiled again.

All the same, I have made one discovery. The essence of snobbery is that you wish to impress other people. The snob is a flutter-brained, hare-brained creature so little satisfied with his or her own standing that in order to consolidate it he or she is always flourishing a title or an honour in other people's faces so that they may believe, and help him to believe what he does not really believe—that he or she is somehow a person of importance.

This is a symptom that I recognise in my own case. Witness this letter. Why is it always on top of all my letters? Because it has a coronet—if I get a letter stamped with a coronet that letter miraculously floats on top. I often ask—why? I know perfectly well that none of my friends will ever be, or ever has been impressed by anything I do to impress them. Yet I do it—here is the letter—on top. This shows, like a rash or a spot, that I have the disease. And I go on to ask when and how did I catch it?

When I was a girl I had certain opportunities for snobbery, because though outwardly an intellectual family, very nobly born in a bookish sense, we had floating fringes in the world of fashion. We had George Duckworth to begin with. But George Duckworth's snobbery was of so gross and palpable a texture that I could smell it and taste it from afar. I did not like that smell and taste. My temptation reached me in subtler ways—through Kitty Maxse originally, I think—a lady of the most delicate charm, of the most ethereal grace so that the great, whom she introduced, were sprayed and disinfected and robbed of their grossness. Who could call the Marchioness of Bath gross, or her daughters, the Ladies Katherine and Beatrice Thynne? It was unthinkable. Beautiful they were and stately; they dressed disgracefully, but they held themselves superbly. When we dined or lunched with old Lady Bath I sat there shivering with ecstasy—an ecstasy that was wholly snobbish perhaps but made up of different parts—of pleasure, terror, laughter and amazement. There Lady Bath sat at the end of the table on a chair stamped with the coronet and arms of the Thynnes; and on the table beside her on two cushions lay two Waterbury watches. These she consulted from time to time. But why? I do not know. Had time any special significance for her? She seemed to have endless leisure. Often she would nod off to sleep. Then she would wake and look at her watches. She looked at them because she liked looking at them. Her indifference to public opinion intrigued and delighted me. So too did her conversation with her butler Middleton.

A carriage would pass the window.

"Who's that driving by?" she would say suddenly.

"Lady Suffield, my lady", Middleton would reply. And Lady Bath would look at her watches. Once I remember the word 'marl' cropped up in conversation.

"What's marl, Middleton?" Lady Bath asked.

"A mixture of earth and carbonate of lime, my lady", Middleton informed her. Meanwhile Katie had seized a bloody bone from the plate and was feeding the dogs. As I sat there I felt these people don't

care a snap what anyone thinks. Here is human nature in its un-
cropped, unpruned, natural state. They have a quality which we in
Kensington lack. Perhaps I am only finding excuses for myself, but
that was the origin of the snobbery which now leads me to put this
letter on top of the pack — the aristocrat is freer, more natural, more
eccentric than we are. Here I note that my snobbery is not of the
intellectual kind. Lady Bath was simple in the extreme. Neither
Katie nor Beatrice could spell. Will Rothenstein and Andrew Lang
were the brightest lights in their intellectual world. Neither Rothenstein or Andrew Lang impressed me. If you ask me would I rather
meet Einstein or the Prince of Wales, I plump for the Prince without
hesitation.

I want coronets; but they must be old coronets; coronets that
carry land with them and country houses; coronets that breed
simplicity, eccentricity, ease; and such confidence in your own
state that you can surround your plate with Waterbury watches and
feed dogs with bloody bones with your own hands. No sooner have I
said this than I am forced to qualify this statement. This letter rises
up in witness against me. It has a coronet on top but it is not an old
coronet; it is from a lady whose birth is no better — perhaps worse —
than my own. Yet when I received this letter I was all in a flutter.
I will read it to you.

Dear Virginia,
I am not very young and since ALL my friends are either dead
or dying I would much like to see you and ask you a great
favour. You will laugh when I tell you what it is but in case you
would lunch here alone with me on [the] 12th or 13th, 17th or
18th, I will tell you what it is. No, I won't. I will wait to know if
on any one of these dates you can see your admirer
                    Margot Oxford*

I wrote at once — though I seldom write at once — to say that I was
entirely at Lady Oxford's service. Whatever she asked, I would do.
I was not left in doubt very long. Soon came this second letter.

Dear Virginia,
I think I should warn you of the favour which I want you to do

* Margot Asquith, Lady Oxford, second wife of Herbert Asquith, Earl of
Oxford (Prime Minister 1908-16).

for me. All my friends are either dying or dead and I am aware that my own time is closing round me. The greatest compliment ever paid me—among few—was when you said I was a good writer. This, coming from you, might have turned my head as you are far the greatest female writer living. When I die, I would like you to write a short notice in *The Times* to say you admired my writing, and thought that journalists should have made more use of me. I am not at all vain, but I have been hurt by being first employed and then turned down by editors of newspapers. This may seem trivial to you—as indeed it is—but I would like you to give me to the Press. Do not give another thought to this if it bothers you, but praise from you would delight my family when I am dead.

Your ever admiring
Margot Oxford

You could send it to Editor of *The Times* as Dawson* keeps and values all contributions upon those who are dead.

Now I was not, I think, flattered to be the greatest female writer in Lady Oxford's eyes; but I was flattered to be asked to lunch with her alone. "Of course," I replied, "I will come and lunch with you alone." And I was pleased when on the day in question Mabel, our dour cook, came to me, and said, "Lady Oxford has sent her car for you, ma'am." Obviously she was impressed by me; I was impressed by myself. I rose in my own esteem because I rose in Mabel's.

When I reached Bedford Square there was a large lunch party; Margot was rigged up in her finery; a ruby cross set with diamonds blazed on her breast; she was curled and crisp like a little Greek horse; tart and darting like an asp or an adder. Philip Morrell was the first to feel her sting. He was foolish and she snubbed him. But then she recovered her temper. She was very brilliant. She rattled off a string of anecdotes about the Duke of Beaufort and the Badminton hunt; how she had got her blue; how she had [heard] about Lady Warwick and the [Prince of Wales?,]† about Lady Ripon,

* Geoffrey Dawson, twice editor of *The Times*, 1912–19, 1923–41.
† 'the' is the last word of the line of type that trails off the page. The Countess of Warwick was a celebrated beauty and member of the Prince of Wales' circle. It is only a possibility that the Prince of Wales was intended here, however.

Lady Bessborough; L[ord] Balfour and 'the Souls'.* As for age,
death and obituary articles, *The Times*, nothing was said of them. I
am sure she had forgotten that such things existed. So had I. I was
enthralled. I embraced her warmly in the hall; and the next thing I
remember is that I found myself pacing along the Farringdon Road
talking aloud to myself, and seeing the butchers' shops and the trays
of penny toys through an air that seemed made of gold dust and
champagne.

Now no party of intellectuals has ever sent me flying down the
Farringdon Road. I have dined with H. G. Wells to meet Bernard
Shaw, Arnold Bennett and Granville Barker and I have only felt like
an old washerwoman toiling step by step up a steep and endless
staircase.

Thus I seem to have arrived at the conclusion that I am not only a
coronet snob; but also a lit up drawing room snob; a social festivity
snob. Any group of people if they are well dressed, and socially
sparkling and unfamiliar will do the trick; sends up that fountain of
gold and diamond dust which I suppose obscures the solid truth.
Here is another letter which perhaps will throw more light upon
other angles of the problem.

It must have been about twelve years ago, for we were still living
in Richmond,† that I received one of those flyaway missives with
which we are now all so familiar—a yellow sheet upon which a hand
bowls like an intoxicated hoop; and finally curls itself into a scrawl
which reads Sibyl Colefax.‡ "It would give me so much pleasure",
it read, "if you would come to tea"—here followed a variety of
dates—"to meet Paul Valéry." Now as I have always met Paul
Valéry or his equivalent since I can remember, to be asked out to tea
to meet him by a Sibyl Colefax whom I did not know—I had never
met her—was no lure to me. If it had been, it was counteracted by
another fact about myself to which I have some shyness in alluding;
my dress complex; my suspenders complex in particular. I hate
being badly dressed; but I hate buying clothes. In particular I hate

* The ts has 'La Balfour' but 'Lord' must surely have been intended.
Arthur James Balfour, philosopher and statesman, Prime Minister 1902–5,
was the central figure of the exclusive, aristocratic and intellectual coterie
known as 'the Souls'.
† The Woolfs lived in Richmond from 1914–24.
‡ Lady Colefax of Argyll House was a well-known London hostess.
Leonard Woolf described her as 'an unabashed hunter of lions'.

buying suspenders. It is partly, I think, that in order to buy suspenders you must visit the most private room in the heart of a shop; you must stand in your chemise.* Shiny black satin women pry and snigger. Whatever the confession reveals, and I suspect it is something discreditable, I am very shy under the eyes of my own sex when in my chemise. But in those days twelve years ago skirts were short; stockings had to be neat; my suspenders were old; and I could not face buying another pair—let alone hat and coat. So I said, "No, I will not come to tea to meet Paul Valéry." Invitations then showered; how many tea parties I was asked to I cannot remember; at last the situation became desperate; I was forced to buy suspenders; and I accepted—shall I say the fiftieth—invitation to Argyll House. This time it was to meet Arnold Bennett.

The very night before the party a review of one of my books by Arnold Bennett appeared in the *Evening Standard*. It was *Orlando*, I think. He attacked it violently. He said it was a worthless book, which had dashed every hope he might have had of me as a writer. His whole column was devoted to trouncing me. Now though very vain—unlike Lady Oxford—my vanity as a writer is purely snobbish. I expose a large surface of skin to the reviewer but very little flesh and blood. That is, I mind good reviews and bad reviews only because I think my friends think I mind them. But as I know that my friends almost instantly forget reviews, whether good or bad, I too forget them in a few hours. My flesh and blood feelings are not touched. The only criticisms of my books that draw blood are those that are unprinted; those that are private.

Thus as twenty four hours had passed since I read the review, I went into the drawing room at Argyll House far more concerned with my appearance as a woman than with my reputation as a writer. Now I saw Sibyl for the first time and I likened her to a bunch of red cherries on a hard black straw hat. She came forward and led me up to Arnold Bennett as a lamb is led to the butcher.

"Here is Mrs Woolf!" she said with a smile. As a hostess she was gloating. She was thinking, now there will be a scene which will redound to the credit of Argyll House. Other people were there— they too seemed expectant; they all smiled. But Arnold Bennett, I felt, was uncomfortable. He was a kind man; he took his own reviews

* 'you must undress' was typed after 'shop' then deleted; it was then written in and partially deleted. The present phrase was the last addition made in the margin.

seriously; here he was shaking hands with a woman whom he had 'slanged', as he called it, only the evening before.

"I am sorry, Mrs Woolf," he began, "that I slanged your book last night . . . "

He stammered. And I blurted out, quite sincerely, "If I choose to publish books, that's my own look out. I must take the consequences."

"Right — right", he stammered. I think he approved. "I didn't like your book", he went on. "I thought it a very bad book . . . " He stammered again.

"You can't hate my books more than I hate yours, Mr Bennett", I said. I don't know if he altogether approved of that; but we sat down together and talked and got on very well indeed. I was pleased to find in some letters of his that have been published that he commended me for bearing him no grudge; he said that we got on finely.

But that is not my point. My point is that this little scene pleased Sibyl, and was the foundation of what I suppose I must call, subject to qualifications, my intimacy with her. I was instantly promoted from tea to meat. It was lunch to begin with; then when I refused lunch, it was dinner. I went — I went several times. But I found by degrees that I was always asked to meet writers; and I did not want to meet writers; and then that if I had Noel Coward on my left, I always had Sir Arthur on my right.* Sir Arthur was very kind; he did his best to entertain me; but why he thought that I was primarily interested in the Dye-stuffs Bill I have never found out. So it was, however. Our talk always drifted that way. At one time I was the second leading authority in England on that measure. But at last, what with Noel Coward on my left and Sir Arthur on my right, I felt I could no longer bring myself to dine with Sibyl. I excused myself. The more I excused myself the more she persisted. Then she suggested that she should come and see me. She came. Again my snobbery asserted itself. I bought iced cakes; tidied up the room; threw away Pinker's bones, and pulled covers over the holes in the chairs. Soon I realised that her snobbery demanded nothing but a burnt bun; as untidy a room as possible; and if my fingers were covered with ink stains it was all to the good. We struck up an intimacy on those lines. She would exclaim, "Oh how I long to be a writer!" And I would reply, "Oh Sibyl, if only I could be [a] great hostess like you!" Her anecdotes of the great world amused me very much; and I drew lurid if fanciful pictures of my own struggles with

* Sir Arthur Colefax, husband of Sibyl.

English prose. As we became more—shall I call it intimate?—can snobs be intimate?—she would sit on the floor, pull up her skirts, adjust her knickers—she only wears one undergarment, I may tell you; it is of silk—and pour out her grievances. She would complain almost with tears in her eyes—how Osbert Sitwell had laughed at her; how people called her a climber, a lion hunter. How vilely untrue this was . . . how all she wanted was that Argyll House should be a centre where interesting people could meet interesting people. And yet she was laughed at . . . abused. Once in the middle of one of these confidences—and they flattered me very much—the telephone rang; and Lady Cunard's butler asked me to dine with her ladyship —whom I had never met. Sibyl, when I explained the situation, was furious. "I've never heard of such insolence!" she exclaimed. Her face was contorted with a look that reminded me of the look on a tigress's face when someone snatches a bone from its paws. She abused Lady Cunard. Nothing she could say was bad enough for her. She was [a] mere lion hunter; a snob. Again, there was Lady Cholmondeley. She asked me to go and see her. "And who is Lady Cholmondeley?" I asked. Never shall I forget the careful and vindictive way in which she pulled that lady's character to pieces. She couldn't understand, I remember she said, anybody being so insolent as to ask another person to dine when they did not know them. She strongly advised me to have nothing to do either with Lady Cunard or Lady Cholmondeley. Yet she had done the very same thing herself. What was the difference between them?

In short there was much to interest me in our intimacy; such as it was. It developed. Soon she suggested a plan which I have never had the courage to make public. It was that there should be fortnightly parties—now at Tavistock Square, now at Argyll House; we were to ask four of our friends; she was to ask four of hers; Bloomsbury and the great world were to mix; she, I rather think, delicately intimated that she would stand the cost. But even I, even at my most intoxicated, saw that this would never do. Once we provided Lytton* for her; the party was a deadly failure. Lytton was very good and very patient; but he said to me at leaving, "Please don't ask me to meet Colefax again."

We reached a kind of frankness. Time after time she threw me over shamelessly; time after time I found out that her excuse only meant that she had a better engagement elsewhere. For example—here is

* Strachey.

one of those excuses—she had invited herself for a particular day: it
was inconvenient; but I had kept it free.

Dearest Virginia,
    I had an unpleasant week of going to my business at 10
instead of 9 and coming back to bed at 6. I thought this would
have mended me by Tuesday instead of which I was summoned
by a difficult lady to see bedroom curtains in Piccadilly at 5:30
and the interview, prolonged till 6:15, sent me to bed altogether! Now I've mended and now you are engaged. Could I
come on the 18th or would you come here on the 16th at 6?
If not the 18th then the 23rd, if you'll have me.
                                    Ever your devoted
                                             Sibyl

    The day after I met someone who had been at a cocktail party at
Madame d'Erlanger's and had met Sibyl. "Was there any talk of
bedroom curtains?" I asked. Apparently there was none.*
    I used to tax her with it; she scarcely prevaricated. But once
when I played the same trick on her—throwing over an engagement,
but giving her three weeks' notice—I got a series of letters which in
the violence of their abuse, in the sincerity of their rage—for she
imputed to me the vilest motives—I had been seduced by a better
engagement—I had been dining, she was sure, with Lady Cunard
or Lady Cholmondeley—reached a pitch of eloquence that was
really impressive. The light all this threw on her psychology, on my
psychology—on the snob psychology generally, was very interesting.
Why did we go on seeing each other? I wondered. What was in fact
the nature of our relation? Light was to be thrown on it in a startling
way.
    One morning last February the telephone rang soon after break-
fast, and Leonard answered it. I saw his face change as he listened.
    "Good God!" he exclaimed. "You don't say so!" Then he turned
to me and said, "Arthur Colefax is dead!"†
    Harold Nicolson was on the telephone; he had rung up to say that
Arthur Colefax had died suddenly the afternoon before; he had only
been ill one day; Sibyl, he said, was distracted. Sir Arthur was dead!

* Typographical errors plus incomplete deletions make this paragraph a
'doubtful reading'. However, the meaning is clear.
† He died 19 February 1936.

A clap struck me full in the face. A clap of genuine surprise and sympathy. It was not for Sir Arthur. For him I felt what one feels for an old cabinet that has always stood in the middle of a drawing room. The cabinet had gone—it was surprising—it was sad. But I had never been intimate with the cabinet. For Sibyl my feeling was different—with her I had been—I was intimate. And for her I felt, as I say, a clap of genuine, unadulterated sympathy. No sooner had I felt it than it split into several pieces. I was very sorry; but I was also very curious. What did she feel—what did she really feel about Arthur?

Now when a feeling is thus mixed it is very difficult to put it into words. In proof of this, when it came to writing a letter of sympathy, I boggled. No words that I could find seemed right. I wrote and re-wrote; finally I tore up what I had written. We were going down to Monks House for the week-end; I picked three flowers; tied them up with a card on which I wrote 'For Sibyl. With love from Leonard and Virginia.' As we passed Argyll House Leonard rang the bell of that now shrouded mansion and gave the flowers into the hand of the weeping Fielding. She at least seemed genuinely heart-broken. That was my solution of the problem.

And it seemed to be amazingly successful. That is, I received a four page letter* a few days later, a heart-broken letter—a letter about Arthur and their happiness; about the old days when they had sat on Greek islands in the sun; about the perfection of their marriage; and her present solitude. It read sincerely; it read as if she were telling the truth; and I was a little flattered that she should tell it so openly, so intimately, even so gushingly, to me.†

When I heard later that she had written letters very like the one she sent me to people whom she scarcely knew at all, I was not so well pleased. When I heard that she had dined out every night since his death, and read in the papers that Lady Colefax had been at this great party and at that first night, I was baffled. Did she feel less than she made out? Or was she being very brave? Was she so

* This letter is included in the 'Monks House Papers' at the University of Sussex Library.

† The following passage is deleted in the ts: "Yet when she asked me to dine with her alone, I could not face it. Again the feeling seemed to break into three separate bits, and when I thought of spending a whole evening alone with her talking about Arthur I shirked it. I thought no. I shall be found out. I made some excuse, and waited till time had passed, and the need for genuine feeling should be less pressing."

tanned and leathered by society that the only thing she could not face was solitude? It was an interesting problem in the psychology of snobbery.

She wrote to me several times. She told me she was leaving Argyll House. She asked me to come and see the May in flower for the last time; I did not go; then she asked me to come and see the tulips in flower for the last time. We were away, and I did not go. Then when I came back in October, she wrote and said that unless I came on Tuesday the 27th of October I should never see Argyll House again. On the 30th she was leaving for ever. She particularly wanted, she said, to see me alone. I was flattered. I said I would come; and on the morning of Tuesday Fielding rang up to remind me; and to say that her ladyship wanted me to come at 4:45 punctually.

It was a wet and windy evening; leaves swirled along the pavement of the King's Road; and I had a feeling of chaos and desolation. At 4:45 precisely I rang the bell of Argyll House for the last time. The door was opened not by Fielding but by a seedy man in a brown suit who looked like a bailiff. He was surly.

"You're too late", he said, shaking his head and holding the door only half open, as if to stop me.

"But Lady Colefax told me to come at a quarter to five", I said.

That rather stumped him.

"I don't know anything about that", he said. "But you'd better come this way."

And he led me not into the drawing room but into the pantry. It was odd to find oneself in the pantry of Argyll House — that pantry from which so many succulent dishes had issued. The pantry was full of kitchen tables; and on them were ranged dinner services, bunches of knives and forks, stacks of tumblers and wine glasses — all with tickets on them. Then I realised that the whole place was up for sale; the surly man was the auctioneer's agent. I stood there looking about me when Fielding hurried in from the kitchen, still in her grey dress and muslin apron, but so flustered and so distracted that I felt she was dressed in sack cloth and ashes. She waved her hands in despair.

"I don't know where Lady Colefax is", she moaned. "And I don't know where to put you. The people are still here. They ought to have gone at four — but still all over the place . . . "

"I'm so sorry, Fielding", I said. "This is very sad — "

Tears ran down her cheeks; were in her eyes; she moaned, as she waved her hands and led me in a fluttering, undecided way, first [into] a scullery, then into the dining room. I sat down on one of the brown chairs in that rich festive room. Last time I had sat there Sir Arthur was on my right; Noel Coward was on my left. Now the chairs were ticketed; there were tickets on the glass trees on the mantelpiece; on the chandelier; on the candlesticks. A man in a black overcoat was strolling about the room, picking up now a candlestick, now a cigarette box, as if calculating what they were worth. Then two furtive fashionable ladies came in. One of them held out her hand to me.

"Have you come to see the furniture?" she said to me, in a low tone, as if she were at a funeral. I recognised Ava Bodley—Mrs Ralph Wigram.*

"No. I've come to see Sibyl", I said.

I thought I detected a shade of envy in her face; I was a friend; she was a mere sightseer. She strolled off, and began looking at the furniture. Then, as I sat there, trying to fix my mind on Sir Arthur and the kindness which he had always shown me—the door half opened; round the edge peered Sibyl who beckoned, silently, as if she were afraid to show herself in her own dining room. I followed her, and she took me into the drawing room and shut the door.

"Who was that?" she said to me anxiously.

"Mrs Wigram", I replied. She wrung her hands.

"Oh I hope she didn't see me", she murmured. "They ought to have gone at four. But they're still all over the place."

The drawing room however was empty; though there were tickets on the chairs and tables. We sank down side by side on the sofa. I used to liken her to a bunch of glossy red cherries on a hard straw hat. But now the cherries were pale. The dye had run. The black brim was soppy with water. She looked old and ill and haggard lines were grooved as if with a chisel on either side of her nose. I felt extremely sorry for her. We were like two survivors clinging to a raft. This was the end of all her parties; we were sitting in the ruins of that magnificent structure which had borne so lately the royal crown on top. I put my bare hand on her bare hand and felt, 'This is genuine. There can be no mistake about this.'

Then Fielding brought in tea—the kind of tea people have when they are starting on a journey; a few slices of thin bread and butter

* Wife of Ralph Follet Wigram, CMG, counsellor in the Foreign Office.

and three parliament biscuits. Sybil apologized for the tea. "What a horrid tea!" Then she began to talk rather distractedly; she told me about her operation; how the doctors said she ought to take a six months' holiday. "Am I Greta Garbo?" she said. Then how she had bought a house in North Street; how she was going to stay with the Clarkes . . . She was always breaking off and saying, "Oh but don't let's go into that." It was as if she wanted to say something, but could not. After all, she had asked me to come to see her alone.

At last I said, "I'm so sorry, Sibyl . . . "

The tears came to her eyes. "Oh it's been awful! You can't think what it's like", she began. Then she stopped. The tears did not fall. "You see I'm not a person who can say what they feel", she said. "I can't talk. I've not talked to anybody. If I did, I couldn't go on. And I've got to go on . . . " and again she began telling me how she had bought a house in North Street, from a madman; the house was very dirty . . . Then the door opened and Fielding beckoned.

"Mrs Wigram wants to speak to you, milady", she said. Sibyl sighed; but she got up and went.

On the whole I admired her very much. I thought, as I sat there, how brave she was. Was she not giving a supper party that very night, here, in the midst of the ruins, in the midst of the chairs and tables that were all up for sale? But here she came back.

"How I loathe that woman!" she exclaimed.

And she told me as she began to eat her bread and butter how Mrs Wigram was a mere climber; the sort of woman who pushed and shoved and she had just played, too, a dirty trick on her. When she heard that Sibyl wanted the house in North Street, she had told the Lyttons, who had bid against her. But she had got the house in spite of them; and very cheap too; for seven hundred pounds less than she expected—"Oh but don't let's talk about that", she broke off. And again I tried to be intimate. I said something rather commonplace and awkward about leaving houses—how much one minded it and so on. Then again tears came into her eyes. "Yes", she said, looking round her. "I've always had a passion for this house. I've felt about it as a lover feels . . . "

Again the door opened.

"Lady Mary Cholmondeley on the telephone, milady", said Fielding.

"Tell her I'm engaged", said Sibyl angrily. Fielding went.

"Who can she mean?" Sibyl asked. "I don't know any Lady Mary

Cholmondeley. Can it be . . . Oh dear," she sighed getting up, "I must go and see for myself. Fielding's the bane of my life", she sighed. "First she cries, then she laughs; and she won't wear spectacles though she's as blind as a bat. I must go and see for myself."

Again she left me. Another illusion had gone, I thought. I had always thought Fielding a treasure—an old servant to whom Sibyl was devoted. But no; first she cried; then she laughed; and she was as blind as a bat. This was another peep into the pantry at Argyll House.

As I sat there waiting I thought of the times I had sat on that sofa —with Sir Arthur; with Arnold Bennett; with George Moore; with old Mr Birrell; with Max Beerbohm. It was in this room that Olga Lynn threw down her music in a rage because people talked; and here that I saw Sibyl glide across the room and lead Lord Balfour, beaming benevolence and distinction, to soothe the angry singer . . . But Sibyl came back again, and again took up her bread and butter.

"What were we talking about", she said, "before Fielding interrupted? And what am I to do about Fielding?" she added. "I can't send her away. She's been with us all these years. But she's such an awful . . . but don't let's go into that," she broke off again.

Again I made an effort to talk more intimately. "I've been thinking of all the people I've met here", I said. "Arnold Bennett. George Moore. Max Beerbohm . . . "

She smiled. I saw that I had given her pleasure. "That's what I like you to say", she said. "That's what I've wanted—that the people I like should meet the people I like. That's what I tried to do—" "And that's what you've done", I said, warming up. I felt very grateful to her, although in fact I had never much enjoyed meeting other writers, still she had kept open house; she had worked very hard; it had been a great achievement in its way. I tried to tell her so.

"I have enjoyed myself in this room so much", I said. "D'you remember the party when Olga Lynn threw down her music? And then, that time I met Arnold Bennett. And then—Henry James . . . " I stopped. I had never met Henry James at Argyll House. That was before my time.

"Did you know him?" I said, quite innocently.

"Know Henry James!" Sibyl exclaimed. Her face lit up. It was as if I had touched on a nerve, the wrong nerve, I rather felt. She became the old Sibyl again—the hostess.

"Dear H.J.! I should think I did! I shall never forget", she began, "how when Wolcott Balestier died in Vienna—he was Rudyard Kipling's brother-in-law, you know—"* Here the door opened again; and again Fielding—Fielding who was as blind as a bat and the curse of Sibyl's life—peered in.

"The car's at the door, milady", she said.

Sibyl turned to me. "I've a tiresome engagement in Mount Street", she said. "I must go. But I'll give you a lift."

She got up and we went into the hall. The door was open. The Rolls Royce was waiting at the door behind the gate. This is my farewell, I said to myself, pausing for a moment, and looked, as one looks for the last time, at the Italian pots, at the looking-glasses, all with their tickets on them, that stood in the hall. I wanted to say something to show that I minded leaving Argyll House for the last time. But Sibyl seemed to have forgotten all about it. She looked animated. The colour had come back into the cherries; the straw hat was hard again. "I was just telling you," she resumed. "When Wolcott Balestier died in Vienna, Henry James came to see me, and he said, 'Dear Sibyl, there are those two poor women alone with the corpse of that dear young man in Vienna, and I feel that it is my duty—' " By this time we were walking down the flagged pathway to the car.

"Mount Street", she said to the chauffeur and got in. "H.J. said to me," she resumed, " 'I feel it is my duty to go to Vienna in case I can be of any assistance to those two bereaved ladies . . . ',." And the car drove off, and she sat by my side, trying to impress me with the fact that she had known Henry James.

---

* Balestier died in 1891; Kipling married his sister Caroline in 1892.

APPENDIX

The following alterations have been made to the text with the aim of correcting what appear to be oversights on Virginia Woolf's part.

Page	Line	Ts or Ms (VW)	Reading Adopted
30	36	tonight	that night
43	25	and sharpness (after 'silence')	deleted
46	5	depended doubtless	doubtless depended
47	39–40	atmosphere merely	merely as the atmosphere
49	19	on	at
49	40	Once your uncle	Your uncle
55	26	they	it
85	11	of the painting	of painting
85	13	I	one
85	35	of course	omitted
87	17	had	and
88	18	are	is
101	17	intimacy formally	to begin again formally
142	19	sobbed	cried
148	4	hostesses	peers
167	8	Turner	him
167	10	who	he
172	1	We true	True, we
172	27	because	that
195	20	and	who

Index

Since Virginia Woolf herself appears on almost every page, she is not included in the Index. Fictional characters are included under the title of the work in which they appear.

Eliot, George 146
English Utilitarians, The 38, 38n
Eton 101–3, 108, 131, 144, 169,
183–4
Euphrosyne 170, 171n
Euripides 127
Evelyns 107–8
Evening Standard 189

Farrell, Sophie 96, 96n, 114, 124,
127, 176
Fayette, Mme de la 70
Fisher, Florence *see* Maitland,
Florence
Fisher, Herbert 100n, 125n, 132
Fisher, Aunt Mary (*née* Jackson)
25n, 38, 89, 100, 100n, 106, 123–4,
125n, 149, 169
Fishers, the 123, 132
Fitzroy Square 96n, 103, 103n, 162,
165n, 171, 171n, 172, 176
Flower, Mrs 163
Forster, E. M. 'Morgan' 139, 176
Fortnightly, The 91
Freshfield, Mrs 159
Freshwater (Isle of Wight) 45
"Friendships Gallery" 25n
Fritham (Hampshire) 121
Fry, Roger 61, 64, 70, 85, 98, 100,
109n, 139, 157, 175; *Roger Fry: A
Biography* ('Roger') 64n, 75, 85,
95, 100
Furse, Charles (Sargent-Furse era)
83n, 163, 173
Furse, Katherine (*née* Symonds) 83n

Galsworthy, John 81
Garsington Manor 68, 68n, 173n,
178
Gauguin, Paul 178
Gertler, Mark 85, 85n
Gibbs, Frederick 73–4, 80, 83, 111,
128, 142–4, 154
Godley, Eveline 128–9
Godrevy Lighthouse (Cornwall)
111–12
Golden Treasury, The 93
Gordon Square 96n, 157, 160, 160n,

162, 165n, 169, 172–4, 176
Gower Street 173n, 178, 178n
Grafton Gallery 163
Grant, Duncan 139, 175–6, 176n,
179n
Grant, Trevor, 'Uncle Trevor' 176,
176n
Grenfell, Mrs William 136, 146

Haldane, R. B. 136, 142
Hamlet 14, 17, 72, 86, 120n
Hawtrey, Ralph 151, 168, 168n, 169
Headlam, Walter 104, 104n, 142
Herbert, Lady Margaret *see* Duck-
worth, Lady Margaret
Hills, Mrs Anna 101–2
Hills, Eustace 102
Hills, John Waller 'Jack' 22, 26, 31,
31n, 35, 47–56, 58–9, 59n, 61, 83,
95, 97, 99–100, 100n, 101–6,
121–4, 137, 143n, 147, 161, 161n,
162, 169
Hills, Judge 'Buzzy' 101
Hills, the 50n
Hindhead (Surrey) 49–50, 100, 161n
Hogarth Press 120
Holman-Hunt, Diana 154n
Holroyd, Michael 64n
Howard, Esmé 143, 151
Hunt, Mrs Gladys Holman 154
Hunt, William Holman 86n, 88,
88n, 154, 154n
Hunts, the Holman 159
Hyde Park Gate 13, 16–17, 25–6,
35, 50n, 51, 61, 63, 83, 87, 90–1,
93–4, 96n, 105, 107, 107n, 117–18,
120–1, 126–7, 142, 153, 157, 159–
160, 160n, 161, 161n, 162–3, 167,
169–70, 172, 181
"Hyde Park Gate, 22" 12, 140, 157
'Hyde Park Gate News, The' 95, 95n
Hylton, Lady 163

Impressionism 163

Jackson, Adeline *see* Vaughan, Adeline
Jackson, Dr John 26, 85, 87–8